"This colloquial telling of many 'insider' Arnold Palmer stories is a joy to read and will appeal to loyal members of Arnie's Army and newcomers to the game alike. . . . This book reveals Palmer as few have seen the man. It is a fine job by a writer who has clearly known Palmer for many years from his sports writing desk at the Orlando Sentinel. Readers will know —and love —Arnie even more when finished reading."

Links: The Best of Golf

"At last, the inside story of one of the most popular figures in sports, superbly reported by the sportswriter who knows him best. Guest, an avid golfer and sports columnist for the Orlando Sentinel, has socialized with Arnie and Winnie Palmer, flown, drank, and played golf with Arnie for years as a neighbor in Orlando. He starts strong, with a chapter characterizing Palmer's relationship with Jack Nicklaus as anything but warm, then goes on to recount several hilarious beer-drinking episodes and harrowing private plane rides. These chapters alone are worth the price."

Steve Hershey, *USA Today*

"There's plenty of Palmer worship in these pages. Yet there's also a good deal of warts, and they are what truly make this a fascinating book. . . . After so much has been written about Palmer the legend, it's nice to read about Palmer the person."

A. R. Tays, *Atlanta Journal/The Atlanta Constitution*

"It's the less serious stuff that makes this book—one of the best I've read on a sports figure—such a delight, little snapshots of Arnie being Arnie."

Ron Green, *The Charlotte Observer*

"Guest notes this now-softened fight (between Palmer and Jack Nicklaus) with a bit of wry insight. It involves Palmer's morning routine, which includes 'gulping down a pitcher of room-temperature water in the healthful, cleansing practice passed down by his great grandfather. After plans for the day are reviewed and the stock options are checked, Arnie excuses himself for his morning constitutional.' Palmer, 'with an impish grin,' refers to this as: 'Well, time for me to go take my Nicklaus.'... Arnold Daniel Palmer is a giver of the highest order. The same can be said of this book."

Jim Jennings, *The Houston Post*

"This book flourishes where others have failed because it takes the reader inside the Palmer kingdom."

Paul Finebaum, *Birmingham Post-Herald*

"Guest's book is by far the most valuable ever written on Palmer. After newspaper clippings and magazine articles are forgotten in the files, something other than the plastic-coated, IMG-burnished Palmer image will remain in the library. A similar effort on Nicklaus ought to be next to it."

John Markon, *Richmond Times-Dispatch*

ARNIE

INSIDE THE LEGEND

ARNIE

INSIDE THE LEGEND

Larry Guest

CUMBERLAND HOUSE PUBLISHERS, INC.
Nashville, Tennessee

Copyright © 1993, 1997 by Larry Guest

All rights reserved. Written permission must be secured from the publisher
to use or reproduce any part of this work, except for brief quotations in
critical reviews or articles.

Published by Cumberland House Publishing, Inc., 2200 Abbott Martin
Road, Suite 102, Nashville, Tennessee, 37215.

Distributed to the trade by Andrews & McMeel, 4520 Main Street, Kansas
City, Missouri, 64111.

Jacket design by Harriet Bateman
Interior design by Joel Wright

Photographs courtesy of Howdy Giles, *The Orlando Sentinel,* Associated
Press

Library of Congress Cataloging-in-Publication Data
Guest, Larry, 1942–
      Arnie : inside the legend / Larry Guest. —2nd ed.
           p. cm.
      Include index.
      ISBN 1-888952-42-3 (pbk. : alk. paper)
      1. Palmer, Arnold, 1929- . 2. Golfer—United States—
      Biography. I. Title.
      GV964.P3G84   1997
      796.352'092—dc21   96-53561
                                CIP

Printed in the United States of America
1 2 3 4 5 6 7—02 03 01 00 99 98 97

To Big Red, *whose indomitable spirit has made her as much a beacon* as a big sister. And to Christa, Dorrie, and Gina, whose childhoods kept getting interrupted by Dad's Arnold Palmer book, which didn't materialize until they were grown.

—L.G.

Contents

Acknowledgments

Grateful and heartfelt acknowledgments to the many who made this once-in-a-lifetime project work, but especially . . . To the editors at *The Orlando Sentinel, Golf,* and *Golf Illustrated* for graciously allowing me to recycle portions of Arnie stories and columns I've written in those publications over the past two decades. To Kaye Kessler, my former World Series roomie and helpful archivist. To Howdy Giles, Arnie, and the Bay Hill Club for sharing some very special photos. And to Dixie Kasper, who doesn't know doodle about golf but could break par on any book-editing links.

Introduction

The first time I embarked upon the project of writing a book about Arnold Palmer, he volunteered to punch my collaborator in the nose. That was in 1975, little more than two years after I joined *The Orlando Sentinel,* and moved to the laid-back central Florida city that Arnie calls home about half of each year.

At that time, I knew him not much better than most. Essentially, I was but another enlistee in the "Army," that enduring global mass that has admired him, appreciated him, from the other side of the gallery ropes. In my role as sports columnist for the *Sentinel,* I had by then interviewed him one-on-one a couple of times, but the friendship and healthy working relationship that later blossomed were still a couple of years away.

That earlier book effort—I was to ghost a tome for Darrell Brown, a bright, engaging chap who had served as copilot and closest confidant to Arnie during most of his glory years as the planet's true king of golf—had been the brainstorm of a loud and lovable guy named Dick Robinson. A mutual friend of mine and Brown's, Robinson was a member and resident at Arnie's Bay Hill Club in Orlando. Recognizing that Brown had, for years, been in a privileged position right there at this great man's elbow in the air, in the next seat at dinner, in the adjacent hotel room, Robinson insisted it was not merely Brown's opportunity but indeed his duty to share with the world his insights into one of the globe's most famous and compelling men of our time. Particularly now that Brown was no longer in Palmer's employ and was presumably free to wax candidly.

Not long after marrying the daughter of former U.S. Ambassador Leonard Firestone, Darrell had resigned to pursue more fulfilling activities than airborne chauffeur and road gofer for A. Daniel Palmer. An accountant by training, Brown had the moxie for more important roles within the Palmer panorama of businesses but was blocked from increased responsibility by Palmer's business manager and budding super-agent, Mark McCormack. Brown was one of many who got too close to Arnie for McCormack's comfort. (See Chapter 6.) McCormack drove a wedge between them; the resultant parting of Brown and Arnie couldn't really be described as icy but nevertheless chilly enough to lower chardonnay to the desired dining temperature.

So when Brown and yours truly paid a courtesy visit to Arnie's quaint little office across the street from Latrobe (Pennsylvania) Country Club a couple of years later to announce what he already knew—intentions of writing a book on him—Arnie closed the door, paced the floor, and exploded. He scowled at me and said he didn't care if I wrote a book. But he didn't want Darrell profiting from his name and their past employee-employer relationship.

"If it's notoriety you want," he bellowed at Brown, "I'll punch you in the nose and that'll give you plenty of notoriety!"

Darrell Brown sat stunned, intimidated by the unwarranted and unseemly attack. Brown's intent, stated up front in our first meeting on the project, was simply to paint a portrait of the Palmer personality through insightful anecdotes and actions behind the scenes. Despite his awkward and disappointing departure, he truly admired Arnie and emphatically mandated to me there would be nothing shocking or scandalous in the book; there would be a few humanizing glimpses of this legend but nothing that would tarnish his immensely marketable image and certainly nothing that Winnie Palmer would be distraught to read.

"I want you to just leave me alone!" Arnie snorted. "Just leave me alone! My life is my own business and I want to keep it that way!"

Darrell was visibly shaken as we drove away in silence to the local motel where we would spend the night and dine with friends. Darrell's friends. Arnie's friends. After Brown had spent virtually every waking hour for a decade with Arnie, those friends were one and the same and therein lay the death knell for Darrell's book.

Within a month, Brown handed me a five-thousand-dollar personal check to cover the time I had already spent conducting interviews and transcribing tapes, thus scrapping the project. Out of my earshot, Arnie has bragged that he got that book stopped. Some have interpreted that to mean he put up the kill money, but I don't think that is correct.

His was a more effective ploy, imploring those mutual friends to lay a guilt trip on Brown. "Darrell, why do you want to do this book on Arnie?" they scolded, as if he were writing a kiss-and-tell epic. They made Darrell feel he was violating a sacred trust. They made Darrell feel like a worm. Unjustly.

Too bad. Darrell Brown's book would have been more celebration than cremation of Arnold Daniel Palmer.

This book has the same intent. I've been writing it for more than fifteen years—in my columns in the *Sentinel* and in feature-length pieces for *Golf, Golf Illustrated,* and other publications here and abroad. Those intimate peeks at Arnie from Augusta to St.

Andrews, from ground-level bars to thirty-five thousand feet, form the basis of this unprecedented profile.

I say "unprecedented" because every book to date about Arnie has been produced with his editorial control and primarily details how he grips a sand wedge or how he played the fourth hole. This leans more toward how he played dinner that night. Or the plane ride home. Or the business meeting the next morning. These are vignettes of a man's man, a swashbuckling risk taker who enjoys life to the fullest, a champion of the so-called moral majority, perhaps the compelling athletic hero of the twentieth century.

How compelling? At the 1987 Bay Hill tournament, Arnie hooked his tee shot on the par-three seventh hole and the ball struck spectator Jane Robinson of Topeka, Kansas, on the shoulder. When Arnie arrived at the scene, Robinson excitedly pointed to her shoulder and gushed: "This is such an honor to be hit by you; this is the greatest day of my life!" Arnie gave her a gallant kiss on the cheek. Then after finishing the hole, he gave her the ball as a souvenir.

You'll recognize some passages and anecdotes; other tales and observations contained here will be new to even the most ardent Arnie-watchers—telling, insightful accounts previously unpublished, most of which likely will make you love the man even more. Some of them, Arnie wouldn't have told himself if he were in control of this keyboard. But most of the warts only serve to forge an even stronger bond with his adoring public.

Orville Henry, longtime columnist for the *Arkansas Democrat,* once stood under the famed tree behind the Augusta National clubhouse, watching Arnie and a fawning gallery making their way from the ninth green to the tenth tee. The topic of conversation was the source of Arnie's appeal.

Larry Guest

"As we become older," Henry said sagely, "we love our parents for their faults. I think that's the same reason so many people love Arnie."

A reasonable theory.

But all else would be academic were it not for the bold "style" that became evident very early in his golfing career.

Exhibit A: Arnie's errant tee shot seemed hopelessly trapped in the right rough, a row of trees blocking his approach to the green. His plastic face contorted first in despair, then to determination as he spotted a two-foot opening between the branches.

He turned to the gallery following him in that major championship and told them he was going to hit it right through the minuscule opening and onto the green. To their delight, he delivered.

"That was always my joy. That put more pressure on me to do it. Sometimes I didn't, but when I did, it was a great thrill for me and the fans," Arnie said, recounting the incident. What is telling is that Arnie was seventeen years old at the time. The "major championship" was a state high school tournament and the "gallery" was a half-dozen relatives and friends.

Arnie's signature "go-for-broke" style, you see, is not one that was developed for tour galleries or TV. The ingredient popularly believed to be the basis for that Palmer charisma—the two words have seemingly become inseparable—was ingrained from adolescence.

Here was a budding hero armed early with a sense of the theatrical. The ham in Arnie pleads guilty.

His only prior experience on stage was a couple of parts in high school plays and standard duty in the church choir. "I remember my mother saying that I had the nicest voice and that she could hear me above everybody else," he recalled, laughing.

But that hell-bent drive for first or nothing and winning with flair was merely the first ingredient. Arnie's appeal goes deeper. He is magnetic because he was a flamboyant winner and because he is both respectful and credible. Peeking out from behind the corners of that exemplary facade of decorum is just the proper mix of human faults to make him believable.

The whole package was first sold through a sporting press corps intrigued by his bold playing style, candor, and "regular-guy" accessibility. In later years, that visibility and appeal have been maintained by a full and richly rewarding portfolio of endorsements.

Arnie himself pleads modesty in attempting to explain his commercial popularity. "The only answer I can give is the honest answer. I use the products."

Although various "Arnie for President" spoofs remain just that, more than a few Republican bigwigs have nudged Arnie to see how his mass appeal would translate in congressional or gubernatorial polls. There have had to be many voters in the most recent presidential elections—given the available choices—who would have welcomed an Arnie option.

Concluding a talk to the Downtown Athletic Club of Orlando in 1988, Arnie opened the floor to questions and was asked about a tongue-in-cheek spread in *Golf* magazine promoting him for the White House. "I thought seriously about the presidency," Arnie said impishly, "but I decided I couldn't afford the pay cut." To those fortunates within Arnie's inner circle, that appeal is accented by a playful, boyish spirit lurking behind that regal bearing.

Exhibit B: The wall phone in Bay Hill Club's nineteenth hole was jangling loudly for the third time one afternoon and none of the regular employees had responded. The bartender had temporarily vacated his post and the grill's two waitresses were busy tending

tables. So the celebrated proprietor dutiful leaped to his feet and snatched the receiver to his ear.

"Hello," he answered, glancing back to where a half-dozen friends were attentively eavesdropping. "Yes, this is the grill. Who'd you want?" he continued, pretending indignation to the delight of his pals.

"This is Arnold Palmer," he announced as the spectators fought back giggles. "Who did you want to speak to?"

Short pause.

"Well, I can't help you unless you tell me what you want," he admonished the caller, winking at the gang. After the curious conversation lasted a few moments more, a seemingly indignant Arnie replaced the receiver and returned to his Michelob and peanuts. "I don't think people should talk that way over the phone," he tersely declared before breaking into a wide grin and adding, "even if it is my wife!"

When the laughter subsided, he explained that Winnie Palmer had been the untimely caller, dialing from their luxury condominium across the street from the club to request a serving of crackers and butter.

He finished his Michelob with the boys, shook hands all around, and disappeared into the clubhouse kitchen. He emerged a few moments later with a plastic container of crackers, a Styrofoam cup of butter, and a sheepish smile.

As the years passed after the aborted Darrell Brown book, I began to occupy, to a somewhat lesser degree, the privileged vantage point from which Darrell came to know and admire Arnie. As the top sports figure and the lead sports columnist of the town, Arnie's and my paths were inextricably bonded. We genuinely hit it off. When Arnie gained control of Orlando's PGA Tour stop and moved it across town to his own Bay Hill Club, he became a more frequent and compelling column subject. I joined Bay Hill. I occasionally played golf with Arnie, occasionally flew with him to and from tournaments. We clacked beer mugs in famous watering holes on two continents. We interacted socially in one another's homes.

His door was always open to me. He and Winnie came to my aid at times of personal and professional crisis. I reciprocated when his name was being sullied by environmental and business glitches not of his doing. He was supportive and sympathetic when my father died. I was supportive and sympathetic when his daughter became seriously ill. Does that make me Arnie's unabashed houseman? Not when you consider I've slapped his hand when warranted—publicly chiding him for being petty in his eternal rivalry with Jack Nicklaus, or tweaking his nose for violating a personal vow never to permit a title sponsor for his former Bay Hill Classic.

But those times have been few. I offer no apologies for a glowing portrait of this man, Arnold Palmer. Sure, he has a few of those faults that Orville Henry mentioned, but on balance he is an exemplary figure, an eminently commendable sports hero for our times. The precise reasons for that can be elusive. A prominent one that had been right there under my nose for years first became truly apparent on the sixteenth tee at the Woodlands Country Club in the 1981 Houston Open. I was serving as Arnie's caddie, a one-week adventure on assignment for *Golf* magazine.

Suddenly and vividly I could see and feel what had been under my nose for years. One of the most important conduits between Arnie and his Army is a simple little statement of mutual respect: eye contact.

As was his habit throughout the tournament, Arnie strolled the tees each time the group ahead had not cleared the fairway. He'd make a tight circle, scanning the faces behind the gallery ropes, nodding here, offering a greeting there. It's a practice that

spoke volumes, a simple, thoughtful gesture that not only brought him to their level but expressed an appreciation for their presence.

On that sixteenth tee at the Woodlands, I came to realize I didn't have to watch him to tell where he was facing during one of those appreciation laps; he was like a beacon producing an afterglow that moved along the row of spectators in a wave. Chests would rise and faces beam as The King made eye contact, acknowledging each person behind the ropes.

In an era when too many celebrity athletes are openly contemptuous of the fans, some could unemotionally sign their way through a nudist colony of autograph hounds, never noticing all the missing knickers. Arnie's prized signature, though executed hundreds of times during each tournament day, is routinely accompanied by an eye-to-eye smile or nod and, often, a compliment or other social amenity.

Unfortunate has been the rule that requires the PGA Tour to pair Arnie for the first two rounds with other past tour winners. Competing alongside Arnie for two days should have been a requirement for each new player, exposing rookies to Palmer's natural style of winning friends for golf.

Of course, it helped that he had the talent to win four Masters and dozens of assorted other titles around the globe. And part and parcel to Arnie's mass appeal have been his middle-class roots and his dashing style of play seemingly forever flirting with disaster. But few superstar athletes have also connected with the populace the way Arnie Palmer has with his simple exchange of mutual respect.

I feel he and I have that same mutual respect. He certainly has mine; his reaction when I told him I'd be assembling this book underscored that I have his. He said he looked forward to the book and even offered some assistance by providing some of the wonderful snapshots that appear in the sixteen-page photo section.

More meaningful, perhaps, he didn't offer to punch me in the nose.

Larry Guest

1

Deke Palmer's Boy

Milfred "Deacon" Palmer, a western Pennsylvania institution, relentlessly instilled in his children the proper respect for others, even if the lesson had to be applied to his famous golfing son at the height of Arnie's global fame. The year was 1964 and the tournament was the PGA Championship in Columbus, Ohio.

THE PALMERS, FATHER AND SON, had just returned from the course and Arnie was attempting to make a left turn into his hotel entrance across two lanes of heavy, oncoming traffic. A traffic cop waved him off and Arnie circled the block, only to find himself in the same predicament.

Arnie, then thirty-four, cranked down the window, poked his head out, and appealed to the policeman. "You know who I am? I'm Arnold Palmer and I need to turn in there to my hotel."

Holding his ground, the unawed policeman tersely instructed Arnie to move along. The car shot forward and smoke billowed from Arnie's ears. But his anger paled in comparison to the sudden eruption from his passenger.

"Son, I don't care who you are—Arnold Palmer or who!" Deacon glowered. "You had no business trying to steamroll that policeman and he was perfectly right to make you go around!"

It was a booster shot of humility that has been only occasionally needed and rarely forgotten by Arnie.

"Deacon taught his son the straight and narrow of life," said Mark McCormack, Arnie's longtime agent, "and wanted to make damned sure his son stayed on it. He had a huge influence on Arnold throughout his career. We all are trying to prove ourselves to somebody or get the approval of somebody, and in Arnold's case that somebody was his father."

Deacon died Friday afternoon, February 6, 1976, in his room at Arnie's Bay Hill Club & Lodge in Orlando after a round of golf with friends.

Arnie was playing at the Bob Hope Desert Classic at the time, finishing his Friday round with a fifty-four-hole total of 214, just four shots behind leader Buddy Allin and three behind Jack Nicklaus. Excitement swept the desert with the anticipation that in the final thirty-six holes, the tournament might offer up a stirring Arnie/Jack confrontation and perhaps even put an end to Arnie's victory drought that was reaching three years that very week.

Naturally, Arnie pulled out and flew home.

To this day, Arnie speaks with ever-growing appreciation for the tough Scottish-Irish values instilled in him by his "Pap." Incidents of boorish or disrespectful behavior by sports' contemporary bad boys invariably move Arnie to suggest the athlete in point should have had someone "to crack down on him like I had."

Deacon Palmer continued to "crack down" on his son, when he thought necessary, right into and through the era when Arnie had

passed his fortieth birthday and was a global celebrity. "He sure did," Arnie says, wide-eyed and nodding.

I had met Deacon Palmer on only two brief occasions, but after years of listening to endearing testimony about the man affectionately known simply as "Deke," I felt I knew him intimately. He was repeatedly spoken of as the guiding light for the personality that would capture the golf world. If there is any one thing that truly kick-started the relationship I have been privileged to share with Arnie, I sense it was this column I felt compelled to write the day after Deke died.

If God has had a—pardon the expression—devilish run of poa-annia in His greens; if He's been getting too much right hand in His tee shots; or if the traps up there are in dire need of raking and weeding—then His troubles are over.

Newest member through the pearly gates, one Milfred J. Palmer, not only has the necessary savvy and energy to lick those problems, he bears the perfect nickname to adorn the heavenly scrolls.

In the short time since ascending late Friday afternoon, "Deacon" Palmer probably has already rolled up the sleeves of his robes and resumed the same work he enjoyed for the last fifty-five of the seventy-one years he spent here on earth. By today, he's no doubt finished reseeding the fairways on the back nine, top-dressed a half-dozen greens, trimmed down the sand traps and repainted the pro shop.

Palmer went to work for Latrobe (Pennsylvania) Country Club in 1921 and was still earning his salary last Friday, when death caught him in his sleep. It was the only way death could. He never slowed down long enough to die when he was awake.

Many modern-day greens superintendents and golf club professionals ride around in a golf cart wearing a white shirt and tie, or sit in their air-conditioned office and tell employees what to do. Not Deacon. He worked right alongside the help, leading by example. Just like he guided his four children.

And while the Latrobe Country Club membership is well-acquainted with Deacon's prowess as a club pro, you've more likely heard of him as Arnold Palmer's father. Even though the designation often made Deacon cringe. Oh, it's not that he minded the second-billing.

"Everybody here is proud of their sons," he once bristled at a gathering when introduced as the proud father of Arnold Palmer. "The thing is, I have two daughters and two sons and Arnold is just one of them. I'm proud of them all." It was perhaps an understandable oversight on the part of the masses who were so familiar with the amazing accomplishments of son Arnold, the charismatic fairway hero who lifted golf from sort of an anonymous floating crap game to an immensely popular and well-heeled sport. And just as Arnold Palmer is largely responsible for making pro golf what it is today, Deacon Palmer is largely responsible for making Arnie what he is.

"Pap didn't just teach me how to play golf," Arnie once understated. "He taught me discipline."

Indeed, Deacon Palmer was a wise and patient man of unwavering principles. He had a face of leather, muscles of iron, and a backbone of steel. But he had a heart of velvet. A man's man. But also a gentleman's gentleman. A saint in golf cleats.

He believed in all the right things: God, country, hard work, respect for others, Lawrence Welk, shots-and-beer, and—most of all—humility.

Larry Guest

The latter was most important in molding the personality that would whip millions of golf fans into frenzied devotion. As greenskeeper at Latrobe, Deacon stressed to his children they had no special privileges. They could not swim in the club pool, and talented young Arnold was not allowed on the course when member play was heavy.

The lesson helped Arnie maintain a perspective on his runaway fame while others in the public eye have been soundly thrashed by their own egos. But even after Arnie had become king of the links, Deacon was still there to give his celebrity son an occasional booster shot.

And while the ranking angels will probably now enjoy the Heavenly Links as they never have before, they'd be advised not to get too uppity when a certain tough old coot comes riding by on his gang mowers.

A few days later, Winnie Palmer went out of her way to express appreciation for the Deke column. In the two decades since it appeared, Arnie has yet to say a word about it directly, though in many other ways his actions immediately suggested he, too, was appreciative of the tribute to the man who most influenced his life.

That is Arnie's way. He rarely reacts directly to the writer of stories or columns about him, whether the epistle is positive or negative. A number of rabbit-eared athletes would do well to adopt the policy, one that Arnie learned from a man named Deacon.

Railing against a journalistic critic or fawning over a favorable report simply wasn't in keeping with Deke's philosophy of maintaining an even keel, of maintaining a grasp of one's roots. That ability to step out of a state house or a limo and connect with the great unwashed—Deke's people—is central to Arnie's enduring popularity.

"It isn't everything to be up here all the time," Arnie recently said, raising his hand eye-level to indicate the upper social strata. "That isn't the whole name of the game to me. It's fun to sometimes be down here with some people that are down to earth and different. I enjoy that. I enjoy hearing them and enjoy talking to them. They are just nice people who are going along and want to have a little fun and drink a little beer and enjoy life.

"My father might be classified as a liberal, though he probably didn't realize what a liberal was until he was much older. I was raised in a different environment from that of most tour golfers and I realize how things can be a little difficult in terms of lifestyle."

Often misstated is the premise that Arnold Palmer is equally at home in a New York boardroom, the Oval Office, or some grungy pool hall. Wrong. Arnie is much more at home trying to bank the eight-ball two rails against a guy wearing a greasy denim shirt and Caterpillar cap, with the next round of beers riding on the shot. There are any number of stories with Arnie circling a green-felt table, stalking his next shot in the back room of a roadhouse, matching his stickmanship against mill workers.

Nearly forty and at the height of his career, this international celebrity millionaire once stopped in at a steel workers' billiards bar twenty miles from Latrobe for a frosty Rolling Rock and a game of eight-ball. The musty neighborhood establishment rarely had a high-fashion visitor wearing designer loafers and a Rolex watch. The regulars, all in work grays, eyed the intruder suspiciously. Arnie and his friends grew uncomfortable with the obvious scrutiny. At last, a crusty old mill hand approached Arnie: "You're Deke Palmer's boy, ain't ya?"

Arnie nodded, the unofficial sergeant-at-arms flashed an approving smile, and the King of Golf became one of the boys. Overdressed a bit, but nevertheless one of the boys.

The pool-hall camaraderie story Arnie likes to share with friends involves a laborers' bar on the west side of Orlando. The beer is cold, the jukebox is loud, and the pool tables become center stage after the four o'clock whistle blows. On a Friday afternoon in 1973, Palmer had missed the cut in the old Citrus Open a few miles away at Rio Pinar Country Club. With his father and a couple of friends in tow, Arnie eased his Cadillac into the row of pickup trucks outside the bar and headed inside to soothe the disappointment.

Arnie picks up the story: "The place had egg cartons on the ceiling and pool tables in the back. It was a pretty tough little bar. You had to sort of get in line to shoot pool with guys who had been digging ditches and putting up power lines and what have for you. You'd work your way through the line for your turn and if you got beat, it was back to the end of the line.

"There was one little guy who was really tough. He didn't know who Arnold Palmer was and didn't really give a crap. My father and the others just watched as I worked my way up and beat this one little guy. Well, I got hot and beat the whole line of guys. We're playing for beers and by now I have a whole row of beers lined up. Now that one little guy's turn comes up again and I beat him again.

"We'd all been there about two hours by this time and had plenty of beer. The little guy walks over pretty deliberately and jams his cue stick to the floor. I figure now I may have to beat him in a fight. But he kinda puts one arm around me and says, 'You can wear my shoes, any time.' To me, it's the greatest compliment in the world. To gain the respect of someone like that is a challenge that many people will never understand."

That, says Arnie, is his definition of charisma, the word many say Palmer introduced to the golfing lexicon.

He acquired the commoners' touch while growing up as the son of a humble greenskeeper during the Great Depression. His playground was the country club, allowing him to acquire the game of his gilded future and rub shoulders with those of political station all the while being reminded of his station. Arnie was just three when Deacon gave him a set of shortened clubs and began teaching him the game. Across the road from the modest green frame house where he grew up was the difficult fifth hole, where as a tyke he earned nickels from women golfers by pinch-hitting their drives across the creek some hundred yards off the tee.

In 1971, Arnie bought the club and was asked if Deke would be retained in his role as greenskeeper and pro. "If he behaves himself," he said with a sly grin.

Despite Arnie's muscular build and affinity for rougher sports like football and baseball, golf would become his game, nurtured and refined by his father's keen eye. Carefully crafted were not only the physical skills of the sport, but the compelling attitude and dashing, competitive spirit still used as the standard by which today's tour pros so often are unfavorably compared.

"Generally, I don't think the tour is on the downslide," Arnie recently said in defense of golf's subsequent generation. "For example, the galleries on site are larger than ever and the purses continue to grow right through the roof. Television ratings have slid some, but I don't know if that's because of—what do you call them—clones? The difference in the late '50s and early '60s was a different kind of TV coverage." The reference was to made-for-TV matches like the "Big Three" and "Shell's Wonderful World of Golf," and the fact that the tour stars of that era played in virtually every tournament that was televised.

"The public got to know the players as individuals," Arnie reasoned. "They got to know them because those players performed as individuals on individual shows. Like, they got to know Nicklaus and Palmer and Player and others as individuals. And all over the U.S., they picked their favorites. And whether they wanted Palmer to get beat, or Nicklaus to get beat, or Player, they had someone to relate to."

But in the '50s and '60s, there was a guy who came along and hitched his pants and took all the shortcuts and challenged the course and smiled and laughed and cursed. In the decades that followed, there were few stars on the tour who exhibited the same compelling emotions and verve.

"You're right," said Arnie, "and that's unfortunate. Today's players are so businesslike. I was having fun. I was enjoying it because I didn't think there would be that much money to play for. And I enjoyed the people. They rooted and they screamed when I'd hit it through the trees. And I still like to play that way for that reason. The fellas today are a little bit different in that they are real businessmen."

Another difference between himself and today's typical pro is that competitive grit.

"I was tough. If I saw Sam Snead was beating me, I watched Sam Snead and I wanted to beat him. And that didn't mean I didn't like him. I never rooted against another player, but I never rooted for them, either. Dow Finsterwald was a helluva player and a friend. And I wanted him to do well. But when he was playing against me, I wanted me to do better. Dow and I competed against each other in Hard Knock City and we are very good friends now. But if we go out and play tomorrow, I'm gonna try my damnedest to beat him.

"I see this today on the tour: These guys root for each other and they do it openly. Well, that's like getting down in the line in a football game and telling the guy on the other side, 'Knock me on my butt. I want you to do good.' I mean, that's bullshit. My father told me many years ago to always figure the guy you're playing is going to make the best shot in the world, or make the putt against you, and just figure you're going to make it better than he is."

Stoic Jack Renner, a journeyman tour player in the '70s and early '80s, once said it was his goal to go out and play eighteen holes without ever changing expression. Arnie was and remains the antithesis of that theory.

"It's no fun if I can't show a little emotion. That's part of life. I don't know why some of these guys aren't more colorful. And maybe they are in their own minds and in their own way. I'm sure Tom Watson doesn't feel he's colorless. And I can see some things about him that are flamboyant. Subtle, but interesting in other ways. A different approach. A more psychological."

Those remarks came in the early '80s when Watson briefly took over as the game's No. 1 player. The colorful, crowd-pleasing likes of Fuzzy Zoeller, Payne Stewart, John Daly and others emerged as stars in subsequent years. Those are players with true charisma, a word seemingly invented for Arnold Palmer, though it took the golfing media a few years to get around to using it.

"In my first few years on the tour, I'm not sure when the press was writing, they knew they were writing about charisma. They were writing more about something that was a little different and more exciting. And the word charisma only really came into it when I wasn't playing and winning as much and the galleries were still following me. That is all a result of the things I did when I was playing well. It didn't matter to me how I won in the early days. It was only later that I became concerned whether I hit eighteen greens. Or how good Sam Snead was because his swing was so picture-perfect and had such great rhythm. Well, I think that's great. But it's not so great if you don't take that swing and win golf tournaments. Unless you do, no one gives a crap.

"I saw guys when I started on the tour, really pretty good players who played in a style like Hogan and Nelson and Snead. They were great players, tee to green, but they never won. Well, I didn't want to be one of those great players. I wanted to be one of the great players who hit it in the woods over here, and then in the ditch over there, and got it in the hole on the next shot. And I didn't care how that happened. And that's what people liked. They enjoyed that. And I enjoyed that.

"I remember playing in the state championship in high school with maybe fifteen or twenty people in back of me. I was in the right rough and there was a row of trees with an opening that big," he said, holding his hands two feet apart. "I turned around and told them I was going to hit it right through that opening. And did. But that was my joy. That put more pressure on me to do it. Sometimes I didn't. But when I did, it was a great thrill."

Most times, young Arnie found the opening. He led Greater Latrobe High School to three sectional titles (1945-47) and was Pennsylvania Interscholastic Athletic Association individual champion in 1946 and 1947. That was a record sufficiently impressive to earn Arnie a berth in the National High School Sports Hall of Fame.

The exemplary and winning attitudes that Deacon Palmer ingrained in his son are now being passed along by Arnie to his own "sons" headlining today's tournament golf. Among the most attentive students is Mark O'Meara, now an Orlando neighbor of Arnie's, who in recent years has come to be recognized as the affable king of the pro-am format.

O'Meara, who won the AT&T Pebble Beach National Pro-Am four times, the Disney World Classic once, and finished second in the Bob Hope Desert Classic—all extended pro-am formats— gives part of the credit for playing easily with amateurs to his own father. But as much as anyone, O'Meara insists Arnie has been the overriding factor in his upbeat demeanor when playing with the Average Als.

"I wish all these pros who resent amateur partners could spend one day at a tournament with Arnold Palmer," O'Meara once said. "Arnold Palmer is the greatest at what he does. He knows how to deal with people. He's a people-person, probably the greatest people-person in the history of golf.

"I've observed the way he handles people. He might be the one most famous person in our sport, but I have never seen him be snobby to anyone, I don't care how bad a golfer that person is or how humble he is. Arnold treats them all the same. He treats Joe Blow the same way he treats any guy in his foursome at the U.S. Open."

After winning at Pebble Beach in 1992, O'Meara said the luck of the draw set his fourth AT&T title apart from the previous three. During the first three rounds of the tournament, O'Meara was paired with Arnie.

"I grew up more in the Jack Nicklaus era and did not get a true appreciation for Arnold's career," O'Meara told reporters afterward. "Now, over twelve years of playing professional golf, I have a tremendous amount of respect and admiration for him. He is so good to everyone. He's a class act, all-around, and was behind me 110 percent. I had a very, very difficult shot out of the bunker at eighteen . . . , and that's really not my forte. I came out of the bunker, and he said, 'That was one great shot.' When Arnold Palmer tells you that, it really means something special. It must have been pretty damn good."

A compliment from Arnie is cherished by virtually every member of golf's family. After Ray Floyd won the 1986 U.S. Open at Shinnecock Hills, Floyd's wife, Maria, proudly unfolded a pink message slip to show a knot of reporters outside the media tent. It was a telephone message transcribed moments earlier by one of the locker room attendants: "I knew it was in the making. It was just a matter of time. —Arnold Palmer."

"This is special," said Maria, carefully tucking the message into her purse.

Months after winning at Bay Hill and Augusta in 1992, rising superstar Fred Couples revealed that two of his most precious letters of encouragement and congratulations came from Arnie. "One was after we won the Ryder Cup and one after I won the Masters," said Couples. "He just said things like, 'I knew you could do it. Many more.' They're probably only four or five lines and his signature. It didn't matter if it was only one word. Those letters are special to me. I think the world of Arnold Palmer. Winning the Masters is truly a special feeling, but I tell you, winning just before that at Bay Hill and having Arnold Palmer hand you the trophy is a fabulous feeling."

Some of the Deke Palmer Credo passed on through Arnie to today's tour stars, however, didn't come in the form that you frame and hang in a privileged spot in the den. An example came in 1982 when Arnie administered a fatherly lecture to Curtis Strange in particular and the entire tour in general about responsible behavior toward fans and tournament volunteers.

There were a number of unsavory incidents during the period that indicated Arnie's young colleagues weren't properly appreciative of the people around them. Strange's tantrum directed at a photographer and an elderly woman scorer during the '82 Bay Hill Classic sent Arnie into action.

Frustrated by a disappointing round, Strange, among other verbal misadventures, scorched matronly scorer Peggy Berry with his patented assortment of purple adjectives. For Arnie, it was the last straw in a wave of churlish actions by rising tour stars. Respect for and appreciation of the masses is at the very core of Arnie's makeup. Now here were assorted tour pros giving that public the backs of their hands. Arnie was mad as hell and wasn't going to take it any more.

Without mentioning Strange by name, he fired off a sharp letter of disgust to PGA commissioner Deane Beman, urging a tighter screw for bad actors. In the letter, Arnie cited numerous instances of "abusive language and displays of temperament" at the Bay Hill tournament. He suggested "suspensions are in order for some of these incidents." After obtaining Arnie's permission, Beman sent copies of the letter to each tour pro and tournament sponsor. The letter soon leaked to the media and the public prints were aquiver with commentary.

"I meant for my comments to remain private," Arnie would say, lamenting his decision to let Beman mass-produce the missive. He said his letter was aimed at a disturbing general trend on the tour and not at Strange in particular. However, it was Strange in particular he confronted two weeks later at the Tournament Players Championship in the straightforward Palmer style. Curtis dropped his head contritely and vowed to shape up.

"Curtis was a perfect gentleman," Arnie said of the man-to-boy lecture. "I think he was very sincere in what he was saying. Only time will tell."

Tour official Dale Antram confirmed that Strange had been fined over the incident but declined to specify the amount. Whispers placed the punishment at less than one thousand dollars, or not exactly capital punishment for a guy who won more than a quarter-million in official money that year.

At first, Strange allowed as how the Palmer letter was "no big deal" and said he couldn't understand why some people think

everything Arnie says is news. Besides, he added with a shrug, he sent the lady a letter of apology and received a letter accepting that apology.

However, the target of those Strange expletives had a slightly different story. "I'm not too happy with his apology, to tell the truth," Berry said. "I've been scoring tournaments for eleven years. This is the first time I've had a player be nasty to me and he was really nasty. He talked to me in tones like I was a dog. He apologized in his letter, but in a backhanded way."

Strange's unfortunate dialogue with Mrs. Berry was reported in *The Orlando Sentinel* a few days after the tournament, with no help from Strange. Asked point-blank about the incident the day after it happened, Curtis, for the life of him, could not recall any unsavory moments. His amnesia was eventually arrested after Arnie talked to Strange as if he were a dog.

Arnie angrily reminded Curtis that he, Arnie, and Strange's late father were close friends. "If he were here today," Arnie snorted, "I think he'd want me to take you over my knee!"

The threat of a spanking apparently worked. In the ensuing years, Strange grew up to become more like a responsible tour pro and less like a country club brat. His bouts of juvenile behavior became only occasional lapses. His relationship with Arnie blossomed as his improved demeanor drew private applause from the old schoolmaster.

Two months after the incident, Strange said: "I said to myself when it all came about how embarrassed I was about it. I'm even embarrassed to talk about it, embarrassed to the point that I will not do it again." Strange said he thought Berry "was out of position, twice. The second time, I got short-tempered with her. It upset her and it should have. It was my fault." He had lashed out at the photographer, claiming camera noise had caused him to miss a four-foot putt. The photographer tried to explain that the camera had shorted out, but Strange stalked off to the next tee, unconvinced.

When Arnie's letter to Beman became public, the press launched into a feverish search of the offending pro and Bay Hill incident that had triggered Arnie's ire, leading to a couple of erroneous reports. One story claimed the letter had been inspired by the circumstances surrounding Tom Weiskopf's being AWOL for the Bay Hill pro-am that year. The report charged that Weiskopf returned two weeks later for a "make-up date" with his amateur partners only as a result of Arnie's letter. In truth, Weiskopf's contrite attempt to reassemble his jilted amateurs for a later game at Bay Hill was set in motion before either Strange's snit or Arnie's letter.

It so happened that I had an interview appointment with Weiskopf immediately following his pro-am round. Thus, I was surprised to happen upon him sitting in the club's grill room only about three hours after his scheduled 8:10 tee time. I sat down and absorbed the amusing story of why his pro-am group had to be assigned an alternate pro that morning.

Tom, one of the tour's more renowned party animals, had snoozed through his wake-up call that morning and was still under the grip of certain strong refreshments when a tour official frantically phoned his room moments before his assigned tee time. Tom begged off for reasons of "illness." In fact, as he sat there across the table, the road maps in Tom's eyes suggested some lingering effects of the malady were still present.

Just then, Bill Knight, a free-lance photographer out of St. Louis, wobbled in and settled into another chair at the table. The roads in his eyes were interstate highways. They exchanged silly grins, and out rolled the story behind Tom's infirmity. The previous evening, Weiskopf and Knight had ventured all the way across

Orlando to Raffles, a lively watering hole where the clientele was only too happy to take turns buying a famous golfer like Weiskopf and his friend innumerable rounds of drinks. This Southern hospitality continued well past midnight until the bartender became emphatic about closing. With considerable effort, Tom rose, managed to slur a thank-you, turned, and walked directly into a wall. The bartender keenly judged it inadvisable for Tom and Bill to attempt driving back to their hotel, the Marriott-International Drive, some twenty miles back across town.

What happened next provided the central theme for a bit of dialogue between Weiskopf and Knight there at the grill table the next morning that ranks among Bay Hill's all-time lore.

Weiskopf: "How'd we get home last night?"

Knight: "You don't remember the truck?"

Weiskopf: "The truck?"

Knight: "Yeah, the bartender had some friend with a pickup truck bring us back to the Marriott."

Weiskopf, wincing in anticipation: "Front or back?"

Knight: "Back."

Weiskopf's pain increased when advised that for the Bay Hill pro-am, amateurs are allowed to "draft" their pro partners. The guys Tom had stiffed had specifically chosen to play with him. Before we left the table that morning, I accepted an assignment from Tom to fetch a list of his jilted teammates and their phone numbers so he could invite them back to Bay Hill for lunch and a round of golf after the tournament. A couple of days before the Tournament Players Championship two weeks later near Jacksonville, Weiskopf made a special trip back to Orlando to play with his team and regale them with entertaining tour yarns over lunch.

Thus, Weiskopf was hardly the source of Arnie's eruption. Arnie was disappointed that Tom had blown the pro-am but properly appreciative of his make-good.

The second misguided focus resulting from the Arnie-Strange caper targeted erascible pro J. C. Snead. During that era, if there were any incident in which a pro was alleged to be less than charming to a fan or tournament official, Standard Operating Procedure was to assume that J. C. was the culprit. The odds were in your favor. Stories of his brusque treatment of pro-am partners were legion.

So, naturally, the army of investigative reporters fleshing out the cause of the Arnie Letter asked one and all what Jessie Carlyle Snead had done this time. What he had done at Bay Hill, as it turns out, was be a perfect gentleman. He not only had been on his best behavior during both the tournament and the pro-am, he even took a couple of his pro-am partners to the practice tee afterward to help correct flaws in their swings.

But while confirming to reporters that Snead hadn't misbehaved at Bay Hill that year, Arnie made the mistake of acknowledging that, yes, he had heard the story of Snead's most infamous pro-am. Supposedly, J. C. had avoided his amateurs throughout the round at the old Florida Citrus Open across Orlando at Rio Pinar Country Club. Fuming at having paid one thousand dollars to play with such an antisocial pro, one of the amateurs surveyed a birdie putt on the eighteenth green. So the story goes, Snead suddenly realized from the scoreboard that the amateur's birdie would vault the team into first place and mean seven hundred dollars for J. C. as pro of the winning team. Snead became quite the chum, rubbing the guy's shoulder and coaching him on the putt. Mentioning the seven hundred dollars, he allegedly went so far as to call the amateur "partner" for the first time all day.

Affronted by the belated show of affection, the amateur narrowed his eyes to devilish turkey buzzard slits and reviewed the situation. "You mean, if I sink this putt, you'll win seven hundred dollars?" he asked. Snead nodded. The amateur purposely slapped the ball across the green and walked off with a smirk of satisfaction.

Snead insists the incident never happened.

The amateur in point, Orlando auto dealer Dennis McNamara, insists it happened exactly as described.

Whatever the truth, it was perfect fodder for the wave of published tour-behavior stories resulting from Arnie's letter to Beman. For months, in every town the tour visited, Snead suffered through week after week of reading that pro-am story. His wife, Sue, fired off an angry letter to Arnie, charging that his role in reviving the infamous pro-am story had hurt the Sneads financially; J. C. was no longer being invited to play in the lucrative Monday pro-ams between tournaments because of his sullied reputation.

Arnie said he responded to Sue Snead with a letter expressing that he was "not responsible for the actions of your husband."

The real tests of Deke's handiwork have been provided by those occasions when Arnie has faced adversity or criticism from other pros. If you want to know the true character of a man, check him in the bad times, not when he's holding the trophy or being lauded by his peers. As the 1988 U.S. Open approached at The Country Club in Brookline, Massachusetts, Arnie faced one of those tests.

The tournament was being staged on the twenty-fifth anniversary of an Open at Brookline when Arnie was involved in a playoff with Jacky Cupit and eventual winner Julius Boros. In re-creations of that 1963 showdown, Arnie was being painted as the bad guy.

Arnie remembered being plagued throughout the Monday playoff with a stomach virus that made frequent trips to the Port-A-Johns necessary. Boros scoffs at the contention, suggesting that Palmer made up the story to conceal another reason for his playoff loss. "We never heard about the virus until he knocked the ball into a stump. Maybe he was just nervous," said Boros. "Maybe he was just nervous about the playoff."

Boros added another dig by referring to Arnie as "my pigeon."

An extremely proud man, Arnie was irritated when he was told of Boros's remarks. He resisted the temptation to publicly retaliate or defend himself. "I'm not going to say anything bad about him," Arnie said. "He can say anything he wants. All I'm going to say is that he was a very fine gentleman. And he was an exceptional player."

Refusing to respond to Boros's charges, Arnie let logic do the talking. How could he have been unduly nervous in 1963? By then he already had won thirty-two tournaments, including four majors. The main reason he lost, he intoned, was simply because Boros played very well. Also contributing, however, was the stomach virus.

Arnie was later asked why he, one of sport's fiercest competitors, rarely utters an unkind word about an opponent. Surely, the inquisitor suggested, he must harbor a deep inner dislike for one or two of the people he has played against in his career. "My father taught me when I was a boy how to be a gentleman," he replied. "It's a lesson that I have never forgotten. I've always wanted to win as much as anybody who ever played this game. But I never wanted to win so badly that I would hurt somebody else. I never did see how it would help my game to be mean to another player."

Though Deke was the principal architect of the golfer extraordinaire, Arnie's mother, who died in 1979, had a hand in some of

the trim work and extra touches. In a telling piece written in collaboration with golf reporter George White for a 1988 Mother's Day spread in *The Orlando Sentinel*, Arnie offered these thoughts about Doris Palmer . . .

When I was a kid, my mother used to take up for me when my dad was getting on me. She's the one who used to take me around to all the golf tournaments. Dad was working. She drove me all over Philadelphia, Detroit, Pittsburgh, every place I had a tournament.

Winnie likes to say that I got my 'ham' from my mother. And it is true that my mother enjoyed being in the limelight. For example, she loved talking to reporters, and when she and Pap went along for some television appearances in New York, he was happy to remain backstage while Doris wanted to be on camera.

She was always rooting—she never had a negative thought. She was such a positive, upbeat influence, always encouraging me.

My father, on the other hand, was always on my side, but he was tough. He was always, "You didn't do it as well as you should have."

I needed a little of that, no question, but my mother was the warm, caring influence that a child absolutely has to have if he is going to make it. I can't express the importance of having her in my life, of how important she was to everything that I have become.

Important, yes, but there was no question that Deke had had the largest influence on Arnie's life, and two stories underscore just how strong this father-son bond remained years after Deke was gone.

Jimmy O'Neal, then Arnie's best friend and partner in auto dealerships and other ventures, accompanied Arnie to the 1982 British Open at Troon. O'Neal and his wife, Sally, sensed that

Arnie was unusually melancholy during the early part of the week. Their friendship was a jocular one, typically filled with playful put-downs and good times. Even heavyweight business deals were transacted with humor and a light air between Arnie and O'Neal. This week, however, Arnie seemed detached, soberly preoccupied.

"I guess Winnie knew why, but it took most of the week for us to pick up on the reason," O'Neal recalled. "Troon had been the one place that Arnie had won the British Open (1962) when his father had been along with him. That made it special and I suppose all of his fond memories of Deke came rushing back. Walking along the eighteenth fairway, he even pointed out the hotel where his father had stayed. 'Pap's room was that one, right up there."

It was at this 1982 Open when the Troon membership decided to make Arnie an honorary member of the club. An ultra-private reception to bestow that membership was held in the clubhouse on that Friday afternoon, at the end of second-round play, with Winnie and the O'Neals among the very few nonmembers allowed to attend.

When asked to respond, Arnie took the microphone, properly thanked the Troon membership for the rare honor and began reflecting on what it meant to have Deke along for that victory in 1962. As he spoke of his father, Arnie's larynx failed. Overcome with emotion, Arnie croaked an apology as he brushed aside the tears that had begun trickling down his cheeks. He began again, only to be overcome again.

"The silence in that room was overwhelming," O'Neal recalled. "Crying in public was something that was just about unheard of for Arnold." Macho king of the globe Arnold Palmer loses to tear ducts. There was the sense that every person in the room was witnessing history, like being there to watch Washington cross the Delaware.

Larry Guest

Then there was the moment after Arnie's oldest daughter, Peggy, was married to Dr. Doug Reintgen, then a medical intern at Duke University, in June 1978 in ceremonies at the Latrobe Country Club. To help accommodate the grand occasion, a porch had been added to the clubhouse on the side facing the eighteenth green to allow more room for reception guests that afternoon. Still today, members of the club refer to it as "Peggy's Porch."

The famous father of the bride kept it together pretty well during the wedding and through much of the reception. But as the guests started dwindling, he stepped out onto Peggy's Porch to share a drink with a friend. His thoughts turned to his father, who had died two years earlier, and he mentioned how much Peggy, as a small girl, adored Deke. He began tearing over again as the friend mentioned how proud Deacon would have been to attend Peggy's wedding.

Arnie motioned with his drink toward the nearby eighteenth green, where Deke's ashes had been strewn, honoring his living request. "He's right here," Arnie said, his voice cracking. "Pap's right here having a drink with us tonight."

"Pap" will always be with Arnie.

2

The Bull and the Bear

O f all the questions about Arnie, the one that comes up far more often than all the others put together is this: How do Arnie and Jack really get along?

HERE BY A LANDSLIDE are the two leading giants of the game over the last half of this century, whose storied duels during the time they were both at the top of their games were the most passionate in sports.

One generally recognized as the greatest player in the game and the other as the greatest player *for* the game, the Jack and Arnie Show offered a distinct contrast of styles on the course and off. Even after the fifteen or twenty years in which they directly competed for top honors on the course, the two legends continued to duel in the areas of course design and corporate stumping, the difference in styles still apparent.

The public's fascination with Nicklaus the golfer was steeped more in respect and awe, much the same as one marvels at the repeating perfection of a buttonhole machine. His game was the work of the gods, not something you and I could hope to emulate. Jack's persona has always been civil and respectful, but rarely warm. His air of superiority built a small but undeniable bridge between himself and the masses. Express permission seemed required before the commoners could cross. His ventures into course design and construction and on-air work as a commentator or corporate spokesman continued to bear the same elite tinge: courses and products intended only for the privileged.

Arnie has been a hero even the great unwashed could embrace. His slash of a swing was not all that different from the same desperate lurch you and I employ on Saturday mornings in an attempt to avoid yet another bogey. Jack, with his yardage book and painstaking perfection, was the anti-Arnie.

"What do you think of Nicklaus?" Arnie was asked in the early 1960s.

"I think he should play faster," Arnie said.

Arnie's rearing as the son of a greenskeeper and his aura of humility created an open door for a public that quickly learned he was as approachable as an insurance salesman. Even in his competitive afterlife, the courses he has built and the pitches he makes on countless TV commercials connect across all demographic lines.

While Jack earned respect and envy, Arnie captured hearts. Arnie relishes signing autographs; Jack endures it.

Fate and their own talents would cast them as the Macy's and Gimbel's of golf, creating a lifetime of competition between the two that ranged at times from friendly and supportive to petty and bitter.

Noteworthy is that the wives of the two golfing superstars remained above the fray, both in public and private. Winnie Palmer and Barbara Nicklaus, two classy and admirable women in every sense, have remained genuine friends and mutual admirers. They often exchange correspondence and have been known to venture off to have lunch and shop when the men are golfing.

So what's with the guys? Arnie resented Jack for coming along and knocking him off the throne he unquestionably held throughout the '60s. He is jealous that Jack's portfolio of golf courses ranks much higher on most lists of the best and most prestigious in the nation and the world. He is jealous that Jack's Memorial Tournament has become more prestigious and erudite than his own Citrus/Hertz/Nestlé's Bay Hill Invitational. He doesn't understand how Jack could be the consummate family man that Arnie became only as a doting grandfather.

Jack resented that no matter how many major championships he piled up, the public still gave their hearts to Arnie, and Madison Avenue still made Palmer its preeminent pitchman.

How do Arnie and Jack really get along? In public, famously. Both are to be commended for keeping a civil, even friendly face on their duel. In private, they weren't so chummy for a long period of time, stretching from shortly after Nicklaus split from Arnie-dominated International Management Group and its hard-bitten chairman, Mark McCormack, to the very recent times when the years finally mellowed their relationship.

"I think our relationship is good," Arnie said one day in 1993. "We're friends. But we are competitive and we will always be that way. Whatever we do, wherever we are, we will be competing against each other. As the years go by and we become less and less factors in tournament play, whatever else we do we'll still compete. And I think we like that and want it to be that way."

Arnie's view of why Jack broke off from IMG?

"I think it started out as a bit of a thing that he wasn't getting the attention from Mark that he felt he should get. He may have been right. But Mark, on the other hand, if it were presented to him, would have said Jack was getting the attention, but that Mark and I were friends and that we started the whole thing of IMG together. Then, I think in Jack's mind, that grew into more than that. It grew into, 'Well, I want to run my own business, anyway.'"

Typically, McCormack is not as charitable in discussing Jack's departure.

"Jealousy," McCormack said bluntly. "Jack was jealous. If I had not decided to do IMG and had personally decided to represent Arnold, Gary, and Jack and become Colonel Tom Parker, if you will, Jack would never have left. But because we signed [Rod] Laver in '68 and [Jean-Claude] Killy in '69 and Jackie Stewart and we're off and running trying to do what we've done, I had to delegate Jack to somebody else and that didn't work.

"Combine that with the fact that when Jack first came out he was fat and a kid with a golden spoon in his mouth, as opposed to being a son of a greenskeeper and the American dream. Jack was born to a fairly wealthy guy in Columbus, Ohio, and had the best instruction, and then he won too quick. He won the Open in '62 and you're not supposed to win it that fast. It's not that easy. The public didn't accept Jack then. They still loved Arnold. So Jack felt Arnold getting all this adulation and him getting short shrift.

"He could only blame two things for that. One, his appearance, attitude, and upbringing. Or two, he could blame me for favoring Arnold. Choosing the latter was the easier thing to do, so he got somebody else to do it. Of course, everybody else he got he's fired. I forget all their names, but he's had a whole string of people and now he's doing it himself and that's fine. He's certainly the greatest golfer who ever lived. But the reason he left me has nothing to do with anything other than he was resentful of Arnold's successes and resentful of what he perceived to be my favoritism toward Arnold and my personal lack of attention toward him."

There is an oft-told story that Nicklaus' departure was hastened by his request in the early '60s for money out of his IMG

account to build a house. So the story goes, he was shocked to discover he had no money in his account and angrily demanded to know what happened to his winnings.

"That's bullshit. It never happened," McCormack recently snapped, shifting to the offensive. "Arnold's the kind of guy that deals in cash, doesn't believe in mortgages. He used to use the phrase that 'if everything goes wrong, I can dig ditches.' Jack was the leverage king. Borrow this, borrow that. The reason Jack had no money is he spent it all, buying planes and houses and borrowings and all that stuff."

Arnie repeatedly exercised two private rituals infinitely telling of the attitude he held toward Nicklaus until the most recent times.

First was on those ill-fated occasions when a friend or member at one of his various clubs unthinkingly showed up in Arnie's presence wearing a golf shirt with Jack's Golden Bear emblem on the chest. Twisting his rubber face into feigned anger, Arnie playfully but firmly assailed the person and often pinched the Golden Bear emblem—usually along with several layers of skin beneath—and twisted hard. "What'cha doin' wearin' that *pig* on your shirt!?" he'd darkly demand.

Indeed, Jack's logo could be confused more with a porker than a grizzly. At least, it used to. In more recent years, the Golden Bear has curiously developed longer legs, making it look less like a pig. Golden Bear insiders say the logo redesign was ordered when the story of Arnie's demeaning "pig assaults" got back to Jack.

The genesis of the pig comparisons dates back to an early Nicklaus golf course project in Japan. Accompanied by aides Jay Morrish and Bob Cupp, Nicklaus met with a potential Japanese client who innocently pointed to the animal logo on Jack's chest and in broken English said, "Ahhhh, a rittle yerrow pig." It was all Morrish and Cupp could do to keep a straight face and, once out of the client's earshot, Jack blew a fuse. When the Palmer camp heard the story, the logo was forever downgraded to pig status.

Arnie's other ritual is even more telling.

On the road, he typically begins the morning by having breakfast in the hotel coffee shop with friends and associates, gulping down a full pitcher of room-temperature water in the healthful, cleansing practice passed down by his grandfather. After plans for the day are reviewed and the stock quotations are checked, Arnie excuses himself for his morning constitutional.

If the group was confined to particularly close associates, Arnie would announce his departure with a flourish, rattling the morning paper back together as he rose and declared through an impish grin: "Well, time for me to go take my Nicklaus."

There is a select cadre of people who have worked closely with both Jack and Arnie on many ventures and thus are armed with the unique perspective of observing the rivalry as "insiders" of both camps. One of those said he has heard both men use the "go take my Nicklaus/Palmer" crack on separate occasions several years apart. "Except that Arnie seemed to be saying it more in jest" said the man, who asked to remain anonymous because he remains a cog on the Nicklaus team.

The same man said Nicklaus is paranoid about the cadre of lieutenants constantly surrounding Arnie and typically avoids using products or people associated with Arnie. He was there for the first Skins Game at the Nicklaus-designed Desert Highlands when Jack stalked into the temporary clubhouse after taping promos for the telecast with Arnie. "I was around the corner from the front door when Jack walked in and was furious, saying, 'Where did all these goddamned Palmer people come from?' Because Arnold had brought along Ed Seay, Ed Bignon, and Dave Harman, Jack was livid." Seay is Arnie's course design architect, Bignon was then

head of Arnold Palmer Golf Course Management, and Harman was then Arnie's primary course builder.

Privately, Arnie criticizes Jack's courses as unplayable and poorly designed in terms of maintenance costs. Privately, Jack likes to sneer that Arnie doesn't even know he's designing a course in, say, Gulf Shores—doesn't even know where it is. Indeed, Jack is typically more hands-on than Arnie in his course projects; Arnie and Seay typically produce layouts that are more user friendly and easier to maintain than Jack's.

For more than a decade, Jack had dealt almost exclusively with Toro—mowing equipment, irrigation systems, everything that Toro does. Toro had reciprocated by pouring sponsorship money and other resources into various Nicklaus tournaments and projects. Toro even provided materials at cost for Muirfield and Glen Abbey, Jack's prized course creations. However, the very day that Arnie signed an extensive endorsement package with Toro, the edict came out of Golden Bear headquarters that Toro products were off limits. The next day, Nicklaus made agreements with Textron, Jacobsen, and Rainbird to supply products previously acquired from Toro. "Jack even went so far," said a Nicklaus camper, "that one of the golf courses we were building had nine holes of Toro irrigation in the ground. He had them rip it out and replace it. That's how far the paranoia went."

Like Toro, Harman was another victim of the rivalry dumped by Nicklaus in 1980 after he started taking too much work from Arnie. A huge, good-natured man out of a California road-building family, Harman is an independent dirt-mover who has become one of the preeminent course builders. He and his bulldozers move in and shape the land according to the designs of Jack, Arnie, and others. For ten years, Jack was his primary client. But when he began signing on for a series of Palmer courses, Jack discontinued using Harman, though writing a glowing letter of testimony to Harman's work and candidly explaining his "Arnie" reasons for finding another heavy equipment man.

In the dozen years after Jack stopped using him, Harman built some seventy-four courses for Arnie but voices admiration for both. "I understand where Jack's coming from," he says. "I've been close to both of them and I have great respect and fondness for both. I'm closer now to Arnold, but I still feel that Jack is a friend, too."

Harman views the Arnie-Jack rivalry as a three-tiered situation: "First, on the surface, they do what they have to do in public to keep up appearances. Then, in anything that has to do with business, it totally falls apart. On that level, they're at each other's throats, which I think is promoted more by their underlings. But then, on the third level, I have also been in the position to see Jack and Arnold sit down together, one-on-one, and have some laughs, talk over old times, and truly enjoy one another. The business side is what gets in the way."

Most of whatever acrimony remained between Jack and Arnie was mostly dissolved in 1992 when a truce was forged in a classy manner. The first olive branch was offered by Nicklaus, who nourishes a tradition at his annual Memorial Tournament in Ohio of honoring some past giant of the game. At each Memorial, Jack convenes his selection committee to choose the honoree of the next year. Typically, the honoree is a former player. But realizing that a certain obvious candidate will play until a tractor drags him off the course, Nicklaus and his Captain's Club committee voted to name as the 1993 honoree an active competitor: A. Daniel Palmer.

"He's going to play golf until he's eighty-five or ninety. You know that," Jack told his committee. "But if you want to honor him while he can still play, while his fans can enjoy it, there's only one

choice." The committee agreed. Whispers persist that the committee had been wanting to name Arnie for years, waiting impatiently for Jack to reach the same conclusion. Whatever the impetus, the good deed was done.

Jack phoned Arnie in Charlotte, North Carolina, where he was playing in a Senior tour event. A man rarely known to make a snap decision, Arnie at first said he would have to think about it. Then he blurted out: "Oh, hell, I'm going."

When the announcement was made, Nicklaus offered up some comments that scraped away years of rivalry, further disarming his elder foe. "He came along when golf needed a shot in the arm," Jack told Bill Livingston of the *Cleveland Plain-Dealer.* "Arnold did it with a hitch of the pants, a fast walk, and a quick swing. It seemed like he hit it where they [the fans] hit it. But Arnold always got it onto the green with a chance to score.

"I don't think Arnold's position has ever been diminished. I was more accepted as time went on. Arnold will always be Arnold. I was the young upstart who came along. People resented that I was going out to beat the king. As I created my own record, I was accepted as more than the kid that's beating Arnold Palmer."

Arnie was moved by the compliments from his long-running adversary. Sometime later, he sent an inquiry through his people to Jack's people asking if Jack would want him to play in the Memorial in addition to being honored. Jack sent word through his people to Arnie's people that, yes, that would be peachy. Arnie sent back word through his people to Jack's people that he was putting it on his calendar.

A short time thereafter, Jack sent word through his people to Arnie's people wondering if Arnie would like Jack to play in Arnie's tournament at Bay Hill. Terrific, came back the response through the chain of fax machines.

Not long after it was announced that Jack would be playing in the Nestlé Invitational at Bay Hill for the first time in nearly a decade. Arnie said some nice things about Jack. He also said his earlier entry into the Memorial was made with no strings attached. Jack had returned the favor voluntarily and Arnie gave the Bear his due.

At Bay Hill, the pretournament highlight was a charming dual press conference with Jack and Arnie, a nostalgic virtual love-in that was given massive national exposure including a wire photo with the two stars playfully pointing at one another. By Friday afternoon of the tournament, both aging stars were battling the thirty-six-hole cut. Jack missed by a single shot, finishing at six-over-par 150 some thirty minutes ahead of Arnie. When Arnie's approach shot safely reached the green in regulation at the difficult eighteenth, thus obviously preserving his plus-five 149 to survive the weekend cut, he was accorded a stirring, standing ovation from the throng in the bleachers around the closing hole.

As the clatter settled into silence, a single voice boomed what no doubt hundreds were thinking: *"At least you beat Jack!"* A ripple of laughter punctuated the outburst. Jack and Arnie can kiss and hug in staged news conferences all they want, but there are those who will never let the rivalry die.

The natural differences between Arnie and Jack have long been reflected in their disparate approach to the sport. To Jack, golf has been his means to an end; to Arnie, golf is his impassioned universe.

In a pensive moment more than a decade ago in his second floor office above the Bay Hill Club men's locker room, Arnie said of Nicklaus: "Jack is the one guy in the history of golf who has put himself above the game and I am going to tell him that if the proper moment presents itself."

Larry Guest

"I never said that," Arnie contended a few years later. When told he had indeed made that statement, he recanted.

"Well, I'll retract that statement. I don't think it's really appropriate. I might have said that in a moment of distress at a time Jack declined to play at Bay Hill or something like that. I was probably overreacting a little. Whenever I said that, I suppose I've taken a different point of view about how people lead their lives. I suppose the bottom line is Jack Nicklaus has the right to do whatever he wants to do. And it isn't my place to be critical of what he does or how he does it. That has simply become my philosophy of 'live and let live.'"

Nevertheless, the lifetime rivalry on the course and in business boardrooms created friction that frequently bubbled up in the inner circle of each. Just as Arnie snidely poked fun at the Golden Bear logo, Jack has been known to make disparaging private remarks about the age and diminishing size of Arnie's Army.

As Arnie alluded, some of the times he has become most out of sorts with Nicklaus were during the early years of the Bay Hill tournament when Jack routinely declined his invitations despite the fact that Arnie was playing annually in Jack's Memorial Tournament. Jack competed in only one of the first three Bay Hill tournaments and his regrets expressed formally by letter in year two, 1980, sent Arnie into a fine fit of anger.

Jack sent word he would not be playing because one of his sons would be competing in a high school basketball tournament during the week of the Bay Hill event. Jack's admirable devotion to family was no excuse in Arnie's eyes, particularly since the eighteenth green at Bay Hill was only about a forty-five-minute helicopter hop from the basketball tournament. "Well, you can tell Jack I won't be at Memorial this year," Arnie fumed to a PGA official, "because Riley is in a show that week!" Riley is Arnie's household pet, a golden retriever.

When my notepad came out to chronicle Jack's decision to skip Bay Hill, Arnie chose his words a bit more carefully, though his ire was hardly concealed. I began the piece thusly:

Thankfully, Arnold Palmer has never been very good about cloaking his emotions. It's one of his strengths as pro golf's enduring superstar.

In a sport where you're often unsure whether to applaud the winner or check his pulse, Arnie's facial gymnastics played a vital role in his twenty-four-karat charisma. A birdie putt and the expression is unbridled euphoria. A bunkered approach and Arnie's countenance suggests a broken back.

True. Arnie never would break par in a poker tournament.

That marvelous bubble gum face would twist into golden sunshine with every three-of-a-kind contort into an unraked trap with a busted straight. After two bets, Amarillo Slim could recite every card in Arnie's hand plus what he had for breakfast and whether he fudged on his 1958 tax return.

That famous face was busy again yesterday when the advisory arrived from Lost Tree Village that Jack would be skipping Bay Hill next week. Written from jowl to jowl was that Arnie was hurt by Jack's decision. And angry.

His knee-jerk response was a hint that the fans at Jack's Memorial Tournament would not have a Palmer to kick around this year. "He [Nicklaus] doesn't give a crap whether I'm there, anyway!

"And you can quote me on that!" he snorted.

Arnie fell in line with that large group of the day that felt Jack was failing to repay his debts to the game and to Arnie.

He had detailed his thoughts days earlier, apparently anticipating a Nicklaus no-show.

"His life is his decision," Arnie said of Nicklaus. "And only when he looks back on it will he know whether he did what he thought was right or wrong. If I felt my decision was right in my own mind, then I would stick with it and I wouldn't look back. And that's the way I'm gonna leave it."

But Arnie couldn't leave it there. No more than he could shrug off a three-putt or stone face a chip-in. There was too much pride at stake.

The Bay Hill tournament was making a nice move up golf's prestige ladder, destined, Arnie was confident, for a revered spot just behind the recognized majors. But the transplanted Orlando tour stop would attain that lofty status only when all of the very top stars of the game indelibly etched Bay Hill into their annual travel plans. Nicklaus, unquestionably, was among those very top stars at the time. And he was the only significant absentee that year.

Arnie recalled the days when Nicklaus burst onto the tour to challenge his crown. The blubbery kid from Ohio State sought tips on playing the tour and turned to Palmer. He needed help with managing his sudden wealth and marketing his instant fame. Arnie led him to Mark McCormack.

"Whether that lasted is not important," Arnie said of the short-lived Nicklaus-McCormack connection. "The fact is that when he needed help and wanted it, he got it.

"He asked if I minded helping him and giving him some insights into professional golf, and I did. Like what to expect and traveling and so forth. And he wanted Mark to help him, which I consented to—even helped him get after that.

"That's what I would do for anybody, really. It's not an exceptional thing. But at that time, I was sort of leading the whole thing," Arnie added, wrestling with modesty to make the point that he was not exactly a Monday rabbit when he assisted young Nicklaus. "The tour was sort of my, uh . . ."

Modesty finally won and Arnie's voice trailed off into an awkward silence—a respite broken by a kidding jab from the interrogator.

"You mean you're not the king now?"

That plastic mug quickly danced through indignation, injury, and laughter before the answer bubbled out. "It depends on what you're talking about," he grinned. "Not if it's golf.

"I'm the king of marathon now," chortled Arnie, at that time a two-miles-a-day recruit to America's jogging craze.

However, Arnie doesn't remember his helping hand to young Nicklaus reaching quite as far in one area as Jack has suggested. The Jack-Arnie rivalry officially began with the 1962 U.S. Open at Oakmont, when rookie pro Jack beat Arnie in a playoff for his first PGA tour victory. According to Jack, Arnie approached him in the locker room prior to the playoff and offered to split the winner and runner-up checks, no matter which of them won.

"A nice gesture to a young kid, but I thought either he should win or I should win," Nicklaus has been quoted. Jack also "revealed" that he and Arnie split the purse for the inaugural World Series of Golf in 1962. "We approached it as just a TV show," he said.

Arnie said to the best of his recollection, neither story is true. He gives Jack the benefit of the doubt by conceding that he possibly could have said something in jest about splitting the Open purse and Jack took him seriously. "But by the time Jack came on tour, the business of splitting purses had stopped," Arnie insists. "That

took place a couple of years in the '50s. Dow Finsterwald and I used to do that. Going into a tournament, Dow and I would agree to pool whatever we made and split it. It was a way of helping one another out. But that only lasted a couple of years. As for splitting with Nicklaus, I just don't remember that at all."

The matter of Jack and Bay Hill had become an irritation several years earlier. The course was Arnie's pride and passion, and he was anxious to showcase it to the world either by hosting a regular tour stop like the Citrus Open long played across town at Orlando's Rio Pinar Country Club or one of golf's nomadic top shows like the U.S. Open or the budding Tournament Players Championship. Before the TPC became anchored at the Tournament Players Club near PGA tour headquarters in Ponte Vedra, Florida, Commissioner Deane Beman's aspiring "fifth major" was played in Atlanta, Fort Worth, and Fort Lauderdale. Arnie had let it be known he would welcome the event at Bay Hill when the tournament, played in 1976 at Inverrary Country Club in Fort Lauderdale, was looking for a permanent Florida home.

Nicklaus won the TPC that year and, in the press conference afterward, drove a stake through Arnie's heart by curtly ruling out Bay Hill as a potential site.

"The only choices in Florida are Doral and here, or build your own facility," Jack said. "I haven't played Bay Hill in years. It's a good golf course, but I don't think it's that good. . . . I really don't know what it looks like now. I don't remember a hole on it. I do remember the greens are extremely large. I don't think the golf course is geared for tournament play."

Jack might as well have slandered a member of Arnie's own family. Saying you "can't remember a hole" on a golf course is the unkindest cut of all, and Palmer was wounded. He fired back, but with a touch of class.

"I'm a little befuddled as to why he would say those things about Bay Hill," Arnie said in reaction. "He's about to have a tournament at his course in Ohio [Muirfield Village] in a few weeks. I'm sure it is a good golf course, and I hope he has a good tournament. I sincerely mean it.

"But I just don't understand why he would say what he did about our club. Why, he hasn't played here in eleven years."

When Arnie did welcome the Citrus Open's shift to his Bay Hill Club in 1979, Nicklaus played in the inaugural but did little to smooth over the rift with his parting comments.

It was a time when Jack and Arnie appeared friendly enough at a glance. When their paths crossed, they'd shake hands and smile for all to see. They'd even team up in a practice round on occasion.

But the once fierce rivalry that headlined pro golf for more than a decade was still smoldering beneath the surface. And it should not have produced widespread palpitations when Nicklaus again practically gave the back of his hand to Arnie's beloved golf course and new tournament. Jack had just walked away from a closing 78 in the first Bay Hill Citrus Classic when an NBC-TV commentator asked Jack what he thought of the course and tournament.

"It's a good golf tournament," he began. "If Arnold wants to keep working at it to make it a better golf course and better tournament, he can."

The widespread instant reaction was that Nicklaus had relegated to mediocrity a course and tournament that were otherwise drawing rave reviews.

"Jack didn't do himself any good with those comments," Arnie said days later. "I've heard from a lot of people—some of them Jack's own friends—who were upset with what he said.

"It doesn't bother me," Arnie contended, turning palms up. "Jack said it, and I have nothing to do with it. I just appreciate his coming and playing."

After the tournament, Arnie received a letter from Nicklaus that generally reflected the remarks the Golden Bear made on the national telecast. "I'm not always sure what Jack is thinking," said Arnie. "I'm not sure what he means sometimes. Maybe that's just Jack's way."

If it is not "Jack's way" to trot out unqualified praise for Orlando's refurbished tour stop, Nicklaus found himself pretty much alone. Despite an early public relations blunder regarding the sale of single-day tickets, the first Bay Hill Citrus Classic ultimately drew enthusiastic applause. Arnie reported receiving "tons" of complimentary mail from competitors and got encouraging feedback from locals.

From the hindsight perspective of a fortnight, Palmer happily admitted he could find little fault with the way the $250,000 tournament came off. He discussed some minor improvements, he regaled in the community involvement, he underscored the prestigious field, and he finally slipped in a strategic dig when mentioning a few possible course alterations to help players and spectators.

"We'd like to add a few spectator mounds, and we might cover over the ditch that crosses the eighth fairway, the one Nicklaus hit two shots in," Arnie noted with a leer.

So the bad seeds already had been sown when, in 1980 and 1981, Nicklaus chose not to lend his presence to the second and third editions of Arnie's Bay Hill tournament, entering instead the Doral and Inverrary tour stops closer to his South Florida home managed by Jack's close friend and business associate, John Montgomery.

The move inspired a haughty but well-placed jab from Alastair Johnston, Arnie's business manager. "I can understand why he would choose to play Inverrary and Doral. Those tournaments need some help, and they are in his back yard," said Johnston. Touché.

Jack's snub of Bay Hill also brought a round of criticism from other prominent pros, among them Gary Player. Gary delivered a personal admonishment to Nicklaus, then took his displeasure public when a reporter asked the globe-hopping South African if he planned to play in Jack's Memorial tournament later that spring.

"Yes," said Player. "I think the players should support one another's tournaments. I think Arnie should play in Jack's tournament and Jack should have played in Arnie's tournament."

Arnie took the advice. He played the Memorial that year, an obvious exercise in one-upmanship.

But his true revenge would be extracted in a sweeter form a month before he reached the Memorial. At the Masters that spring, Arnie and Nicklaus survived the thirty-six-hole cut but found themselves at the bottom of the field following Saturday's third round. Nicklaus completed the first three rounds at 218, Arnie at 219. Though the two aging adversaries hopelessly trailed the leader and eventual champion Seve Ballesteros (203), a nostalgic and compelling undercard was created for Sunday's final round when Arnie and Jack fell together in the pairings.

Arnie's zeal for the rare face-off with his longtime arch rival was apparent from the moment he learned of the happenstance pairing that Saturday night. Dinner at the Palmers's rented home in Augusta had included agent McCormack, Player, and a few close

friends. As after-dinner drinks were served, Winnie phoned the club for Arnie's Sunday tee time.

She literally danced back into the dining room, eyes sparkling, and made a sing-song announcement: "You're at 11:32 . . . with guess who!"

Arnie at first shrugged quizzically, but McCormack caught on instantly. "Jack Nicklaus!" the agent half-shouted, and Winnie confirmed with a grinning nod.

Player rattled the room with a robust burst of laughter.

Arnie's jowls widened into a soft smile, his eyes narrowing in determination. He swiped the air with his fist and declared: "I'll whip his ass!"

He repeated the vow early Sunday morning when Masters pairings cochairman Montgomery "Gummy" Harrison intercepted Arnie to assure that the much anticipated coupling had not been contrived. "That's fine, Gummy," Palmer comforted. "I'm just gonna beat him."

And he did. One more time, with feeling.

That morning, Augusta National officials should have erected a marquee on Magnolia Lane advertising the day's first act as "The Bull & Bear Show."

It was the first time Arnie and Jack had been paired together at Augusta since 1975. It was the first time they had gone head to-head in the final round of any tournament since way back in the 1973 Bob Hope Desert Classic when Arnie last won on the regular tour.

As it turned out, Nicklaus vs. Palmer was no closer than the day's main act, Ballesteros vs. The Field. But Arnie's decisive 69-73 victory in this little renewal of yesteryear was no less cherished by the thousands who scrambled to the course early, ignoring ominous skies, to form easily the largest gallery of the day. It was just like old times, only three hours earlier.

Unlike another era when Jack and Arnie often teed off after Sunday lunch and dueled for yet another tournament title, their meeting this time was a midmorning match with not much more on the table than nineteenth place in this green-swathed annual spring rites of golf. They didn't even have a little side Nassau bet going, Arnie once again insisting he has never had a personal side bet working during a tournament round.

"We were playing for much more than money," he beamed an hour after the match.

The man younger pros affectionately refer to as "The Bull" was playing for pride. The competition between him and Nicklaus was well-documented; their keen personal rivalry was thinly veiled in the weeks after Jack's no-show at Bay Hill. After Arnie seized command with birdies at two and three, he was obviously enjoying the dream pairing as the monstrous gallery thundering through the Augusta National shrubbery pulled for their respective man in this clash of titans.

As Jack and Arnie left the ninth tee, reigning three-time Player of the Year Tom Watson stood in the adjacent first fairway, nodding and smiling at the awesome merger of Arnie's Army and Jack's Pack. With only a modest gallery following Tom and Hubert Green, one could imagine Watson asking: "If I'm the new king of golf, why are all those people over there with those two old guys?"

"Both Jack and I were proud to see that many people," Arnie would say later. "It's a tribute to the game and to the fact that we've both played a long time and accumulated so many friends along the way. I feel a great deal of gratitude for that and for the game."

Arnie, giving up ten years and huge chunks of yardage, captured this nostalgic little mini-tournament in the Arnie style of old,

Larry Guest

scrambling for par from deep trouble in the woods, slashing out of traps to save par, and ramming home long putts just when it appeared the enemy was about to overtake the fort.

"This is like the '60s," gushed a veteran scribe, "when it seemed Arnie could get it up and down in two from the deck of a sinking ship."

He was, indeed, a man inspired. "Arnie plays good," Winnie would gush afterward, "when he's got something like this to light his fire." Only once in his prior eighteen Masters rounds had Arnie broken 70.

When the two international fairway celebrities were ushered to the press building and perched side-by-side on the interview stand, Nicklaus attempted to low-key the day's confrontation. "It's difficult for anyone to get pumped up when you're twenty shots behind," said the slump-ridden Nicklaus.

Arnie, who also won the press conference, was having none of it.

"I had a little more incentive to play a little better today," he declared.

Asked to elaborate, he fixed that famous puss into a coy smile and said: "I don't think I have to elaborate."

Minutes later, he did anyway.

"I don't think we've ever played together that we weren't playing each other a little bit. Whether we were playing for the National Open—or last place in the Masters."

Then he zinged his fallen foe with one of several well-placed needles. "And I think it will always be that way," he added wryly, "at least until Jack gets too old."

A hundred reporters howled and Nicklaus smiled in good sport.

▼

Over the next decade, Arnie and Jack shared only a handful of rounds. There has been the occasional practice round, like at Bellerive in St. Louis two days before at the 1992 PGA when, as Arnie put it, "We met in the parking lot, and neither one of us had a game. So we just went out together." Some five thousand fans happily plodded along, forming the largest gallery of the day.

Occasionally, officials have rigged Jack and Arnie in the same pairings during tournaments, though Jack seemed to resent that. Such a pairing was contrived for the first two rounds of the 1987 PGA Championship at Palm Beach Gardens, with Tom Watson thrown in to sweeten the pot.

Arnie, Jack, and Tom, 8:51, No. 1 tee. It was a grouping of the gods, a threesome thrown together by the PGA Championship for the benefit of history and ticket sales.

Indeed, the ploy moved a few daily admissions, but history wilted in southern Florida's August heat. It became tangled in the dense rough bordering the Champions Course at PGA National. It was frittered away on the blight-stricken greens.

Never in their long and illustrious careers had these three giants of the game been amassed as a threesome in tournament competition. The historians were atwitter at what was expected to be a sweet occasion suitable for framing. It was, however, a day more for survival than history.

Watson carved a courageous 70 after recovering from a shaky start. Arnie and Jack staggered to disappointing 76s, and the entire exercise was thwarted by steamy conditions that limited the gallery and left players soaked in perspiration. The weather bureau's numbers—93 degrees and 66 percent humidity—hardly reflected the sultry discomfort in the midmorning still.

When finished, Tom and Arnie wanted to talk more about heat than history. Nicklaus didn't want to talk at all.

Sensing the moment, the media asked tournament officials to convene all three into the interview room after the round. Nicklaus slam-dunked the request and even attempted to avoid reporters waiting in the locker room by using an alternate exit.

When scribes caught up with him at his car, Nicklaus down-played the historic pairing. "I've played a lot with them," he said irritably. "I didn't feel very good about it. I feel like getting in my car, going home, and cooling off. It's a hot day."

With that, Nicklaus disappeared up the club's driveway and headed for his Lost Tree Village home eight miles away.

Watson seemed most aware of the significance of the grouping, maybe even affected by it at the outset. "It was fun. It was unique. It was a different feeling at the first tee," said Watson, who promptly bogeyed the first two holes.

Watson's weather report: "It was 140 degrees out there. The heat got to me today more than any other round I can remember. By the eleventh or twelfth hole, I felt rubbery out there."

Arnie sweats profusely even in moderate warmth. It's partial-ly because of a family tradition. As a lad, he often had breakfast with his paternal grandparents who began each day by downing large quantities of water. For all these years, Arnie routinely has gulped four large glasses of water with breakfast. On this day, all that *agua* was coming out in torrents.

On the front nine, he went through six golf gloves trying to maintain a dry grip. He avoided touching his cream slacks, which were wet with perspiration "all the way to the cuffs. In my fifty-seven years, I've never been this wet. Even my socks were soaked."

So was his Bay Hill visor. Standing over a four-foot par putt on the eighth green, Arnie actually tried to time his stroke between the drops of sweat falling from the bill of the visor. A drop fell right on the ball just as he began the stroke. He flinched, and the ball lipped the cup. He stepped back and laughed.

Walking to the next tee, he caught the attention of Ed Seay, president and principal architect of Arnold Palmer Golf Course Design Company, and requested two aids: sugarless gum ("My mouth is like cotton") and sweatbands.

Arnie would wear the wristlets on the back nine for the first time in his career only as a result of Seay's resourcefulness. Seay scurried to the PGA National pro shop where he was advised the vast inventory did not include sweatbands.

Undaunted, Seay was struck with an idea. He hustled off to the tennis pro shop, only to discover that it was closed during the tournament. Through the glass, however, he could see a secretary seated in an adjacent office and began tapping on the door.

"We're closed!" she shouted.

"It's an emergency!" Seay shouted back. The secretary came to the door.

"I need to buy two sweatbands. They're not for me. They're for Arnold Palmer."

The secretary rolled her eyes skeptically but took Seay's $6.80 in exchange for a pair of sweatbands. "I'm only doing this," she said, "because your story is so original."

A footnote: Two months after the tournament, addressing the Downtown Athletic Club of Orlando, Arnie, who'd just turned fifty-eight, recounted that steamy day and playfully expressed empathy for Jack, then forty-seven. In the news was Jack's same aging hurdles—blurred vision, putting yips, back trouble, etc.—that Arnie already had experienced. Quipped Arnie: "You know you're getting old when the names in your little black book all have 'M.D.' at the end of them."

There was a time when Jack and Arnie were genuine friends, often traveling together and even sharing a hotel suite on occasion.

One of those occasions was the filming of the old "Big Three" TV series in the '60s at Royal Montreal Golf Club in Canada. Jack, Arnie, and Gary Player were assigned a three-bedroom suite for the two-day shoot. "They weren't using video then. They were using film," Arnie recalls. "They moved the cameras with every shot. It usually took one full day to do nine holes. We stayed together all the time when we were shooting one of those matches, in Hawaii, Scotland, or wherever."

On the final night of their stay, the three famous golfers ordered room service to their posh suite. Arnie was on the phone checking in with Winnie when the food arrived. One of the others spilled a drink on Arnie and from there, the particulars become hazy.

"I took a bottle of something—probably ginger ale or beer— and shook it up and squirted Gary and Jack. Then the whole thing went crazy," Arnie said, breaking into laughter.

Instantly, a full-scale food fight broke out, the three grand exalted giants of golf hurling whipped cream and baked potatoes at one another like mischievous lads at summer camp. Alternately, they ducked behind furniture and hurdled beds to avoid flying food, then returned fire until all three collapsed in laughter.

"The room was a mess," Arnie said, obviously still greatly amused at the recollection. "It was crazy. We got a bill for demolishing the suite. That was funny. Gary brought that up just the other day. We had to pay for new drapes. Actually, IMG paid for it. We sent the bill to them. There was always something going on. There were other pranks, some not printable. Something happened at St. Andrews when the 'Big Three' was filmed there, but I can't remember what it was.

"I just know we ended up the series tied—all three of us for the whole series on total score. So then we went to Puerto Rico, Dorado Beach, to play it off. And I won, but only after that tied too. After eighteen, Jack and I were tied, so we played it off in sudden death. And Jack duck-hooked it on the first hole, and I won. They ought to show that series again."

Royalties on today's scale would eclipse the original fee Arnie, Jack, and Gary commanded for filming the "Big Three" shows. "In those days it was quite a bit. But by today's standard, it was nothing. It was something like ten thousand dollars a show, as I recall."

Player often tells the story of the Montreal food fight as an insight to the relationship Jack and Arnie enjoyed in those earlier years. "The food fight was silly and uncalled for," Gary muses sheepishly. "But it shows how famously we all got along in those days, even Jack and Arnold. Too bad it didn't last between those two."

3

The Big Five-Oh

Orlandoan or Latrobean?

While central Floridians like to claim Arnie as their own, the heartbeat of the Palmer empire remains at the end of a private drive just across from the Latrobe Country Club. Three homes— Arnie's and those of two high school chums—flank the little winding drive that climbs a gentle, wooded hill overlooking the golf course and dead ends at the door of Arnie's office.

THE QUAINT STRUCTURE could be mistaken for a fourth home on the little street. But once through the white screen door, there is a tidy configuration of cozy offices for Arnie, two secretaries, "Man Friday" Donald W. "Doc" Giffin, and Arnie's copilot. A short hallway leads into a spacious golf workshop where hundreds of clubs, bags, shoes, and gloves are clustered in barrels and stacked against walls, workbenches, and machinery.

The double doors to Arnie's personal office are almost always open, giving an instant view of this international celebrity and making one privy to his nonstop telephone conversations.

A slight hearing deficiency pushes Arnie to a volume several decibels above the norm and his resonant basso profundo reverberates throughout the small building.

". . . and one of these days," he boomed into the receiver on one milestone morning, "I'm gonna learn how to play golf again and make a comeback."

On the other end of the line was a man in Dallas, one of a long list of friends and admirers who called on this particular day and well into this particular night to extend best wishes to Arnie on the occasion of his fiftieth birthday.

For Arnie, September 10, 1979, marked a bittersweet milestone. Birthdays are just as special to Arnie as the rest of us, but his macho molecules were refusing to submit to the fact he had just become, by official golf standards, a senior citizen.

"Fifty!!??" he rebuked one caller, playfully feigning indignation. "There's no way I can be that old. Actually, I'm just thirty today. Somebody must have made a mistake." He laughed heartily. Doc, secretaries Carole Constantine and Carole Higgins, and an intruding columnist echoed a chorus of chuckles.

Arnie sat behind his memorabilia-laden desk looking something like a Christmas present. The casual green corduroy slacks and red pullover contrasted in Yule colors against his thinning locks that are almost white now. No small child ever enjoyed a birthday more than Arnie on his half-century mark. He laughed and joked with the staff and battered lightheartedly with callers and chased away the few quiet moments with a bar or two of whatever song came to mind. Once it was a shaggy-dog joke punchline set to

Tony Bennett's signature ballad: "I left my haaaaarp," Arnie warbled, "in Sam Frank's Discoooooooo . . ."

His day had begun and ended like all days when he was in Latrobe during this time in his life. The sun was barely peeking over Chestnut Ridge when Arnie took his then-usual two-mile jog through the golf course's early morning mist. He panted back through the door in time to complete the ritual by watching Arthur Smith pick his banjo from Charlotte—Arnie's favorite TV show at the time.

"I was born at 5:30 on a Tuesday morning and I'm still getting started about that time every day," he mused.

Fourteen hours later, he would be commanding the bar in his comfortable basement den where some combination of neighbors, friends, and employees assemble nightly when Arnie is in town.

The festivities had moved outside onto the driveway two nights earlier for a not-too-surprise, western-style birthday party, complete with a hay wagon ride for the fifty guests. What did surprise Arnie was the appearance of Arthur Smith, who had been flown in by Winnie Palmer to perform. Smith, as much a fan of Arnie's as vice versa, refused Winnie's offer of pay. She had considered Glen Campbell, but "that would have meant an orchestra to back him up and I wanted to keep the whole thing as low-key as possible."

It was as low-key as any other party where half the guest list is fetched from around the country by executive jet.

The invitees were restricted to a few International Management Group associates and Arnie's closest friends. The latter includes ageless harness driver-trainer Del Miller, sixteen years Arnie's elder, who tried to comfort his aging golf pal and trotter partner. "One consolation," grinned the dwarfish Miller, "is that the years after fifty don't go as fast as the ones leading up to fifty."

When a photographer for the Latrobe newspaper posed him over a configuration of golf balls forming the number fifty, Arnie snorted: "Christ! You'd think fifty is ancient or something!"

A well-wishing telegram from Pennsylvania Governor Richard Thornburgh began: "As your age creeps closer to par . . ."

"*Par??!!*" Arnie protested with a scowl, "Par is 72. Hell, I'm a long way from that!"

He told one long distance well-wisher he felt "better than I did when I was forty and probably better than I did when I was thirty. But that's as far as I can go," he added with a laugh. "I can't remember what I felt like when I was twenty."

That evening in his basement den, he managed to relocate his fountain of youth.

"I don't feel fifty now," he told one caller after a couple of boilermakers, "and I'm feeling younger with each drink."

Arnie's birthday was darkened by only two circumstances — one serious, one frivolous. His seventy-one-year-old mother was hospitalized, although the nightly report from Dr. Tom Moran, one of the neighbors, was more encouraging than it had been.

The other thorn was that his country club was closed to play that day, as it is every Monday.

Arnold D. Palmer, intergalactic hero, multimillionaire, and all-around swell guy, was celebrating his fiftieth birthday on a delightful late-September day in western Pennsylvania and was itching to play golf. Although it most certainly would have been overlooked, the club owner took no special liberties.

Perhaps it was a leftover vestige from his late father, Deke, once the club's revered groundskeeper who taught his son that whatever applies to the members doubly applies to the pro and his family.

By midafternoon, Joe Tito, Rolling Rock brewery executive and lifetime pal, perched on a stool in the workshop while Arnie fiddled with golf clubs and took more telephone calls. The long spiral cord from the wall-mounted phone tracked Arnie's movements from the vise to the saw and back to the workbench as he tinkered with a driver while conversing and battling a heavy decision.

Arnie wanted to go find a place to hit a few balls. Tito, a dapper little man, who at the time drove a white Corvette with white fur upholstery, preferred to steer Arnie to the Rolling Rock tap in the Palmer basement. The tap won.

Much of the remainder of the afternoon and evening — between more calls — was spent futilely trying to teach a sportswriter how to operate the sensitive tap in such a manner that a glass contained more than one inch of Rolling Rock liquid and less than six inches of Rolling Rock foam.

Lee Trevino called from the head table at his Pittsburgh induction into the American Golf Hall of Fame on a speakerphone hookup that allowed the banquet to eavesdrop. "Lee, do you have your papers to be in this country?" Palmer jabbed.

"Arnie," the Mex jabbed back, "I met a lady today who said she was using Lee Trevino clubs and was still scoring bad. I told her she must be using Arnold Palmer golf balls." The banquet audience could be heard howling in the background.

"Listen, the way you guys are playing, I may come back on the tour," retorted Arnie.

Bob Hope called from Chicago.

But no word from the Jimmy Carter White House.

"Wrong administration," said the golfing partner of four Republican presidents.

For the host and birthday honoree, the delightful day came to an end with the fourth quarter of the Falcons-Eagles Monday

Night Football Game flickering on his new two thousand dollar, forty-eight-inch TV—a birthday gift from Winnie.

What he had really wanted, he said, was a helicopter. So Joe Tito gave him one: six inches long and plastic.

The evening was afflicted with only one serious moment.

Somewhere around the fourth boilermaker—"shots-and-beer" to residents of this steel mill town—I asked Arnie for his birthday wish.

The man so gentle in nature and rugged in build rocked back from the bar. His much photographed mug was a study in reflection. "My wish," he said, pausing to assemble the right words, "would be for another fifty just like the last fifty. I like competition and people, and I've been lucky enough to have plenty of both."

In golfing terms, Arnie's birthday qualified him to play in seniors events—a door that held little attraction for Arnie at the time. The budding PGA Senior tour was for old guys, and Arnie was not ready to accept geriatric status for himself—even though he hadn't won on the regular tour since he was forty-three.

Days earlier, he rejected his first opportunity to compete in the PGA Seniors Championship, mailing his regrets. He stiff-armed promoters offering him "a really significant amount of money" to be commissioner and main gate attraction for a proposed satellite tour of top-name senior pros.

Asked which entry he would make if given the opportunity to play in a regular tour event or a seniors tournament of equal prize money, Palmer vowed without hesitation he would tackle the tougher challenge of the "junior" tour. "That's what I'm more interested in. I enjoy that more," he explained on his fiftieth birthday. "I'm not ready to play seniors' tournaments."

For more than a year, he didn't. Except for an appearance at the unofficial World Seniors Invitational in Charlotte, North

Larry Guest

Carolina, Arnie passed on all fifty-and-over events for the first fifteen months after he became a senior. Insiders suspect part of his motivation was fear of what might not happen.

Winless since 1973, it was all Arnie could do at that stage of his life to convince himself he could still be competitive on the regular tour. Imagine the cold slap it would have been for him to begin playing often on the Senior tour and discover that he couldn't whip the old guys, either.

So it was with more than a little trepidation and adventure that he finally entered an official Senior tour event the first week of December 1980. There was a pulsing mix of joy and relief in the cabin of his plane after Arnie won that 1980 PGA Seniors Championship at Turnberry Isle Country Club near Miami.

The champagne stopper popped with a bang into the headliner of N1AP as it climbed through thirty thousand feet, startling the famous pilot. Within moments, the eight passengers were hoisting monogrammed glasses in a bubbly salute to the man flying the Orlando-bound executive jet. From his command seat, Arnie grinned over his shoulder, acknowledging the toast.

"Cheers!" laughed the revived King, accepting the congratulations with a hearty thumbs-up response.

An hour earlier, he had been bathed in the warm applause of some five thousand worshippers on the eighteenth green at Turnberry, when Arnie won his first United States golf event of any significance in nearly eight years.

It had been so long, his closest friends had forgotten the celebration ritual. "We used to have these parties all the time after Arnie had won a tournament," said Latrobe insurance man and Palmer pal Danny Bonar. "We'd present him with something from Joe Tito, owner of Rolling Rock brewery.

"It was some damn thing," Bonar said, adding with a chuckle: "But it's been so long, I can't remember what it was."

The 1980 PGA Seniors Championship was not exactly the Masters or the U.S. Open. It wasn't even the Danny Thomas Memphis Open. And the events of the day had offered only brief flashbacks to those gilded days when Arnie had kicked down the door of various final rounds, claiming trophies like a baron recovering his rightful jewels.

Arnie sort of slipped up to the back door and loaded this one through the tailgate. He won in large part because everyone else in contention fell over and clutched a lily to their chests. Arnie and silver-haired Paul Harney struggled over the closing holes, falling into a playoff against one another for the first time in seventeen years. They had similarly gone overtime in the 1963 Westchester Open, Arnie winning on the first playoff hole. Just as he would this time.

The difference, however, was that this time, Harney, away from competitive golf and its Sunday pressures for more than a decade, wobbled through the final five holes three-over-par. And Arnie "charged" to victory with a final-round 75, sliding in a five-foot birdie on the first playoff hole after missing one of the same length on the final hole of regulation.

At the awards ceremonies, Arnie's excitement was tempered by the knowledge that his putter had kept Harney and other contenders in the game. "I'm very happy to have won. I've finally won a PGA Championship, even if it is the seniors' championship," he laughed, alluding to the fact that the "regular" PGA Championship is the only one of golf's four majors not among his sixty-one regular tour victories. "But I'm disappointed without doubt about my short game, which all week was not up to the standards I want it to be. I lost ten to twenty shots around the green this week." He missed eight putts of ten feet or shorter in the final round alone.

But if this long-awaited American victory was something less than nectar for those lifetime members of Arnie's Army, it was not apparent on the beaming faces of the South Florida faithful on this December Sunday afternoon. Or on Arnie's, either.

There had been a couple of 1975 victories across the Atlantic in some Spanish crapshoot and an English tournament filled mostly with guys who sell Vardon grips and molded golf balls most weeks of the year. And there was that drought-buster in Edmonton, Canada, the previous summer when Arnie only had to whip Isao Aoki, Gary Player, and a bunch of Canadian club pros in the hundred thousand-dollar Canadian PGA.

That one also had come with some missteps at the finish. A three-shot lead over Aoki had dwindled to just one when Arnie suffered a three-putt, double-bogey six on the next-to-last hole. "I almost dropped dead out there," Arnie would say later. "I was trying to gather myself up and remember what to do. It had been so long, I forgot how to act."

Walking to the eighteenth, a tight, 410-yard par-four at Edmonton's Mayfair Country Club, Arnie recalled an early-week game plan. "I remembered thinking that if I ever got to that hole with a one-shot lead, I would play it safe with a 2-iron off the tee," he said. But the trademark go-for-broke Palmer persona just wouldn't allow that, even at a juncture in his life when he might have swapped all the shots-and-beers in western Pennsylvania for just one more victory.

"I just couldn't do it," he recalled. "I wasn't going to be chickenshit. That's just not the way I play. I had to do it my way."

Arnie's way has always been to go for the gusto. And any golf pro who went for anything less irritated him. Some months earlier,

Arnie had stomped around his garage/workshop reeling in disgust at the words of a young tour player who intoned he was satisfied to make the cut, knowing he would collect a decent check.

"Can you imagine that?" Arnie snorted. "I mean that is really unbelievable. It's like doing something that doesn't excite you. Asked for his wish, one of these guys told somebody, 'I just want to make the cut every week.' You've gotta be kidding me. I'd rather win one tournament in my life than make the cut every week. I'd rather be able to say I've won a golf tournament, but I haven't made the cut the rest of the time. When you get old and you can't win and you're just out here, then that's something else. You might say, 'Hey, just let me make the cut.' But when you're young and charging, winning is the name of the game."

So there on the eighteenth tee at Edmonton, Arnie drew back and blasted a driver straight down the heart of the fairway, leaving easy work of the par he needed to secure the trophy.

But until a blustery Sunday afternoon four months later on a Miami playground for overprivileged adults, Arnold Palmer had not won under the Stars and Stripes since the 1973 Bob Hope Desert Classic. The little off-Broadway Canadian event had been welcome balm for the frustrated old trouper; the triumph in the PGA Seniors that December against an array of household names was news.

Spectators and tournament officials and the lean, graying guy himself were popping buttons all over the place. The PGA Senior, only the second tournament for seniors that Arnie had entered since his fiftieth birthday fifteen months earlier, became an event because of his mere presence. Making a return engagement at Turnberry, the tournament attracted galleries smaller than the typical tour event, but more than twice the size of a year earlier when Arnie had passed on his first chance to play with the old guys.

His name at the top of the leaderboard for the final three rounds meant the tournament was played on page one of the nation's sports pages rather than relegated to a few lines of small print as it had been when Don January ran away with the title the previous year. Spectators were so few in number then, only the tees and greens were roped off. Tournament officials quickly realized that would be insufficient when Arnie's exuberant Army overran the place during the opening round. Overnight, ropes were added to most fairways and the marshal force was doubled.

A PGA official even confided that a tape-delay telecast of the final round on ESPN was made possible only after the network was assured of Arnie's entry in the tournament.

All of those in the Palmer inner circle sensed what was coming when Arnie surged into the second-round lead with the low round of the day, a windswept three-under-par 69. When N1AP was dispatched that Sunday morning to fetch Winnie and the wives of Arnie's Orlando pals who had joined him for the Miami event, the plane had been stocked with wine and champagne.

Winnie refused to open the bubbly. "I'm too superstitious," she laughed.

There would be a proper time for the uncorking on Sunday evening, no matter what the altitude.

Still to unfold would be yet another even more touching champagne salute to the winner hours after the little jet had landed in Orlando. That evening, an electric silence would settle over the dining room at Arnie's Bay Hill Club as longtime pal and tour colleague Dow Finsterwald proposed a toast.

Arnie, friends, and all who happened to be in the dining room that evening were provided a glass of bubbly by Finsterwald, who revived the words of a famous athlete. "Fame is but a vapor," Finsty quoted, "popularity may be an accident, and money has wings. But the one thing that endures is character.

"Arnie, my friend," Finsterwald said, dramatically raising his glass along with everyone in the room, "You're a champion and your character will always endure."

Little by little, Arnie came to accept his status as a senior tour pro, slowly increasing his playing schedule with the fifty-and-over set, enjoying some tasty success that included winning the 1981 U.S. Senior Open. Still, he refused to give up his link with the regular tour, making regular appearances with the younger pros in the belief there was still that magical week somewhere out there where he could again string together four golden rounds and beat the kids.

It was May 1981, and Arnie was making his seventh appearance of the year on the regular tour at the Houston Open. I was along for the ride on an assignment from *Golf* magazine to pinch-hit as Arnie's caddy and write from that privileged, pointblank perspective about this great man at his own golfing crossroads. It was a lifting, though not completely pretty experience to watch Arnie endure not only his eroding skills but the insensitive critics beyond the ropes who were sneering at his dream.

His Houston Open third round already had been soiled by five bogeys when Arnie approached The Woodlands' seventeenth green. A poor 2-iron approach into heavy rough blanketed the largely adoring gallery with a melancholy pall—ideal acoustics for a swarthy little man with an oil-black moustache and foghorn voice.

"Give it up, Palmer!" the man shouted. "You're gettin' too old, just like me!"

The gallery gasped, shock and embarrassment turning to white hot disdain. Five hundred pairs of eyes narrowed to ominous pencil strokes and shot lasers at the disrespectful fan. On the collar of the green, playing partner Craig Stadler, his bushy eyebrows

forming an angry V, edged closer to Palmer's caddie and growled a wish that Arnie take out his sand wedge and use it on the offending loudmouth. Behind the ropes, a distraught Missy Alford, a member and resident at The Woodlands, scurried about trying to obtain the name of the dastardly little man.

In a sport where hecklers are considered in the same general social strata with child molesters, the crime becomes doubly offensive when the target is that beloved, pants-hitching motor oil salesman from Latrobe, Pennsylvania.

Graphic evidence of Arnie's enduring, ageless appeal could be collected from assorted venues that year.

It was boisterous and beaming from behind the gallery ropes of the Senior Open in July, when more than forty-three thousand spectators frolicked about Oakland Hills near Detroit as Arnie won the tournament that had drawn just four thousand a year earlier without him in the field.

It was tender and moving on the eve of the Houston tournament when Missy and Larry Alford's seven-year-old son gave thanks at an informal dinner in his home with Arnie among those with bowed heads around the table. "Thank you, Lord, for this food and for our guests," Larry Jr. began, speaking extemporaneously as his parents had taught. "Thank you for Arnold Palmer, the greatest golfer in the world. Amen."

(Ten years later, Larry Alford Jr., who grew up to be a national-class junior golfer, lost an arm in an automobile accident. Within months, he launched a remarkable competitive comeback with the help of a special prosthesis and words of inspiration and encouragement from Arnie.)

Arnie's eyes blinked open at the end of the boy's blessing and a soft smile spread across that famous countenance. The seven year-old's candor was perhaps the most touching, but just one of the countless indications at Houston that the love affair between Arnie and his Army was passionate as ever.

That was the conclusion I reached while straining at the weight of Arnie's sixty-three-pound bag during the Houston Open. The neophyte caddie was a weeklong journalistic intruder that Arnie had agreed to tolerate. The assignment was to observe this legend-in-crisis from the proximity of the guy carrying his bag.

The competitive flame within Arnie was still crackling sharply at age fifty-one, and his ability to perform under the most suffocating pressure had not totally dissipated. He would prove that at Oakland Hills two months later, but first against the flatbellies at Houston, where he birdied two of the final three holes of the second round, knowing nothing short of that would survive the cut. "That was just as hard," Arnie conceded, "as winning the tournament."

If he could somehow arrest the disturbing fluctuations in his confidence and concentration, he reasoned, the notion of another regular tour victory was not the pipe dream widely embraced. But even in the process of winning the Senior Open, Arnie's self-esteem would take a roller-coaster ride. Down after a second round 76 that had him talking of withdrawing from the following week's British Open. Up again after a solid 68 on the demanding Oakland Hills layout. Down after bogeying two of the last three holes to force the tournament into an eighteen-hole playoff. And, finally, up again after charging from six shots down to win the playoff.

The Houston heckler's dark pronouncement merely reflected the hushed whispers of many. Give it up, Arnie, they silently implored. Enjoy your jet and the seniors and surface on the regular tour only for cameos at the Masters and Bay Hill and maybe another spot or two to bathe in the nostalgic applause you so richly deserve.

Larry Guest

Palmer devotees, bolstered by an occasional round in the 60s, remained blindly confident that the slashing swing and dogged resolve would produce one more champagne toast for old times' sake.

But Arnie himself offered a startling and unprecedented hint at surrender during the Houston event. For the archives, it came at 7:04 A.M., May 1, 1981, in the coffee shop of the Woodlands Inn, in the company of his investigative caddie, players Dave Stockton and Bob Murphy, and scrambled eggs. "I may be about to hang it up except for a very, very few tournaments," he blurted suddenly. Stockton and Murphy very nearly dropped their muffins; the caddie reached for a small notepad to record the time and place of this significant juncture in golfing history.

Later, Arnie would say his words were steeped in the agony of the moment: His two-over-par opening round the previous day had placed him in danger of missing the cut for the second tour event in a row and had doubtless sentenced him to a 157th consecutive tour non-win since the 1973 Hope Desert Classic.

"That was the combination of a little frustration and being ready not to play as much," Arnie would later elaborate, sipping a beer in his hotel suite. "I still enjoy it and I still want to play, but I'm getting to the point where I'm about ready to slow it up."

The hope of another regular tour victory is eroding, then? "Oh . . ." Arnie began with a sigh and a long pause, torn between objectivity and psychology. "I suppose it is a little bit. But I never really let it go away. When it goes away totally, then you won't see me out here very much.

"You've heard me talking about playing in Fort Worth (Colonial) in two weeks. If I thought there was no chance of my winning that tournament, there would be no chance whatsoever of my entering." Note: He didn't enter.

Arnie concedes the ebbing of self-belief but is at a loss to explain it. Extensive time spent with him either during or immediately after several tournaments during this time frame foster a theory: While doggedly shielding the flickering flame of optimism from the winds of reality, Arnie was buoyed by the belief he could step over onto the new Seniors tour and dominate the old guys as he did twenty years earlier. But his first few senior appearances produced as much consternation as conquest.

Even in his first two seniors victories—the '80 PGA Seniors and the '81 U.S. Senior Open—Arnie uncharacteristically faltered in the stretch. He won both events in playoffs created by his bogeys during the final nine. And in between, in the Michelob Seniors in Tampa, he bogeyed six straight holes on the final nine for a shattering loss after playing superbly into an "insurmountable" six-shot lead.

Arnie bristled when reminded of such checkered performances.

"I don't know why you and all other writers want to push the business of choking," he snapped. "If you want to say I choked, say it. To me, that's bull. People don't even want to read that.

"I have said I had trouble getting the ball in the hole, no question about that. In Tampa and one other place it was bad and it bothered me. It bothered me in Canada and I still won the tournament," he said, alluding to an unsanctioned Canadian PGA Senior event. "On the last hole, when I really needed to make four and I damned near made three, it restored some of my confidence. But the fact is I hit some bad shots."

Recovery time from those clunkers was lengthening with age for Arnie—a baffling tendency. He was four under par through seven holes in the final round at Tampa and running away from the field when he was dreadfully short with an eight-foot birdie putt

and promptly fell apart. He was two under par through six holes in the first round at Houston and about to go to three with a short birdie putt. He missed it and, before he could sweep aside the disappointment, bogeyed four of the next five holes.

The last bogey came when he completely missed the hole on a three-footer and his frustrations boiled over as he walked up the next fairway. "I can't understand why I can play so good for seven holes and then turn around so completely," he said, his face contorting in anguish.

Larry the psychologist/caddie lurched into action. "Don't let that putt get to you. They'll fall."

"It's more than that. It's my system," he replied. "I'm going to see my doctor when I get home. I'm playing good. I know that's not it. It's like at Tampa. I have a certain feeling after a bad shot. It's not that I'm having negative thoughts."

"No thoughts, maybe?"

"That's it exactly," he blinked with a matter-of-fact nod, pausing in the middle of the fairway for a phantom swing.

If Arnie's mind occasionally went blank during play, it was a flurry of frenetic activity during warm-up. No less than four drivers accompanied him to the practice tee each day at Houston and as many as six putters were among the final eliminations mere minutes before tee time.

Blithe spirit Fuzzy Zoeller walked across the putting green one day and, scanning Arnie's inventory of semi-mallets, mallets, and blades, unsheathed the needle. "Arnie," Zoeller called out with a laugh, "you're gonna have to buy a bigger jet just to carry all the putters."

"How many putters do you have?" chimed in Jerry Pate.

"We counted them the other day at home," Arnie said, "and didn't have as many as we thought—only about two hundred."

Pate shook his head and smiled knowingly. "I don't even have that many clubs."

Arnie's frustrations with putting over the last couple of decades became fodder for locker room quips, particularly when his book in collaboration with British writer Peter Dobereiner hit the shelves in 1986. The title: *Arnold Palmer's Complete Book of Putting.* One of the tour's most renowned one-liner comics thought that was such an irony he was heard to suggest: "Next up must be *Greg Norman's Handbook on Humility.*"

Ouch.

Journeyman tour pro Tim Norris coughed up this funny after a putter switch carried him into the first-round lead of the 1989 Anheuser-Busch Classic: "I was using an Arnold Palmer blade putter, and that's like buying a ship from the people who built the Titanic."

Double ouch.

Various pros privately lamented that Arnie's inconsistency on the course could be traced to his reluctance to stick with a putter long enough to develop a feel for it. Arnie pleads guilty. "That's true. Absolutely true," he said. He said that in 1981 during the Houston Open, but added that was fun to him. He didn't really resolve to change the counterproductive habit until the start of the 1993 season, after another dozen years of erratic putting.

"I'm changing putters so often," he said a few years ago, "that I'm not giving myself a chance, or the putter. I'm going to stop doing that. I'm going to come to the golf course with one putter. I may have a bunch before I get there. But when I get there, I'll have just one."

One for that day. Not to say there might not be a different one the next day.

"Exactly. I won't argue with that."

His earlier admission at Houston came during what was to have been the fourth round of that '81 tournament. As heavy Sunday rains flooded The Woodlands course, Arnie paced his suite, alternately putting to square "holes" of two-sided tape stuck to the carpet and tinkering with clubs. He'd dismantle a wire coat hanger to install a double reminder grip on one of the blade putters or replace the rubber grip on one of the candidate drivers with a spiral of leather.

"What bugs me," he blurted, "is some of the things I don't understand about what is happening to my game. I don't feel that much different than I ever felt playing golf. Except I know that at times I can't really let it fly the way I really want to. My body is the same as it was twenty years ago. I watch the kids swing a golf club, and I just think about why I can't do it the way I used to."

Arnie wasn't conceding much to the flat-bellies, perhaps, because he had more or less become one himself. A program of jogging had rehoned his body to a firm 174 pounds, down from a high of 206 in his mid-forties. Running at dawn, however, did not recapture the Power of Palmer Positive Thinking. *Los Angeles Times* columnist Jim Murray once compared Arnie's arrival at any PGA tour event to a swashbuckler jumping onto the deck of a pirate ship, knife clenched between his teeth. In his later years, however, he'd ease up the gangplank cautiously, seemingly resigned to an inevitable and fatal ambush.

Many insist Arnie still plays like a contender from tee to green and might yet win again if he whips the mental gremlins tethered to his putters. If mind-over-putter is the hurdle, might he consider a dose of positive attitude from a hypnotist or any one of the new wave of sports psychologists?

"No, I would rather let my game and my life take its own course," he said. "And I'm not going to try to put something into it superficially that couldn't or shouldn't be there. If I couldn't quit smoking on my own, I would never be hypnotized into quitting. And the same thing is true in my golf. If I can't call on my own mind and my own ability to make me play the way I feel I should, I'm not going to 'X' means to try to recall it. If it's meant to be, it's meant to be. If I work hard enough it'll come back. If I don't, it won't."

If that last theory had proven true, the millions who still, dearly love this man would have had another PGA tour victory to celebrate. Never, said some longtime Palmer-watchers, had he worked harder on his game than during the first couple of years after he turned fifty. At Houston, Arnie may have led the tournament in time on the practice tee where, one by one, fellow pros would pause at Arnie's spot on the firing line to offer suggestions.

"The fact that the guys are interested and concerned and want to see me play well, that's great," said Arnie. "It's nice to know they feel that way. But, still, the bottom line is that you want to do it yourself for your own satisfaction."

The tip he offers in return—by example—is his unequaled galleryside manner. The devotion he elicits from his Army is due, in no small part, to his animated enthusiasm and unfailing sense of thoughtfulness.

That was never hammered home more convincingly for Senior tour pro Rives McBee than during the 1989 Senior Open at the Laurel Valley Country Club in Ligonier, Pennsylvania, just a few miles from Arnie's Latrobe roots.

"In the few times I had played with and observed Arnie during my days on the regular tour, I learned to admire the way he treated people and never made excuses. I've always tried to pattern myself after that," McBee said. "For example, I never heard him make an excuse for a bad round, saying the course is set up too tough, or they put too much water on the greens or whatever. The rest of us use those excuses, but I never heard him do that. Not

once. So I was already a fan of Arnie's when he did something at Laurel Valley that made me truly appreciate him."

Wanting more than ever to play well in his backyard in front of lifetime friends and former school chums, Arnie staggered to an 82 in the third round of the tournament and would have loved nothing better than a quiet place to agonize. Humiliation and a muggy July afternoon conspired to test his manners and patience.

"But there were so many people wanting his autograph, I swear it took him forty-five minutes to get from the scorer's tent to the clubhouse," McBee recalls. "He signed everything and was gracious to everyone. Finally, he said he just couldn't stand up anymore. There was a clubhouse patio that has been fenced off as a little VIP compound. He went there, sat down at a table next to the fence, and spent the next hour signing things the fans passed over the fence."

His every gesture and word directed to the fans, collectively and individually, is an unmistakable statement that the guy over there on the other side of the ropes is a human being of equal importance and every bit as worthy of the same consideration due even the king of golf pros. It's a genuine doctrine with Arnie, ingrained by his late father, Deacon, and transmitted to the fans through conduits as basic as simple eye contact.

As was his habit, he strolled the '81 Houston Open tees during waiting periods, scanning the faces in the gallery, nodding here, offering a greeting there. The collective afterglow often reached sufficient candlepower to illuminate the Astrodome.

This basic respect and empathy for others extend to the private Palmer, even during moments of extreme emotion. During the champagne flight home six months earlier after his PGA Seniors victory, Arnie's first U.S. triumph of any kind in almost eight years, he frequently drifted from the celebration to express remorse for sixty-five-hole leader Walker Inman, whose game crumbled in the stretch. "I kept wanting to tell him something that would help. But I didn't know what to say," Arnie kept saying somberly.

Four months later, Arnie would suffer a similar final-round disaster at Tampa. And even while consumed with frustration and embarrassment over the day's depressing turn of events, Arnie repeatedly shoved aside his personal grief during the ninety-minute drive home to Orlando after discovering one of his passengers would be celebrating a wedding anniversary that night. At a time when he could be excused for being concerned only for himself, Arnie instead kept detailing and expanding the offer of an anniversary dinner for the couple at his Bay Hill Club.

More visible are beyond-the-call human courtesies Arnie routinely extends on the golf course. The traditional taboo on autograph requests during tournament rounds, for example, is generally honored by adult fans. However, young novices frequently thrust paper and pen toward the pros as they make their way from one green to the next tee. Typically, Arnie will say politely, "After I'm finished," take two more steps, then reach back toward the rejected youngster. "Well, here, give it here," he'll say, smiling, then sign his name and playfully muss the youngster's hair.

Departing one green at Houston, he was intercepted by a lad of about ten who requested a tee. "After I'm finished," came the Palmer reflex and the bill of the boy's baseball cap dropped toward the ground. Upon reaching the next tee. Arnie instructed his ersatz caddie to give the boy a tee.

"No, wait a minute," came an afterthought, and Arnie dug into a pocket of his bag for a tee with his name on it. He waded back into the gallery and handed it to the boy.

The four-alarm smile it produced suggested that baseball cap was probably launched through several low-flying clouds upon the happy news of Arnie's next victory. Even if it wasn't a regular tour victory.

Larry Guest

▼

Arnie gave up few concessions to senior citizenship, most notably the shorter tees used on the Senior Tour, the practice of using electric carts in tournaments, and the shift by many other erratic-putting seniors to the controversial elongated putter.

Always an advocate of playing a golf course to its fullest, Arnie and tee placements became a cause celebre during the 1989 Tournament of Champions at the LaCosta resort in California. By then, the tournament had become a dual event with separate but simultaneous competitions for winners on both the senior and regular tours of the previous year. Arnie had not competed for several years because he didn't win on the Senior tour in 1986 or 1987. His victory in 1988 sent him back to LaCosta for an embarrassing moment.

The tournament utilized two sets of tees on most holes. The younger champs from the regular tour played from the championship tees at LaCosta, while the senior champs competed from the shorter, member tees on most holes.

On the second hole of the second round in '89, Arnie, out of force of habit ingrained by nearly forty years of professional competition, stopped at the longer, championship tee and whacked his drive. Playing partner Harold Henning followed suit and both were assessed two-stroke penalties for playing from the wrong tees.

"That's the closest I've ever come to walking off the golf course," Arnie fumed afterward, making it clear his anger was not over the penalty but was directed at the unique situation under which seniors played from shorter tees on nine of the eighteen holes. "Ridiculous! This is the only tournament I've played in my entire career where there are two sets of tees. I've complained about it from day one. It's a second-class-citizen sort of thing. You shouldn't have two tees. If you're going to do that, they ought to make us wear skirts."

The next day, Chi Chi Rodriguez playfully wore a skirt onto the putting green to needle his longtime pal. As serious as he was about the issue, even Arnie couldn't resist a belly laugh.

But for all his protestations, tournament officials stayed with the dual-tee policy until Ray Floyd forced a change. In 1992 he became the first in history to win on both the regular and senior tours. Single tee placements were used for the '93 tournament to allow Floyd to compete simultaneously in both divisions.

Arnie's discomfort with the practice of using electric carts during Senior tour events led to an even louder confrontation. Then fifty-four, Arnie forced the issue in 1983 by implying he would curtail his Senior tour appearances unless the use of carts was either eliminated or severely limited.

Cornering Senior tour guru Brian Henning and commish Deane Beman, Arnie insisted the matter be placed on the agenda of the tour's advisory council meeting in conjunction with the World Seniors Invitational at Quail Hollow Country Club in Charlotte, North Carolina. Arnie was one of seven members on the Council.

He argued the carts detracted from the public image of the tour and proposed a provision that would allow cart use only by the most elderly players, like Sam Snead, then seventy-one, or those with medical infirmities, like Julius Boros, who had undergone quadruple bypass heart surgery.

One crotchety senior pro made it clear that Arnie couldn't impose his will on the group. "If Arnold thinks he can bowl over the council next week, I think he's in for a butt-kicking. I'd be happy to see him play every week. But we can't run this thing for one guy. The Senior tour is growing and drawing good crowds every week whether Arnold is there or not," said the advisory council member.

Larry Guest

Arnie already had inspired a rule requiring that either the player or his caddie walk, thus allowing the galleries to keep pace. But getting the carts virtually eliminated was another matter.

"We had a lot of fun with that one," recalled tour star Don January, another advisory council member. "Arnold would bring it up at every meeting and I kept telling him how we couldn't do that. Finally, I decided the only way to get him off of it was to join him. When he brought it up for about the sixth time, I said, 'Okay, I agree. Let's get rid of the carts.' His eyes got this big around. I figured the only way I was going to get him off of it was to let him see what it would stir up. So we passed the rule."

The rule, something of a compromise, provided that the seniors, with certain exceptions for Snead, Boros, et al., would no longer be permitted to use carts during the final two rounds of tournaments. The so-called "Arnie Rule" was set to be announced to the membership at the 1986 opening tournament in Fort Pierce, Florida and go into effect at a tournament later that year, giving the old guys time to get their legs in shape.

On the Sunday evening approaching that thunderclap announcement, Arnie looked ahead to the week when the Senior tour would be, so to speak, put back on its feet. From the idyllic vantage point on the deck of his third-story Bay Hill condo, with the setting sun kissing both Lake Tibet Butler and his evening highball, Arnie needed just three words to assess the situation. "The party's over," he said, eyebrows raised for emphasis.

"What this will do, I think, is clean up the last rounds of our tournaments. You know I have always felt pretty strongly that if you play professional golf, you shouldn't be riding golf carts." The idea was to make the Senior tour events look a little more like a serious competition and less like the West Memphis Four-Ball.

With that, Arnie headed for Fort Pierce, but not before I offered a weather forecast: sunny and warm on the course, icy breezes in the locker room.

Indeed, when the notice went up on the locker room wall at Fort Pierce for the Senior tour players to see, you'd have thought somebody put poison in their Polident. After assorted howls, most of the top players assembled that Tuesday night in angry conclave and voted 36-6 against the new rule. At first, Arnie insisted the rule would stick, referring to the Tuesday night meeting as an unauthorized kangaroo court.

"Their vote is unofficial," he said. "They can only suggest what is to be done. If we [executive board] had made a bad decision and the players voted against it, we would reconsider. But here is a case where we made a good decision. The decision will stick. The rule we put in is there to stay."

Within days, it was reversed.

"Before we could put it in for a tournament, the players raised so much hell, signing petitions and so forth, that it was revoked," said January. "Arnold never brought it up again. He just needed to hear from the people."

Part of Arnie's subsequent silence on the issue may have been inspired by the realization that some in the public mistakenly thought his motivation was to gain a competitive advantage against the Senior tour field, few of whom had kept themselves in the sort of physical condition that Arnie was in.

Typical of the dissenting voices was this letter reprinted in Arnie's hometown *Orlando Sentinel* on February 20, 1986:

It may be sacrilegious, or at least irreverence, to question the "Arnie Rule" concerning the use of golf carts by contestants in the

last two rounds of any Senior PGA tour. Arnold Palmer says, "If you play professional golf, you shouldn't be riding golf carts."

Most golf course professionals now force us to use golf carts to protect the lucrative income derived from such rentals.

We of the old folks generation who support the seniors really do not care how or whether the tour players walk or ride, but rather the golf enthusiast cares about the finesse these seniors demonstrate when they get to the ball. Is it possible that, by forcing the seniors to walk, some of Palmer's competition is eliminated before the match begins?

Is it possible that those who control golf appear to be talking out of both sides of their mouths—that is, ride when they want you to so they can make the megabucks from those who support golf, and don't ride when they tell you not to or you won't look professional?

Charlie Owens may not have a classic golf swing, nor is he able to walk eighteen because of an injury while he was a paratrooper, but he proved recently in winning a tour event in Fort Pierce that he can compete with the seniors—if he is allowed to.

Charles R. Johnson
Longwood

Say this for Arnie: If he was going to do it, he was going to hold out as long as possible, doing it his way to the last dying gasp. No hypnotists. No carts. No member tees. No long putters. Arnie was not an old washed-out geezer, by God, and he was trying to keep it that way. If the other guys were willing to run up the white flag to Father Time, well, that was their problem.

You see, Arnie may have become as much a captive to his own macho pride as his business distractions, the common excuse offered by so many for his flagging play. Several of the Senior tour stars who, like Arnie, had suffered from putting lapses, have turned with success to the new elongated putters that are anchored with one hand against the player's chest.

Most insiders felt a similar switch by Arnie, who remains largely effective tee to green, would return him to regular title contention. The first time he gave the odd implement a try on the putting green, he startled himself by holing putt after putt.

Several railbirds took note, silently figuring Arnie might be inspired to swallow his pride and take it to the course. He looked up and saw their eyebrows high-jumping. He began chuckling out loud and shaking his head. "No, no, no. No way," he answered, though no one had had to ask the obvious question.

"I think the long putter will be around for a while as a part of the game of golf," he said recently. "But it's not as strong as it was. We're going back to more conventional style putting, for the most part. But the long putter has kept a number of players in the game who might have given up because or poor putting. The closest I would come would be a little longer conventional putter, permitting me to stand more upright like Ray Floyd."

As this book went to press, he had never even used the long putter in a friendly round with cronies. "It's been to the putting green, but that's as far as it gets," he said. "It's not in keeping with how I envision golf."

Bulldroppings. Not in keeping with his macho self-image may be closer to the truth. But then, maybe that's why diehards wearing little umbrellas on their collars still gather to conjure one more victory celebration for their favorite golfing businessman, who is still very much on his feet, stiff-arming the calendar.

Larry Guest

4

90-Proof Palmer

When the time has been just right at Arnie's Bay Hill Club in Orlando after one of the club's storied daily "shootouts," a shots-and-beer contest has been known to break out in the locker room—more often than not at Arnie's playful urging. He'll buy a round and goad friends into participating.

YOU GRUDGINGLY AGREE to have "just one" to affirm your manhood there in front of all the boys. Then somebody else buys a round, then another. Arnie leers, knowingly.

If you're like me, it only takes about three. They go down like they're attached to a blowtorch. Your eyes water and your nose gets runny and in a few moments the worst seems over. Then you can just feel your whole system dissolving, dropping back to slow motion. The room starts taking high-banked Daytona turns, your tongue turns into a bowling pin, and you wonder why Arnold Palmer is sitting there laughing at you instead of sending for a stretcher.

Arnie sucked me in twice. Never again. Not after the last time, when my wife and I had a dinner date with Bay Hill member Paul Polizzi and his wife, Norma. By the time I wobbled home from the sound defeat in shots-and-beer, showered, and dressed, I lapsed into a state that might be described as wide-eyed comatose. I could see and hear. And I could walk, though it required summoning up every functioning fiber in my being to move forward in an upright position. But I couldn't talk.

At dinner, I was a zombie. An unblinking mannequin.

My wife was not amused. Once off the critical list, I apologized for days to the Polizzis. Paul just laughed. He had witnessed enough of Arnie's shots-and-beer contests and their victims to understand my condition.

A similar victim was Greg Norman, who resided at Bay Hill for several years until his move to south Florida in the late '80s. By his own definition, Greg Norman is not much of a serious drinker. A little wine with dinner. A few beers after golf, of course. You have to give him the latter. After all, he is Australian and part of the Down-Under citizenship requirements are a couple of Foster's five times a day.

Shots-and-beer was new and deadly to the Great White Shark the afternoon Arnie reeled him in after a Bay Hill shootout. Norman made the mistake of sticking around after the ritual, rapping with other members while the whiskey was sneaking up on his brain. What Norman can remember happening from that point on is this:

It took all the concentration I could muster to put one foot ahead of the other from the locker room to the parking lot and flop down in my little red Ferrari. I lived only about four blocks from the club at that time and somehow managed to make it home. But in concentrating on getting my feet to work, I had forgotten to take off my golf spikes. I don't know why I forgot to take off my spikes.

When I stepped out onto the concrete floor of my garage, the spikes shot out from under me and I fell flat on my back.

Norman's wife, Laura, heard the commotion and threw open the door to discover old Greggie Boy, suave and dashing international golf figure that he is, lying on his back looking at the ceiling and laughing his head off.

"Boy, did my head hurt the next morning," says Norman.

The most infamous of Arnie's shots-and-beer sessions actually was a contest to see who would be the last man standing. This remarkable little competition broke out during one of the annual Bay Hill Member-Guest tournaments sometime in the early '70s. In the shots-and-beer championships, it was Arnie against a field of five. The field never had a chance.

A neat row of six shot glasses was lined up across the bar and each man stepped forward to take his turn at bat. With all still standing, someone would tell a story or a joke and they proceeded to round two. One by one, the foolish local challengers began to drop out on the third round until just Arnie, Latrobe insurance executive Danny Bonar, and Latrobe foundry owner Chris Adams remained.

Bonar was dismissed somewhere about round six and was carted off to Dow Finsterwald's nearby condo, where legend has it he lost his cookies on one of Dow's flowered sofas. "Not so," said Bonar. A chipper sort, he alternately laughs and winces at each retelling of the Great Shots-and-Beer Death Match.

Legend also has it that Adams, an extremely large man, went out on round eight in dramatic fashion. He tilted his head back, tossed down shot No. 8, and never returned his head to the locked and upright position. He keeled over backward, his fall caught by a couple of spectators. Arnie laughed, threw down his own No. 8, then dragged Adams into the showers, fully clothed.

Incredibly, Arnie delivered a brief welcoming address at the Member-Guest dinner that evening, appearing to be only slightly tipsy at worst.

The danger of including anecdotes focusing on strong drink is the natural tendency to interpret that to mean that Arnie has a hidden drinking problem. He has no such problem that I know of, hidden or otherwise. The old saw that comes to mind when you suggest someone doesn't have a drinking problem is this: He drinks. He gets drunk. He falls down. No problem.

The difference with Arnie's drinking is that he doesn't get drunk—at least not perceptibly so—and he never falls down. In that respect, he is not dissimilar to many of the other men who grew up in the steel mill towns of western Pennsylvania. There, they practically have shots-and-beer for breakfast. A deadly combination for outsiders, but just a part of life in Latrobe. A shot and beer for those folks is about like the rest of us having a Nehi Grape.

Arnie and the business people around him are unusually sensitive to yarns about the boss and liquor, though they really shouldn't be. In 1989, coinciding with Arnie's sixtieth birthday, I wrote a two-part series of never-told anecdotes for *Golf Illustrated*. The series contained some humanizing anecdotes that Arnie wouldn't necessarily publish himself, but nothing that would appreciably dent his global popularity. The one portion of that series I figured would bring repercussions from Palmer Central was an account of his first, naive brush with a homosexual while a seaman in the Coast Guard. (More about that later.)

Oddly, the only complaint was about the inclusion of the following story, which implied that Arnie consumed a beer or two

while driving a carload of pals from Tampa to Orlando after he had blown the lead in a Senior tour event. The day that downtrodden Arnie and several buddies answered the call of nature at a deserted roadside not far from Disney World speaks volumes on Arnie's immense respect for his fellowman and the unfailing sense of kindness and thoughtfulness that has bonded him to millions. This was a moment when Arnie might have been forgiven for not thinking about his fellowman, especially an unseen stranger totally unaware of Arnie's concern.

It was a Sunday afternoon in 1981, and Arnie had just blown the Michelob Seniors in Tampa in flameout style reminiscent of his infamous collapse in the 1966 U.S. Open at Olympic Club. Like at Olympic, when he handed the title to Billy Casper, Arnie had a seven-shot lead turning to the final nine holes of the Tampa tournament. He may as well have played that final loop with a shovel and hoe.

Don January was the gleeful recipient this time as Arnie inexplicably bogeyed his way to the clubhouse, his huge lead steadily slipping away in excruciating Chinese water-torture fashion. After blistering the front side with a 32, Arnie closed with a six-over-par 41 to miss a playoff with January and Doug Ford by one tantalizing stroke.

He had used a new putter and a new putting tip. Ageless senior pro Jerry Barber had worked with Arnie on the putting green early in the week, firming up Arnie's grip and shifting his weight more to the left side. The putter was a black Spalding blade putter Arnie had extracted early in the week from a barrel in the Carrollwood Country Club pro shop. It still had the thirty-dollar price trig taped to the shaft when he angrily jammed it back in the bag beside the eighteenth green and stalked into the scorer's tent.

Barber, his own final round completed earlier, had ventured out to the eighteenth to watch Arnie finish after hearing news of the great man's unseemly collapse. Barber asked a reporter how Arnie had bogeyed six holes on the incoming nine and was told that four of the six were the result of three-putting. "That," Barber said wryly, "wasn't part of my instructions."

His wounded scorecard signed, Arnie retreated to the clubhouse dazed. The first time he had approached the locker room that week, an amusing exchange occurred with seventy-two-year-old rookie doorkeeper Don Ruff. Suspiciously scanning Arnie's clothes, Ruff had stepped in front of the legend, blocking his path. "Sonny, where's your badge?" he demanded.

Arnie, thinking the part-time security guard was joking, replied: "Uh, well, I don't have one yet."

Ruff: "Well, you can't go in here."

An embarrassed tournament official quickly stammered that this was Mr. Arnold Palmer and he was a player and permitted inside. Ruff laughed at his own failure to recognize the marquee star of the week, and Arnie laughed along with him, shook his hand, and signed his pairing sheet.

Five days later, there was no frivolity when Arnie approached the locker room after the tournament had slipped through his fingers in such embarrassing style. He and Ruff made eye contact, both shaking their heads somberly, and Arnie disappeared into the building.

Within moments, Arnie sat hollow-eyed at the arm of baseball great Stan Musial in a VIP lounge. Stan the Man sympathetically wore a grim, remorseful expression usually reserved for funerals, firings, and 41 on the final nine.

A telephone sitting between the two legends rang and Stan answered. Apparent from Musial's responses was that the caller

had departed the tournament early, was checking in to confirm Palmer's final margin of victory, and was now stunned to learn he had crashed and burned on final approach.

"No, no, he didn't win," stammered Musial, ". . . uh, January . . . In a playoff. . . . What happened? . . . Well, uh, uh . . ." Stan the Man squirmed uneasily, what with the disaster victim sipping a Michelob right there at his elbow.

Arnie, his eyes narrowing, leaned toward the phone and finished Stan's play-by-play report. "He got something caught in his throat," Arnie shouted into the receiver, "and choked on it!"

Musial emitted a nervous little laugh that he cut short when noticing that the others in Arnie's entourage were still dutifully brooding out of respect for the dearly departed victory. That same despondent tone remained intact during the first few moments of the ninety-minute ride home to Orlando. Arnie had commuted to the final round from his Bay Hill Club in a nine-passenger carryall stuffed with friends and associates who had gone along for the Sunday ride expecting an old-fashioned Palmer celebration.

Among the traveling squad was courtly fellow senior pro Dow Finsterwald, Bay Hill Classic tournament director Jim Bell, your faithful historian, and a few affluent cronies including Arnie's lifelong pal and playful antagonist Joe Tito. One spot was left open for an extremely large cooler of beer.

As always—whether in jet, helicopter, powerboat, golf cart or Chevy Suburban—Arnie was in the command seat, this time still sulking even halfway through the first round of beers. When Tito laughed at something said by another of the passengers, Arnie shot him a scowling laser glance.

"Look, pal," Tito snorted, "we're not the ones who blew a seven-shot lead, so there's no reason for us to pout all the way back to Orlando!" Arnie's wonderfully plastic mug quickly progressed from anger to pained remorse to a sheepish smile. He threw a half-filled can of beer on Tito and everybody laughed. The gloom was broken.

The next hour on Interstate 4 became a cacophony of good cheer and beer cans snapping open. By the time Arnie steered the Good Ship Michelob onto a back-road shortcut near Disney World, there was a great clamor for a pit stop. Arnie wheeled off onto a lonely dirt road for several hundred yards and, thankfully, jolted to a stop.

The assorted golf legends and industry captains tumbled out and deposited ninety minutes of beer consumption. Unbeknownst to Arnie, Jim Bell, always trying to please the boss, corralled the considerable pile of empty beer cans that had been rattling around in the Suburban's rear luggage area and created an impressive mound of aluminum in the roadside ditch.

Arnie was not aware of the disrespectful dumping until the journey had been resumed. A good two miles after the whiz stop, somebody expressed awe over the size of the beer can mountain back there in the ditch. Arnie began asking questions until he realized what had happened. "Jim, I can't believe you did that," he scolded. "That's some man's property. We'll be at Bay Hill in just a few minutes and you could have put the cans in a dumpster."

Arnie scowled another moment, pondering the offense, then hit the brakes. He wheeled the carryall around on the two-lane road and returned to the impromptu "dump." The next scene begged for a photographer. Or Norman Rockwell. There was the international celebrity king of golf, Finsterwald, and an assortment of wealthy corporate heads returning the mound of beer cans fire-bucket fashion—from the roadside ditch to the back of Arnie's Chevy Suburban.

Presumably, the property owner never knew his rights had been dutifully protected by a world-famous golfer just hours after the superstar's most debilitating collapse.

That noble respect for others and their property was one of the admirable qualities instilled in Arnie by his father, Milfred "Deacon" Palmer. The popular and proper greenskeeper and pro at Latrobe Country Club, Deacon taught his son to respect authority and appreciate the rights and pride of others no matter their station in life.

For many Christmases after he became a global celebrity and man of infinite means, Arnie expressed that appreciation to the blue-collar men of Latrobe through a holiday ritual. He would load up several drinking buddies at midmorning and set off for a day-long tour of the pubs frequented by steel mill workers. Deacon had taught him that these tough, hard-laboring men—many of whom had been Arnie's schoolmates—were armed with too much pride to accept charity, even at Christmas. Showing up each year to buy them all a round of drinks would be seen unacceptably as pretentiously flaunting his riches. So he devised a scheme involving the one-dollar punch cards popular in taverns during the '60s. Arnie would declare that if he hit the jackpot, all in attendance would drink on the jackpot until depleted.

While he renewed old friendships with small talk, the bartender kept punching out numbers under secret bankrolling from Arnie until the jackpot was found. Somewhere beneath it all was an earthy man-to-man bond that was strengthened through the mill-town tradition of hoisting a whiskey together.

Time flies when you're having fun. Winnie often had to send a neighbor to roust Arnie and pals out of some festive tavern as they went through dozens of punch cards each Christmas. It's dark and dirty work, but somebody had to do it.

On Christmas Eve '68, the tour ended at the Youngstown Volunteer Fire Department, about a quarter-mile from Arnie's house and office. (Latrobe Country Club is actually closer to Youngstown than Latrobe.) In the back of the firehouse is a grubby little bar that helps defray the operating costs of the fire department. When the steel mill clanked to a stop each day, some of the bastions of middle America, their cheeks charred with honest labor, filled the firehouse bar. They were unshaven and crusty, but proud, and daily in need of a liquid attitude adjustment. They were Arnie's kind of guys.

The traveling squad that Christmas Eve included Arnie's man Friday, Doc Giffin, Deacon, and Arnie's next-door-neighbor, Kenny Bowman. They entered the firehouse at dusk and out came a punch card. And a second punch card. And a third . . .

Assuming these Christmas angels had been gone a sufficient number of hours to spread their annual cheer, Winnie dispatched a search party of one, family friend Dr. Tom Moran. He hardly got out of his driveway before spotting Arnie's new Mark III in front of the firehouse and wheeled in.

Fresh funds for the punch cards.

Not clear is how much more time elapsed before the angels, mill workers, or the punch cards were exhausted, but when the group emerged, the Mark III was covered in snow.

Each evening typically ends with Arnie in his den sharing drinks and laughter with friends. It is said you can tell much about a man by checking the titles of his books. In Arnie's basement den, the most prominent volume atop a bookcase next to the bar is a

large, leather-bound book titled, *The World's Greatest Book*. It opens to reveal a tiny bar with an assortment of miniature liquor bottles secreted away inside.

In Arnie's environment, you see, liquor was simply a fixture of the landscape, part and parcel to most every activity as indicated by the story of his foray into the Pennsylvania tradition of bear hunting.

Jack Nicklaus is not the only variety of bear that Arnie has stalked in his lifetime. On an infamous November weekend in 1968, Arnie and two other Palmers set out for the Alleghenies of upper Pennsylvania in ill-fated and madcap pursuit of a grizzly. This bear hunt was the brainchild of one Michael Francis "Spooks" Palmer, Arnie's uncle and a foreman at Latrobe Steel Company.

"Actually, Spooks was the favorite of the owner of the company. Everybody loved Spooks," Arnie testifies. "Spooks was a good man and good worker. Played a little golf. Drank a lot of whiskey. If you ever meet a Michael Palmer, don't challenge him to drink. I've never known any Michael Palmer who couldn't drink a lot."

Arnie, Spooks, and Deacon set out that Sunday afternoon bound for a friend's cabin near Ridgeway, Pennsylvania, armed with several rifles, several fifths of Canadian Club, overnight gear, several fifths of Seagram's VO, playing cards, several sixpacks of Rolling Rock, dice, and—rumor has it—perhaps even some ammo for the rifles. The latter has never been confirmed.

The plan called for the brave hunters to spend the night in the cabin, arise before daybreak on the first day of bear season, spend that Monday in mortal combat with the bears, and return to Latrobe loaded (pardon the pun) with all the bear pelts Arnie's brand-new 1969 Lincoln Continental Mark III could transport.

The Mark III had progressed only a few blocks when the first bottle of VO began making the rounds, quickly pursued by a can of

Rolling Rock. From the crack of the first pull-top, the warning was sounded to all bears of northwest Pennsylvania that the dreaded Boilermaker Express was on the way. Despite several refueling stops at the liquor cabinets of assorted friends en route, the Palmer Bear Hunt covered the 110 miles from Latrobe to Ridgeway in a mere seven hours.

With no open eatery to be found on a Sunday evening, dinner was acquired at the Ridgeway Elks Lodge, where several locals were only too thrilled to rap with the famous golfer and share tips on how to mount a bear head. There was the usual spate of autographs, plus a special request. A fellow Elk reputed to be the most fervent Arnie fan in the Alleghenies lay seriously ill in the local hospital. Just a brief visit from his hero might do wonders for his recovery.

Despite a heavy rain and gathering darkness, Arnie agreed to visit the stranger, forty-two-year-old Laverne Smith, who was suffering from ulcer surgery complications. Smith, who returned to his job as a tool shop superintendent and has since retired, still clings to the golden memory of that inspirational surprise visit by Arnie and the autographed photo that occupies a prominent position in Smith's living room.

"We finally made it to the cabin shortly before midnight," says Arnie, picking up the story, "where we drank whiskey, shot craps, and nearly froze to death."

Around three A.M., the Palmer trio went straight to bed to rest up for the big day ahead. At four A.M., the owner of the cabin awakened his guests and announced breakfast.

On foot, the three Palmers were dispatched one by one to bone-chilling outposts in the Allegheny National Forest that was yet to be illuminated by the morning sun. Shivering and trying to think of warm Hawaii fairways, Arnold Palmer, golfing legend, sat

in a hollow, squinting into the darkness for large, furry silhouettes. As light began to filter through the trees, he saw a figure moving in the distance. Then another. And another. Hunters. There were hundreds of hunters out there, sifting through the forest as if it were Amen's Corner on the second Saturday in April.

The way Spooks Palmer remembers it, he toughed it out until about 7:30 that morning before growing restless. He abandoned his station and found Arnie gathering firewood. The law against open fires in a national forest gave way to the law of survival. In minutes, Arnie and Spooks had a life-giving blaze that attracted Deacon and the precious remains of a fifth of VO. Two laps around the campfire, however, and the bottle was as empty as their chances of bagging a bear.

They returned to the cabin for hot showers and a premature exit for Latrobe. Let it be duly recorded in the annals of big-game hunting that by nine A.M. on the first day of bear season, 1968, the Palmer assault on the grizzlies of Pennsylvania ran up a white flag and retreated in the Mark III. "The only bear we saw," Arnie likes to say, "was each other's 'bear' ass in the shower."

Although Arnie never has exhibited anything close to a drinking "problem," it is nonetheless noteworthy that his last regular tour victory in 1973—and his best chance of adding one more regular tour triumph in the last twenty years—came when he took brief breaks from alcohol. The latter foray into abstinence—or something close—came in what could be considered the most important week in his career over those last two decades.

It didn't involve a major championship. It didn't even involve a victory. But it had a huge effect on his continued play in tournament golf since that week in 1983 when he very nearly turned back the clock in the Los Angeles Open. The sports world froze in excited expectation that week when Arnie, then fifty-three, surged into the lead and found himself a mouth-watering ten holes from ending a ten-year victory drought on the PGA tour.

That eventful and far-reaching week in early January began routinely enough with Arnie climbing aboard his Citation II executive jet at Orlando International Airport. Masking his ongoing concerns about the state of his unproductive golf game was a sporty ensemble of elegant suede slacks—a Christmas gift from Winnie—and a bright yellow cashmere sweater with a noticeable hole in the back.

Winnie chuckled at the hole and quipped: "Maybe it'll make him play harder."

A smart-aleck sportswriter, poking fun at the fancy pants, wondered aloud if the plane was bound for San Diego and Los Angeles—or San Francisco.

"What is this," he shot back, feigning rejection, "Pick On Arnie Day?" He kissed Winnie good-bye, and Arnie, copilot Lee Lauderback, and the sportswriter were off, hardly imagining the landmark turn of events that lay ahead during the next seven days.

The first item on the itinerary went off as expected. On that Monday in San Diego, Arnie would be receiving the NCAA's prestigious Theodore Roosevelt Award at the outset of the association's annual convention. Arnie's name was being added to a distinguished list of previous Teddy winners. Gerald Ford. Art Linkletter. Dwight Eisenhower. Jesse Owens. Bill Cosby. All onetime student athletes who went on to become the kind of high profile role models that allows the NCAA to stick out its chest even in times of controversy and scandal.

First rehearsal of Arnie's acceptance speech came at thirty-nine thousand feet somewhere over the barren moonscape of west Texas. Having delegated the controls to copilot Lee Lauderback, Arnie began trying out his talk. Reading from four-by-six note-

cards, his basso profundo thundered about the plush but snug cabin.

"President Frank, friends, honored guests, ladies and gentlemen . . ." To his practice audience, he opened with a small joke, tying the NCAA's Theodore Roosevelt Award to his own golfing image as a man with "a big stick." Not speaking softly, Arnie waded through a grateful mention of his experience as a Wake Forest underclassman, a melancholy reference to the death of his Wake roommate during their senior year, a statement of concern over the possible effect of pro sports strikes, and finally, a salute to the aims of the NCAA.

The stilted, five-minute spiel completed, Arnie twisted his pliable mug into the sort of contemptuous scowl usually reserved for a buried lie. "That's no good," he snorted. "I've got to work on it tonight. This just isn't what I want to get across."

He worked on it during an overnight stopover in Palm Springs. He scribbled last-minute adjustments the next morning in San Diego. But by the second notecard when he actually stood before 1,400 delegates at the seventy-seventh annual NCAA convention, he drifted from the prepared text to do what Arnie does best. He lapsed into simply being himself.

Totally abandoning the notes, he fondly recounted the adventure of departing Latrobe on a bus bound for North Carolina and the unknown mysteries awaiting him at what was then Wake Forest College. "I remember walking across the campus with a set of golf clubs and a bag in each hand and neither of them fully loaded. Two young ladies walked by and said, 'Hi!' Being from Pennsylvania, I dropped everything to see what they wanted, but they kept on walking. My education began right there."

When the burst of laughter died off, what followed was an easy patter of recollections and patriotic challenges, delivered from the hip. Maybe the analogy embraces the wrong Roosevelt, but Arnie's acceptance of the NCAA's revered "Teddy" award became something of a fireside chat.

Playing to the collegiate officials, Arnie made it sound almost as though he never could have hooked a 2-iron through an opening in the trees if not for his collegiate grooming.

"The greatest influence in my life—other than my parents— was my college. The things that happened to me there, the people I met there, still influence my life to a great degree."

Though flying solo without notecards, he did remember to mention Buddy Worsham, the ill-fated roommate whose body Arnie had to identify one tragic morning. Worsham had tried to entice Arnie that autumn evening to attend the Wake Forest home-coming dance. But Arnie had celebrated a bit too energetically at the football game that day and maybe even participated in the old ritual of consuming certain fluids believed to help your team win. Whatever, Arnie fended off Worsham's invitation in favor of a nap, a fateful decision that may have saved a golf legacy from being wasted in a North Carolina roadside ditch.

Arnie's golf coach strolled somberly into the dorm around midnight to break the grim news: Driving back from the dance, Worsham and another athlete careened off the road and perished.

Now, three decades later, the Palmer legacy was facing anoth-er crossroads of sorts. That next morning after receiving the Teddy, he would be checking in at the Los Angeles Open for the first of three early-season PGA tour appearances that carried special pur-pose for Arnie.

Embarrassed by his game's continued decline—he had mined less than ten thousand dollars in each of the '81 and '82 seasons from PGA tour purses—Arnie was declaring that his play in the L.A. Open and Bob Hope Desert Classic would determine whether

he would continue to regularly pursue the main tour or retreat into semiretirement. If he wasn't truly competitive in one or more of the three tests, he was vowing he would drastically curtail his subsequent playing activity to "Bay Hill, some majors, and a few seniors events."

The doubters were suggesting his skills, at age fifty-four, had too greatly eroded to compete with the tour stars of the day. The faithful were clinging to the notion that he could summon one more hurrah if only his concentration were not so subdivided by myriad business interests.

I had tagged along to observe the Teddy presentation, with plans to remain in California to cover the convention's closing days and an NFL playoff game that next Saturday between the New York Jets and Los Angeles Raiders in L.A. Coliseum. In between, I would rejoin Arnie for the first two rounds of the tournament, being played that year at fabled Rancho Park. After the Jets-Raiders game, I was to hop an early flight out of LAX that Sunday morning to cover the Cowboys-Packers playoff game in Dallas.

But Arnie's stunning run at the L.A. Open title turned out to be a much larger story for Orlando readers, causing me to cancel my Sunday morning flight to Dallas and detour, instead, to Arnie's suite at the Beverly Hills Hotel, a fashionable hideout where the parking lot suggests a nearby limousine factory must have sprung a leak.

He swung open the door to his suite and yours truly blinked for a moment at yet another bold ensemble: jet-black slacks and a bright orange golf shirt. "Did I lose track of the months? Is today Halloween?"

Once again, Arnie's plastic mug twisted into playful pain as he retreated to a full-length mirror. "Is this too much? Maybe you're right," he judged, peeling off the shirt. He replaced it with a soft yellow.

"This is better: Wake Forest colors," the Demon Deacon alumnus said, returning to putting practice across the brown pile carpeting.

On the coffee table stood a significant symbol of this significant week. A bottle of Chivas Regal, placed there six days earlier, compliments of the hotel management. The significance was that it was still unopened.

During the cross-country flight the previous Sunday, Arnie declared he would have nothing to drink during the L.A. Open. He recalled a similar decree traveling west to start the 1973 season, after going winless in '72 for the first time in his tour career: He would lay off the booze until he won a tournament. Abstinence quickly assisted Arnie to the 1973 Bob Hope Desert Classic that winter, and he had not won again on the regular tour.

Underlings say that 1973 venture into abstinence was something short of cold turkey. Cold turkey no, cold duck yes. Arnie made an exception for cold duck, the cheap purple wine craze of that era, and showed up in his condo for the first night of the L.A. Open with a bagful of cold duck. During the course of the tournament, a nearby liquor store's entire stock of cold duck was exhausted and the owner came by Arnie's condo on Saturday of that week to leave a note saying he had just gotten in a special shipment of cold duck.

Now, ten years later, he was back on G-rated liquids again, with no escape clause even for cold duck. Don't listen to eyewitnesses at the hotel's famous Polo Lounge or at the trendy Palm Restaurant who may have thought they saw Arnie imbibing during the tournament week. That was Perrier water and a wedge of lime in Arnie's hand.

The Palm, on Santa Monica, is an unpretentious little diner where the lobster started at forty-eight dollars, even in 1983. Its walls and ceiling are covered with caricatures of famous faces, some of which also can be seen sitting in the open booths on most any evening.

Arnie was halfway through the L.A. Open and still in serious contention that Friday night when he took the sportswriter/hitchhiker/wiseacre and copilot Lauderback to dinner at the Palm. "Right this way, Mr. Palmer," the maitre d' called out the instant we stepped through the door. None of the dozens awaiting a table seemed to mind.

Arnie instantly became the star attraction that evening in the Palm. Diners at nearby tables sent notes, applauding his position in the tournament. A man and his son approached the table and thanked Arnie for his round of 69 that day. Combined with an opening-round 66, Arnie was just two strokes out of the lead.

A woman being led to her table suddenly recognized Arnie's familiar mug and jolted to a wide-eyed stop. Her three companions crashed into her, accordion-style. Just like in the cartoons.

Arnie and pals were almost through dinner when Johnny Carson arrived. Noting his old golfing friend, Johnny announced his presence with a loud one-liner for the enjoyment of all: "I wondered whose tractor was double-parked outside!"

Carson and Palmer embraced and exchanged pleasantries. Johnny, seated at the adjacent booth, took over as the star of the Palm. Arnie was ready to leave.

Saturday morning's sun had not quite made it to the West Coast as Lee Trevino shivered in the Rancho Park Golf Club's locker room, sipping coffee from a white Styrofoam cup. He had barely survived the thirty-six-hole cut, thus relegating himself to one of the earliest tee times. His thoughts were on the legend tied for third, who would not have to tee off for another five hours.

"If Arnold wins this tournament," gushed the Merry Mex, "they'll have to close the course two weeks for repairs. People will tear it up."

Young pro Mike Sullivan, overhearing the Trevino Theory, playfully asked: "Arnold who?"

"The Arnold who's kickin' our butts this week, that's who," Trevino shot back, laughing. "He's the guy back in the hotel sleeping while we're out here groping around in the dark!"

Some of the tour's other noted philosophers offered diverse opinions on the impact golf and the tour might feel from a Palmer victory. Older players, with vivid memories of the excitement Arnie once brought to any tour event, generally foresaw a resurgence of interest. The younger players were more conservative in their remarks, angering ageless Charlie Sifford.

"If it wasn't for Arnold, some of these scraggly wimps would be out pickin' cotton today," snorted Sifford, a cigar stub bouncing with each word. "If they realized what he's meant to golf, they'd get down and kiss his feet."

Said veteran pro George Archer: "It would be great for Arnie to win. But I think it would mean more to him than it would to the tour or to golf."

Tour publicist Tom Place speculated that a Palmer win, had the tournament been on network TV that week, would be the main topic of Monday morning conversation, upstaging the NFL playoff games of that weekend. "Maybe even without TV," Place said after a moment to reconsider.

"It would be fantastic," said vet Gene Littler. "Everybody would like to see it happen."

Larry Guest

However, Keith Fergus, then a twenty-eight-year-old pro from Texas, had a firm grip on his pulse rate. "It would be nice," he said with a shrug, "but everybody would go about their business and forget about it the next week."

Huh? Earth to Keith! . . . Earth to Keith! . . .

Friday night at the Palm, I had announced my revised game plan for the weekend. I would check out of my hotel Saturday morning, cover the Raiders' game, and fly to Dallas that night only if Arnie had fallen more than three strokes behind at the close of Saturday's third round. If he led or was within three strokes, I would check back into the hotel and remain in L.A. to cover Arnie's final-lap attempt to alter golf history.

"Now it would be a lot easier," I deadpanned, "if you can assure me you'll be within three strokes tomorrow night, so I won't have to pack and check out of my hotel."

Arnie returned a soft smile and after a moment of thought, finally said, "I think you'd better check out just to be safe."

"Jeez, how can we have any confidence in you if you don't have confidence in yourself?" ol' wiseacre here needled, laughing.

The next evening, after the Jets had dispatched the Raiders in a Coliseum brawl, a phone call to my newspaper determined that Arnie had shot in the 60s for the third straight day. His 68 gave him a ten-under-par total of 203 and hoisted him to within one slim stroke of the fifty-four-hole lead. Gil Morgan, Mark McCumber, and Lanny Wadkins were tied at 202.

My next call went to the Beverly Hills Hotel, room 221.

"Arnold? This is Larry. Nice goin' today."

There was a pause.

"You callin' from Dallas?"

You can't tell the wise guys for all the wise guys.

During Sunday breakfast in the Polo Lounge, the maitre d'
arrived at Arnie's table with a phone on a long cord. Just like in the
movies. Arnie reached out in anticipation, but the man asked if a
Larry Guest was at the table.

I took the phone as Arnie's face contorted in minor irritation.
The caller was Myra Gelband, an editor at *Sports Illustrated*. Like
the rest of the world, the magazine had not anticipated this would
be the weekend Arnie would find his fountain of youth and thus
had not assigned a staff writer to cover golfdom's second coming.
She asked if I would accept the assignment and began discussing
deadlines and other particulars.

As we talked, the maitre d' returned to the table to announce
another call, this one for Arnie. He was sorry, he said, that the only
long-cord telephone was tied up at the moment. Arnie would have
to take the call on a phone at the reception desk. Arnie's face
advanced to major irritation as he pushed out of the booth. Here
was his chance to take an important call at his table in the Polo
Club like Edward G. Robinson or somebody and the only long-
cord telephone was tied up by a sportswriter. The nerve.

Two hours later, the man they call the king was on the putting
green moments before his final round, jabbing erratic putts toward
a cup six feet away. Fewer than half were falling in.

"You nervous?" I asked.

"Do I look nervous?"

"Not really."

"Are you nervous?" he inquired.

"Yes," I admitted. "I feel a little like I'm back in college and
about to pitch a big game."

He laughed. "I'm nervous, too," he confessed, eyebrows raised
for emphasis. "I've been nervous for fifty-three years."

Bill Kratzert, one of the younger tour pros who developed a strong friendship with Arnie, strolled over to wish his aging pal good luck. Off in one of the first pairings of the day, Kratzert had just completed a fine, closing round of 66.

"I wish I could give it to you," he said.

"I'd take it," Arnie said with a smile that gave way to an afterthought. "No, I don't think I should, come to think of it. I'm anxious to see what happens."

So were thousands ringing the first two holes—tee to green already sending cries of *"Go get 'em, Arrrr-nie!!"* reverberating across the hills of west Los Angeles.

The cries grew to a guttural roar on the fourth hole when Arnie's thirty-foot birdie putt rolled strong and true, its famous owner punching the air with a clenched fist as the ball toppled over the lip and disappeared into ecstasy. Resurrected was a yellowed legacy. Arnie had turned back the clock twenty years to when life was a series of similar birdie putts and frenetic roars.

In the final round of a regular PGA tour event, Arnold D. Palmer, fifty-three and winless for ten years, was at that moment tied for the lead. He followed with yet another birdie, snatching the solo lead after fifty-nine holes of the Los Angeles Bleeping Open, and a decade of pent-up adoration burst from Arnie's Army, Southern California Battalion.

The sound that he jerked out of the masses packed around the fifth green by rifling a 4-iron to within a foot of the cup was more wrestling roar than golf cheer—a *yaaaaa-booooo* outpouring of love for the man who had not, by damn, been dispatched to a rocking chair after all.

They were certain they were witnessing a page in history. A woman selling programs, sensing the same, shouted advice of a bar-

---

gain as Arnie and his throng thundered through the clubhouse turn. "Get your programs! Three dollars today, ten dollars tomorrow!"

Alas, the programs became devalued after all the booklets could commemorate two hours later was that Gil Morgan outdueled Mark McCumber for the title. Morgan won on the strength of a final-round 68 for a fourteen-under-par total of 270. Arnie's closing 72 left him with a 275 total and tantalizing thoughts of what might have been.

The brave bid had died at the onset of the back nine, where the mortal wound was a string of three bogeys. The stirring epic was left with a bittersweet final act. Arnie didn't win, but he rekindled the notion, even if only briefly, that he still could. And he showed a new generation of bland, young tour pros his special talent for turning something so staid and tranquil as a golf tournament into a quivering, hooting mass of emotion.

Just that he was near the lead after the first round was enough to exhaust all the Friday daily tickets that tournament officials had printed. They had to use leftover pro-am and practice round tickets. Thousands of extra Saturday and Sunday tickets were hastily printed, but they still ran out.

On Sunday, Arnie's Army began occupying two holes at a time—one division lining the hole he was playing from tee to green and another staking out the best vantage points on the hole ahead. Even after he fell out of the chase, the Army stood firm, leaving a gallery of only about a hundred tagging along with the final threesome just behind, where the championship was being decided.

Saturday night dispatches heralding Arnie's contending position brought the nation's media in droves. Sports columnists from New York, Chicago, Philadelphia, Dallas, Kansas City, and Washington quickly convened at Rancho Park. In addition to *Sports Illustrated*, *Time* magazine hastily arranged coverage in the event Arnie could pull off the impossible.

Larry Guest

Though he didn't win, his overall play in the tournament, if nothing else, upgraded impossible to improbable.

"This has answered some of the questions in my own mind about playing," he told a packed press tent afterward. "I had gotten to the point I didn't feel I was hitting the ball strong enough to compete. And now I think I am.

"I know that being physically better has helped my golf," he said, not mentioning the untouched bottle of Chivas Regal. "And if I'm going to win, I'm going to have to get better, physically. I had to be strong throughout my round and I wasn't as strong on the back nine today as I wanted to be."

Trim and fit, Arnie had begun the day with a two-mile dawn run. But roadwork has little to do with his inconsistency on the greens, and there was some symbolism there in his hotel room that morning as he putted into a yawning, brass trash can. "If the holes were that big, I could make a lot of putts," he mused.

He would miss putts of three, ten, and four feet on consecutive holes on the final nine to leave him talking about what might have been. As he addressed the media, Morgan and McCumber were dueling out in the privacy of the eighteenth hole. Departing the tent, one writer, seemingly more out of curiosity than any sense of urgency, asked who had won the tournament.

But all that mattered was who hadn't.

A few feet away, Arnie emerged from the tent, his face reflecting none of the happy consolation that his frustrated legions had gained from their man's strong showing. He walked directly to the sportswriter/hitchhiker/wiseacre and stopped, his face twelve inches from mine. His expression was stern. "Shit!" he said.

Coming close has never counted for much with Arnold Palmer.

5

Face-off with Father Time

The galleries are still very important to me. They're one of the reasons I'm still playing. Arnie's Army has changed a lot over the years, but it's still there, and I appreciate that. But there are other reasons I'm still playing. I still enjoy the game as much as ever. And I still have the drive to win.

Arnold Palmer, quoted in the
Atlanta Journal-Constitution, October 1986

IN THE YEARS FOLLOWING that brush with victory at the L.A. Open, the debate became a constant in Arnie's world: Should he continue to please himself and the enduring "Army" by playing regular tour events in his role of virtual ceremonial entrant? Or should he bow out—except for an annual pilgrimage to the Masters and a smattering of Senior tour appearances—so as not to risk coating a mahogany career with a plywood finish?

Didn't Kareem stay too long, a sad victim of his financial collapse? The galleries whisper snide jokes at the sight of pathetic old Doug Ford struggling to yet another 85 at Augusta National each spring, stubbornly exercising his lifetime exemption as a former (1957) Masters champ. Is Arnie flirting with the same derision? He should be too proud, goes the standard argument, to risk drawing sympathy rather than respect from all those lingering worshippers on the other side of the ropes.

Arnie is proud. And he is stubborn. And he is determined. And he is going to play and work and train and condition and retool to stay out there on the course until the calendar leaves him no corner, no ray of hope that another victory is somewhere around the bend. Not just on the Senior Tour, where, at press time for this book, he had not won since 1988. But even on the regular PGA Tour, where he has not won since 1973.

To give up that premise is to stop living life to the fullest for this old charger. Other sexagenarians can search out a creek bank if they want, but Arnie is certain there is plenty of fuel left in his tank to build another golf course, fly around the world, sell some more motor oil, and yes, win another tournament.

Those unyielding standards have provided global inspiration throughout the autumn of Arnie's career. Long after others have retreated to career alternatives, Arnie stubbornly has kept alive the flame of hope that he still can compete with the kids. In recent years he has found allies all about him in the battle against the calendar.

For example, in 1986—the Year of the (Gray) Panther, an old geezer named Nicklaus won the Masters, and then one of the littlest senior citizens by the name of Shoemaker rode a long shot to Kentucky Derby roses. Those dramatic feats put a bounce in a lot of rickety old steps, Arnie's included. He fired off a telegram the day after Nicklaus turned back the clock, congratulating his then-forty-six-year-old archrival and adding: "Maybe there's hope for a fifty-sixty-year-old."

"That just proved," Arnie said of Jack's stunning victory, "that you can pull yourself together and do something like that. I think we all have a tendency to start feeling a little sorry for ourselves when we get older. As a result, we look for excuses and say, 'Well, I don't need to do that. I'm getting too old.'

"That's a lot of baloney. I don't say you can do everything you want to, but I certainly feel you can do a lot of things that you don't even try—if you try. If you have it in your heart that you can, then certainly there is that possibility. And Nicklaus proved that, too."

Girding him in that resolve have been the occasional spurts of good play against the talented kids on the regular tour—encouraging booster shots to revive the memory of that near victory in the 1983 L.A. Open. There would not be anything else so dramatic or sustained—at least not on the regular tour—but enough to keep that flame flickering against the winds of advancing age.

One such booster shot was injected by the 1989 PGA Championship at Kemper Lakes outside Chicago, where the first round suggested it was the Time Warp Open. With the leaderboard bearing such relics as Arnold Palmer, Jack Nicklaus, and Tom Watson, what year is it? Anybody seen Elvis? You figured Ben Hogan had to be home kicking himself for not entering.

Watson, nearly forty and a winner just once in the previous five years, opened with a fine 67, only one shot out of the lead. Nicklaus, forty-nine, was just one more shot back at 68. Sharing that lofty rung on the leaderboard was the Latrobe Legend, just a month shy of his sixtieth birthday.

Arnie had rattled to the forefront in dramatic style, rolling back the calendar with a string of five birdies on the Kemper Lakes front nine. The streak was announced as a bulletin in the tournament press center just as first-day leader Mike Reid was concluding his post-round interview session. Reid, a wisp of a pro with a delightfully wry sense of humor, immediately sensed the news angle of the day. "Oh, no," he said playfully, "now you guys will throw away everything I've said."

At least that comment was preserved before reporters clamored out of the media center and onto the course to witness this time capsule named Palmer. They were there to record the shock waves on the par-five fifteenth when Arnie birdied to pull even with Reid at six-under-par. Three closing pars and Arnie would have led not only the PGA, but the national news. This was, after all, the only one of golf's four majors that Arnie had never won. And he had given little indication that year that he could still compete in a major. In two rounds each in the Masters and British Open, he had failed to break 80 and missed the cut in each. Arnie's Army, Kemper Lakes Division, was growing and becoming more vocal in its support with each hole.

But there the fairy tale ended. Arnie bogeyed two of the three finishing holes to settle for a 68 and drifted out of contention for good with a two-over-par 74 the next day. An 81 in the third round brought full cycle, in just thirty-six hours, the ecstatic hoots and euphoria with his five-birdie start on Thursday to the return of retirement pleas after his Saturday embarrassment.

The time has come—and may actually be overdue—for Arnold Palmer to quit something, his empathizing critics were declaring. If not quit, at least severely cut back—tournament golf or globe hopping to build courses or jamming his work schedule with corporate appearances in the name of piling millions on top of the millions of dollars he's already earned. (Or in the name of International Management Group, the Mark McCormack representation giant that insiders lament has Arnie under whip-and-bridle like some aging plowhorse.)

"Arnie, you're almost sixty-two," began this sage ol' busybody one day over beers in the Bay Hill locker room. "Why don't you just enjoy playing the Senior Tour, do a couple of commercials a year, and tell the guys at IMG to go make their own living?"

Though he said nothing, his wide-eyed grin and nod seemed to say it all: "You're probably right. I should, but I probably won't."

That conversation came a few days after Arnie's continued disappointing play in the 1991 U.S. Senior Open at demanding Oakland Hills Country Club outside Detroit. He had missed the thirty-six-hole cut for the second Senior Open in a row and had been relegated to a TV set in his Latrobe den to watch Jack and Gary and Chi Chi and his other contemporaries battle for the title.

Ten years earlier, Arnie had won the 1981 Senior Open at Oakland Hills. But this time, he flew home on Saturday morning. Greater Detroit groaned when Arnie missed the cut. The faithful Army jammed the grandstands around the eighteenth late that Friday afternoon only to shake its head in sadness as Arnie bogeyed to miss by a shot. That night's local newscasts were speckled with laments of Arnie's premature exit.

The last thing this twentieth century hero needs is to have his swashbuckling career punctuated by pity. What he needed more at the moment, he argued, was focus. He needed to concentrate more on his business or on his golf. One or the other.

The records show that Senior tour events are won largely by players while in the fifty to fifty-five age range. After fifty-five, the skills, the strength, the desire begin ebbing too fast to cling to the leaderboards. Only in the past decade has Arnie begun to hint that maybe—just maybe—he can no longer compete with the kids on the regular tour. At the '91 Senior Open came hints that resignation was also creeping into his Senior tour self assessment.

At that time, Arnie had won just one senior event in the previous six years, none in the previous three. Heading into Oakland Hills, he was No. 61 on the 1991 Senior tour money list, trailing the likes of Dudley Wysong, Bob Betley, and Jack Kiefer.

Jack Kiefer?

Arnie mentioned noticing an erosion of his effectiveness more in the prior five years than in any other five-year period before. "One of the problems is I'm not out here enough. I still enjoy it, and the fires are still there, though I don't know if they're as hot as I think they are."

Each time his confidence surged, his mind seemed to wander, he said, and another clunker of a shot would throw him back to square one.

"As you get older, it gets tougher to maintain concentration," Arnie said. "Anything can come to your mind—anything that might be troubling you. In the other years, I didn't let those things enter in. I find I'm giving myself hell more and more for allowing that to happen."

"That was certainly understandable considering his off-course activities entering the '90s had become an entanglement of litigation. Those soothing beers after play were now accompanied by yet another stack of pink telephone messages like the batch that awaited him after he missed the Oakland Hills cut. Easing onto a long bench between two rows of lockers, the great man sorted through the stack silently and shook his head.

I flashed back to a day two years earlier in the Jacksonville offices of his golf course design company as an example of the three-ring circus that is Arnie's golf/business treadmill. This was in the middle, mind you, of the Senior TPC at the Players Club, two miles inland from the offices. His tee time for the second round was a mere two hours hence.

He had just finished a half-hour interview with a magazine writer working on one of several national pieces that would coincide with his sixtieth birthday that September. Next in line was a volunteer official of the Nestlé Invitational, Arnie's PGA tour stop at Bay Hill Club. The man had papers to execute. Two of Arnie's staff architects had design work ready for his approval and fine-tuning on one course being built in Ireland, another in Italy. Ed Seay, fun-loving and gifted president of this busy outpost in the Palmer empire, had a long to-do list on a yellow sheet to go over with the boss.

Nine holes or eighteen for the ceremonial course opening next month? "Let's say nine, and leave it so I can change my mind if we have time for eighteen that day," said Arnie, rolling his index finger to keep Seay moving down the list.

A prospective client in North Carolina wanted Arnie's company to build his course but preferred not to tie in Arnie's club management firm to the deal. Get the guy on the phone. "How many more?" Arnie finally asked, rubbernecking to inspect the list. "I should already be at the golf course."

There was a time when the minions of Arnold Palmer Enterprises were under strict orders to handle all business with their famous CEO on the early days of the week, leaving him free to think birdies and eagles when the tournaments began. But like so much else about his golf, that was another time in Arnie's life.

The business had become too lucrative, too far-reaching now to be handled on Mondays and Tuesdays. Arnold Palmer Enterprises is a maze of companies including three aviation firms, a half dozen auto dealerships, the course design and club management operations, apparel merchandising, land development and more. Competitive golf—Arnie's nostalgic play days on the PGA Senior Tour—was relegated to second position.

He accepts that reality and the effects it has on his passion to win again. In a sport of fluctuating effectiveness, Arnie's peaks have been shorter, his valleys deeper, strapped by his divided attention.

So there in the Oakland Hills locker room, with Arnie rummaging through the stack of phone messages from assorted outposts of his empire, there was little reason to wax hopeful about the next victory. When asked earlier that week if he still felt he could win on the increasingly competitive Senior Tour, he told reporters: "I feel fairly confident I can. I think I can win now. I'll continue to play only as long as I think I can compete."

Arnie may have been more candid on the subject upon encountering one of his former caddies, Ernest "Creamy" Caroline, still toting a bag there at the Senior Open well into his seventies. Arnie shook his head and smiled fondly as the weathered and colorful caddie toddled off lugging some pro's golf bag. "Creamy is just like me," he said, chuckling. "It'll take a tractor to pull both of us off the golf course."

Perhaps all of us who so tenaciously cling to our cherished images of Arnie as a champion don't have the right to push him behind the ropes. We like to think there is something noble in the way Koufax and Hogan and certain other immortals knew when to quit. But then, maybe Arnie has the right idea in pursuing the gusto on every front at an age when the rest of us reach for that cane pole.

The first guy who beat Arnie at Oakland Hills chose the cane pole. In a 1946 national amateur tournament there, Arnie lost to a fellow teenager named Mac Hunter in the thirty-six-hole final. Hunter played briefly on the PGA tour, then settled into a successful club pro career. Did Arnie know whatever became of Mac Hunter?

Larry Guest

"Yes," he nodded. "Mac retired from Riviera Country Club [in Los Angeles] a few years ago and is now lying on the beaches of Hawaii."

"What does that tell you?" a friend asked.

"That tells me," Arnie shot back with verve, "he doesn't know about life."

One of Arnie's most notable and reluctant concessions to life was erasing the U.S. Open from his annual schedule. It didn't go without a helluva fight.

After Arnie no longer qualified for a berth in the Open under the normal criteria, the United States Golf Association, which governs the Open, gave him a special exemption in each of the four years running through 1983. That gave him thirty-one Opens in a row.

For the 1984 Open at Winged Foot, the USGA ended Arnie's free passes, setting off a hail of public protest. For the USGA, the timing was unfortunate: The same year Arnie's exemptions were discontinued, one was given to veteran Japanese star Isao Aoki. The resulting revival of World War II by many of the troops in Arnie's Army was predictable.

In subsequent years, other players debated the USGA's decision to end Arnie's exemptions, among them Gary Player. "Arnold Palmer has played such an enormous role in the history of golf," Player argued. "I think he should be allowed to play in the U.S. Open as long as he wants to. He subjugates himself to the qualifying every year, simply because he loves this game. He shouldn't have to do that. The game of golf owes him more than that."

But if he wanted to go for a thirty-second Open, Arnie would have to earn a spot in one of the one-day, thirty-six-hole sectional qualifying tournaments like any other nonexempt player.

"You have to draw the line somewhere," Arnie said in defense of the USGA. "You can't continue to invite people when there are young people who can play and are trying to make a career for themselves."

Instead, Arnie simply saddled up for the grueling qualifier in an attempt to earn his way back into the Open. Off he went to a sectional qualifier at Sharon Golf Club in Akron, Ohio. His thirty-six-hole total 146 was two strokes over par and two strokes short of qualifying for one of the eight spots available to sixty competitors at Sharon.

"This may be the end for me," Arnie, fifty-four, said of his Open aspirations that day. Any who believed those words were unfamiliar with the man's almost limitless determination.

1985: Arnie zips back home to Orlando from playing in a seniors tournament in Denver to compete in Open sectional qualifying at his own Bay Hill Club the very next day. "I'm giving it this one last try," he says. He misses by four shots after a double-bogey-bogey-bogey start.

1986: Arnie, fifty-six, reasons that he hadn't given himself a proper chance to qualify in '85 by flying in right after the Denver tournament. This time, he takes the week off leading into the sectional qualifier at Bay Hill to prepare. "I just figured that if it's worth the effort to try to qualify, then it was worth giving yourself a chance," he explained. "This will be the last one. The last attempt to qualify. Whether successful or not. I guess fifty-six is the limit — even by my standards." By best estimates, the second oldest in the field of sixty-one contestants is fifteen years younger than Arnie. He shoots 80-74, missing by a mile. As he taps in for par on his thirty-

sixth hole, a loud clap of thunder booms overhead. Arnie looks skyward and tips his visor.

1987: Arnie doesn't listen to God. He shoots a creditable one-under 143 but misses qualifying at Disney's Magnolia Course by five shots. By the boards is a return to an Open at Olympic Club, where in 1966 he lost a seven-shot lead on the closing nine and the next-day playoff to Billy Casper. You know what he says. All together now: *This is the last time.* "You can only chase the dream so long," he sighs.

1988: Despite a painful rib injury, Arnie, fifty-eight, suffers through an opening-round 79—including a sextuple bogey 11 on the par-five sixth hole in the sectional qualifier at Bay Hill, then decides not to put himself through the ordeal of playing the second eighteen. Afterward, he announces—guess what?—this was the last time he would try to qualify for the Open. "I've, had good times with the Open—I've won one and should have won four or five others," he says. "It's been a fun tournament, a good tournament for me, but I think this is it. I'm going to schedule something for this week next year, just so I won't be tempted again."

1989: "I discussed it with Winnie. She encouraged me to take another shot at qualifying. So, I'm doing it," Arnie says on the eve of sectional qualifying at Disney World's Magnolia Course. He shoots two-over 146, missing by eight strokes, and declares: "I think this is it. I said that last year, didn't I? And the year before. But I really think this is the last time."

1990: Although the sectional qualifier at Bay Hill is set with one noteworthy name missing from the lineup, observers half expect

Arnie will come running out to the first tee, flapping his arms and saying he has changed his mind. But Arnie, now sixty, had given up the ghost a month earlier, somewhat reluctantly allowing the Open entry deadline to pass. (However, he hadn't quite thrown in the towel on the "other" Open, the one set later that summer over on The Old Course at St. Andrews. Arnie had quietly accepted the Royal & Ancient's invitation, incorrectly predicting it would be his last fling at the British Open. He confessed he couldn't resist one more because of the historic venue.)

U.S. Open sectional qualifiers are staged at assorted sites scattered about the country and players are free to choose a location. Except for his 1984 qualifying attempt in Ohio, Arnie chose to try his hand at qualifying in Orlando. It was not a choice for the faint of heart. Orlando has proven to be the toughest route to the Open. In addition to the covey of regular tour players who make Orlando home, Central Florida is stuffed with par-busting mini-tour pros. Thus the Orlando sectional qualifying fields are among the strongest in the country, a fact that is overlooked by the USGA, which assigns no extra spots to Orlando as it does at each year's sectional located in the city where the PGA tour happens to be playing. So despite a lineup of inordinate talent, the Orlando qualifier—usually staged at Arnie's Bay Hill Club—is assigned one Open berth for every eight to ten competitors, just like Kalamazoo or Sioux Falls where even-par on some garden-variety course is a solid bet to earn a roster spot in the Open.

At Bay Hill—on one of the toughest layouts in the country—a qualifier must be several shots under par to harbor hopes of playing in the Open. Throw in the usual Central Florida summer heat and humidity and you wonder why a man in his mid-fifties would put himself through thirty-six holes of one-day torture at any site, let alone at the course even tour pros refer to as "Bay Long." But to Arnie, it's a mountain and it was there.

I tagged along to record for *The Orlando Sentinel* one of those mountain-climbing expeditions, June 4, 1985 . . .

▼

Qualifying entrant No. P3691 in the U.S. Open Golf Championship headed out of the circular clubhouse driveway and turned onto Masters Boulevard at 6 A.M., the headlights of his personal golf cart slicing through the darkness. His morning paper in tow, he stopped to pick up a hitchhiking reporter before continuing to his condo residence just past the Bay Hill Club's tennis courts.

Arnold Palmer's longest day had begun.

The once and always king of golf would spend the next twelve hours attempting, for just the second time in three decades, to qualify for the Open. What lay ahead were thirty-six grueling holes of golf in heat-wave temperatures that would reach 100 degrees. At age fifty-five, he would be the oldest of the fifty-five contestants tackling the elements and two laps of demanding Bay Hill Club in pursuit of seven precious berths in the Open field two weeks later at Oakland Hills just outside Detroit.

6:13 A.M. — With the invigorating scent of sausage and eggs wafting from Winnie Palmer's kitchen and the first rays of sunlight filtering into the breakfast nook, a large thermometer on the patio says this June Tuesday has awakened to a balmy 78 degrees. Scorpions are already scurrying for shade.

6:32 A.M. — Arnie: "Winifred, you think I should take a vitamin?" Winnie: "A double dose." Arnie (playful, pained expression): "Whaddaya think, I'm an old man or somethin'?"

7:10 A.M.—Arnie sits in front of his double lockers just inside the door of the Bay Hill men's locker room, lacing on a pair of golf spikes. He is trim and natty in gray slacks and sky blue shirt. He says he doesn't plan to change to fresh clothes at the midday break between rounds. "Nah, I want to smell good when I finish," he says, laughing. Three locker room attendants and two business associates laugh in chorus. "Besides," he adds, "I remember doing that once, and I shot 600 in the afternoon round."

A Bay Hill member bolts through the door, smiling brightly when he sees the proprietor. "What's this I hear? You guys walking thirty-six holes in this heat today?" the member jabs.

"Only us young guys. The older guys will quit," Arnie jabs back.

7:28 A.M.—After just ten practice shots, dark splotches of perspiration are already polka-dotting his shirt. "One thing about it. It doesn't take long to warm up today," Arnie laughs. Two dozen early-rising lifers in Arnie's Army laugh with him. They wipe their brows. He rips a drive long and pure, the ball cresting against the morning haze, then falling into the distant dew, dead center on the driving range. "Another like that," Arnie says brightly, "and we go to the putting green—where the important stuff is." The next drive lurches to the right. The putting green has to wait.

8:10 A.M., second hole—Arnie blinks in despair as his shot from a greenside bunker skitters across the putting surface, trickles down an embankment and disappears into a lake. Starting on the back nine, he has opened bogey-double-bogey to soar three strokes over par. His attempt to qualify has effectively ended. He would plod on, stubbornly determined, too proud to run up a white hankie, for thirty-four more holes. Somewhere it is etched in stone in this man's makeup: Arnold Palmer does not quit.

9:07 A.M., sixth hole—The score and temperature have climbed to four over and 82 degrees. Squinting into the sun, Arnie produces a sky-blue hat in the style of an incumbent movie hero. "Indiana Palmer" promptly rolls in a twenty-five-footer for his first birdie of the day. A hundred spectators applaud and trudge off to the next hole, confident the kids in this qualifier are now in jeopardy of a patented Palmer Charge.

9:50 A.M., ninth hole—An urchin of a man in worn loafers and carrying a tattered, rusting lawn chair arrives as the growing gallery flows onto the front nine. "Didn't think there'd be this many out here. Must be lots of people who don't work for a living " he says to no one in particular. "How's Palmer doin'?"

"Three over," says no one in particular.

"Hmmmmmmmm," says the urchin. "Well, guess I'll follow him a few holes. Just to watch him suffer."

10:50 A.M., fifteenth hole—Arnie *is* suffering. His shirt is completely wet. His slacks are soaked down to his hips. His second shot is even wetter, lying at the bottom of the lake fronting the green. Double-bogey. Score and temperature: six over par and 91 degrees.

11:20 A.M., seventeenth hole—Stepping onto the tee, Arnie tries at pep talk. "All right, Rolls," he says to his caddie, Royce Nielson. "Time to get something going . . . or send in a pinch hitter." He pushes the drive into the stand of thin young pines protecting the corner of the dogleg.

"The reason those trees were planted," he announces in deadpan disgust, "is so if anyone drives it there, he'll be in trouble."

"I wonder," says a fan, "who did that?" Arnie manages a tight-lipped smile.

Noon—Standing bare-chested in front of a locker-room mirror, Arnie towels off and combs his graying hair. "I feel pretty good—better than I should after shooting seventy-bleeping-seven!"

he snorts. Bolstered by a BLT on whole wheat and early reports of high scores by most other qualifiers, Arnie revives hope that a good afternoon round could still get him in the Open.

Recanting his wardrobe plans, he has decided to change his saturated clothes. Rolls Royce is dispatched to the condo for another pair of slacks while Arnie waits in the locker room in only his undershorts and a fresh shirt. "Maybe," he jokes, "I'll play like this." He doesn't.

2:10 P.M., twenty-third hole — After missing the green, Arnie chips in for a birdie to go one under for the afternoon round. The gallery, now three hundred, squeals with delight. Is there still time?

2:40 P.M., twenty-sixth hole — The temperature has reached 100 degrees. The collar of Arnie's newly soaked shirt has reached 110 degrees. He stalks off the green and glares at a friend. "Sonuvabitch!" he mutters. He has just missed his third straight makeable birdie putt. If there is time, it is rapidly running out.

4:20 P.M., thirty-fourth hole — A merciful thundershower arrests play, arrests the thermometer, and sends Arnie fleeing to the clubhouse on a golf cart straining under the weight of Rolls and four business associates clinging to various umbrellas and bumpers. A check of the scoreboard yields the bad news that scores have not run high after all. "I've got no chance," Arnie sighs. "I get a week's vacation [during the Open] to rest and spend with the kids."

5:45 P.M., thirty-sixth hole — Rain delay over, Arnie completes a solid afternoon round of 71. Too little, too late. His 148 total is five shots too many. A promising but winless tour sophomore named Paul Azinger is medalist at 141.

As Arnie somberly signs his scorecard, comic relief arrives. Two-year-old granddaughter Katie toddles onto the eighteenth green as the next three players approach, sending Winnie Palmer

in frantic pursuit. The face that launched a thousand Pennzoil cans melts into laughter.

"What's wrong, Granny?" he teases Winnie.

Granddaughter corralled, Arnie extends his arms, but the tot shies away. "Just because I miss the cut," he says in baby talk, "you don't love Gumpy anymore?" Katie smiles sheepishly and gives Gumpy a tight hug.

Smart girl, Katie.

Just because he had given up chasing the Open should not have been taken as a sign he was ready to strike the tents in any other area of his circus.

Just five days after dodging a cardiac bullet, Arnie pulled back the yoke on his private jet one Saturday in early 1992, embarking from Orlando International on a twenty-five-day itinerary that did not read like a sixty-two-year-old man trying to step off the merry-go-round.

During that span, he would play in the Bob Hope Desert Classic in Palm Springs, dash on to Hawaii to compete in the Senior Skins Game, and return to the mainland for a third tournament in three weeks, the AT&T National Pro-Am at Pebble Beach. Before the sun set on the Del Monte Lodge that Sunday night, he was off on a three-day detour through the South Pacific to check on two golf courses one of his companies had under construction in Jakarta, Indonesia, then huddled in Singapore with the Crown Prince of Malaysia before returning home to Orlando. Whew!

"Slowing down? So far I haven't," he said, somewhat sheepishly, while autographing a stack of photographs, magazine covers,

Pennzoil cans, putters, etc., on the eve of that junket. "I really do hope to do some slowing down this year."

A week earlier, Arnie had feared he might have to pull the emergency cord and hop off the Palmer Express for an extended pause. A cardiac stress test taken during the '91 Christmas holidays had sent up a warning flag and Arnie checked into a Latrobe hospital for an angiogram. The procedure calls for the introduction of a dye into the bloodstream, enabling X-rays to check for blockages in the heart's main blood vessels.

The test turned out fine; doctors said the earlier warning was a false positive, so it was back to a hardy pursuit of life.

Did it scare him?

"Sure, when they tell you you might have to be ballooned or have open-heart surgery, it gets your attention," he said. "You don't know until they see the tests. They said probably the worst they would have to do is an angioplasty. But it [the angiogram] was good. Very good."

Arnie whipped a copy of his angiogram out of a handsome, leather briefcase to verify the happy conclusion. "Clean. Very clean," he said, his tones suggesting the kind of pride you might use when showing off photos of the grandchildren.

Of course, the fact that Arnie's dad died of a massive heart attack during a visit to Bay Hill when he was seventy-one "was another reason to get checked out," Arnie admitted.

The brush with mortality having been conquered like just another bold 3-wood recovery from deep rough, Arnie charged forward declaring a singular, pulsing goal for 1992: "Win."

A determined glare underscored the one-word vow.

But those damned statistics were talking again. And not in support of his case. Just one of his ten victories on the Senior tour had come in the previous six years, none since he won the 1988

Crestar Classic in Richmond. He had humbly finished sixty-fifth and forty-sixth on the Senior tour money list in 1990 and 1991, only reluctantly admitting that a series of controversial and draining legal entanglements might have contributed to his slide. Those distractions—Isleworth Country Club falling into receivership, the ugly dissolution of ambitious Arnold Palmer Automotive Group, and the aborted sale of Bay Hill to a Japanese group—had been all but resolved.

"I don't guess everything will get totally settled to where you have total freedom," Arnie was saying. "But it is better. No question about that." Arnie shifted his focus to reviving his golf game. Bay Hill's new head professional, Jim Deaton, and Arnold Palmer Golf Academy instructor Brad Brewer were sought for "constructive critiques," and a couple of slight swing changes brought quick and encouraging results. From the tips at demanding Bay Hill, Arnie blistered the front nine for a 31 and talked about shooting his age for the first time. Alas, he "only" managed a 67. A week later, in high winds, he reeled off an impressive 69.

So this most dogged opponent of Father Time was embarking on a hopeful 1992, his spirits lifted, his focus renewed and one of the strongest competitive hearts the sports world ever has known pumping along just fine, thank you.

Arnie's golf game was back on course. Off the course, however, it was a different story. He was still recovering from a few bogeys he'd racked up in his game with guys carrying briefcases.

6

Darth McCormack
and the Evil Empire

There hardly has been an occurrence of more than modest significance to golf that is not commemorated by a brass plate bolted to the spot. Engraved plaques clutter the world's golfscape, permanently recording the deeds and misdeeds that forged new chapters in the game.

THERE'S ONE ANCHORED in the rough where Jerry Pate launched a gilded 5-iron approach in Atlanta, another erected beside the ninth tee at Rancho Park to enshrine Arnie Palmer's septuple-bogey 12. There's a marble marker preserving the spot on the eighteenth at Bay Hill from which Robert Gamez struck one of those sudden-death miracle shots Greg Norman tries to forget. And a memorial beside the first tee at Cherry Hills etching the legacy of Arnie driving the green in the '60 Open.

There was another crossroads of golf that summer of 1960 more deserving of bronze than any other contemporary moment in the sport. Historians would be more than justified in erecting a plaque on the spot in Cleveland where Arnie first asked attorney Mark McCormack to review an endorsement contract. It was a simple act that would forever change the scope of capitalism not only in pro golf, but in myriad other sports. Drawing on one another, Arnie would become the preeminent athlete pitchman; McCormack would become the preeminent athletes' agent.

Parlaying Arnie's natural appeal and bold play with McCormack's imagination and tenacity instantly produced exhibition and endorsement fees that were unprecedented and set the cornerstone for the largest multinational athletic representation firm the world has known—McCormack's International Management Group.

Actually, their meeting in 1960 was a renewal of their friendship. They had competed years earlier when Arnie was at Wake Forest and McCormack was on the golf team at William and Mary. Now Arnie had blossomed into a revered national superstar and McCormack had become a bright young attorney for the Cleveland firm of Arter & Hadden.

Little could Arnie have imagined that teaming up on that first endorsement would be the genesis of a lifelong business relationship with McCormack that would make both of them millionaires many times over. But neither could Arnie have imagined how completely he would come to depend on McCormack and his ever-expanding legions of IMG sports power brokers.

Arnie's complex business involvements, his endorsements, his staff, and his tournament scheduling are almost totally controlled by IMG. To a lesser degree, even his social relationships are framed

by the barrage of influence and advice flowing from the brusque McCormack and his mercurial top aide, Alastair Johnston.

"I feel sorry for Arnie," said one of his closest and truest friends. "Supposedly to have total control of what's going on around him and he has no control."

At first, McCormack represented only Arnie. Then, a gifted little South African named Gary Player was added. Dow Finsterwald recalled being in the hotel room with Arnie at the Baton Rouge Open when McCormack called to gush about Player's potential and ask if Arnie minded him handling Gary's contracts, too. Again with Arnie's permission, young Jack Nicklaus was added. And race car driver Jackie Stewart and skier Jean-Claude Killy. International Management Group had lifted off on a rocket ride to world sports domination.

Until recently a part-owner of the firm, Arnie remains a showcase client of IMG. But the energetic McCormack has built it into nearly a billion dollar-a-year conglomerate that represents athletes and celebrities, manages resorts, owns and manages sports events, negotiates TV rights for mega-events such as Wimbledon and the Olympics, produces television shows, builds golf courses, peddles books and tapes, and now probably even represents the virtuoso baritone who headed the marquee at the last concert you attended.

"We . . . have . . . no . . . competition," McCormack boasted, pausing between each word for emphasis, "on a worldwide basis across the spectrum of our activities. There are people in certain pieces of our business that compete with us in certain geographical places. We have fifty-one offices in nineteen countries and there is no other bona fide multinational company in this business, today.

"We represent more NFL players than Steinberg, Woolf, and Demhoff, combined," he noted with pride during a 1993 interview, alluding to three top football agents. "We represent most of the hockey superstars. In golf and tennis there is nobody even close to us. In figure skating, skiing, broadcasting, there is nobody close. In basketball, we're probably third. In baseball, we're good, but not huge. But there is nobody within light years to us by any comparative standard you would want to draw—financial gross, number of clients, whatever."

As IMG has expanded, it even competes now with the star client that got the company going. Arnie's course design and management companies have been duplicated by similar firms under the banner of IMG, which has positioned itself to seek new course clients. Instead of Ed Seay dealing directly with potential clients about building a course, IMG Course Design now often does the sales pitch. Before, if the client balked at Arnie's standard $1.25 million fee, Seay was free to negotiate, trim this or that, and still get the job for Arnie's company at a compromise price. Then IMG begin shuffling the clients down its own rate-card list of budding pro/designers to Nick Faldo's nine hundred thousand, or Bernhard Langer's eight hundred thousand, or to the economy tier—Ian Woosnam, Ray Floyd, or Curtis Strange—at about two hundred and fifty thousand. (In 1996, Faldo and Langer joined the big-name IMG defections that already included Greg Norman and Nick Price.)

Also, if IMG lands the client for Arnie, IMG controls the revenue, backing out its own commission and a healthy list of expenses, before the remainder filters back to Arnie and Seay's company. Some of Seay's underlings say the bottom line to Arnie's company for a course project, once typically in the neighborhood of seven hundred and fifty thousand dollars, more recently comes in at about half that after the fee is filtered through Cleveland. "Some of our people have a problem with that, but I don't," said Seay.

In little more than a decade, IMG became so large McCormack could no longer devote much attention to Arnie, whose care and commercialism was turned over to an ambitious young Scot named Alastair Johnston. An accountant by schooling in Glasgow and London, Johnston is a tall, handsome man whose Scottish brogue can thicken at the drop of a couple of eyelashes. In McCormack's mold, he became a senior vice-president at IMG and Arnie's shadow. As the endorsements and royalties continued to spiral through more commas and zeroes, Johnston developed enormous clout and credibility with Arnie.

In almost daily contact, Arnie saw Johnston as a charming, talented advisor. Arnie's staffers and friends, however, came to see a manipulative, ruthless side of the ambitious Scot.

It's not clear exactly when the adjectives for McCormack, Johnston, and the rest of IMG switched from "creative and aggressive" to terms like "arrogant" and "vicious" and "Machiavellian."

No one seems to have a date when IMG began to stand for International Money Grabbers or I.M.Greedy in derisive locker room banter. Golf media guides don't list the season when McCormack first earned *St. Petersburg Times* columnist Hubert Mizell's apt description as "a man impossible to like." When did former U.S. Open champ and IMG client Curtis Strange first notice that, "to a lot of people, IMG is a four-letter word"?

Whenever it was that McCormack and his company earned black hats, an Arnie/IMG paradox was born. Here was the unlikely mix of Arnie's winsome persona and Mark's abrasive nature. An odd hybrid of Arnie's honor and integrity tethered to IMG's shadowy stealth.

McCormack airily sniffs that IMG became an evil empire when it arrived as the New York Yankees, the Notre Dame

Fighting Irish, of sports representation. When it became a runaway No. 1 in all the polls.

"I think people resent success. So people shoot at us," he reasoned during a rambling interview at the 1993 Nestlé Invitational at Bay Hill. "People can get mad at us and not like our methods and say this or that. But our greed—if we are called greedy and grasping—is really on behalf of our clients. When we say we'll do something, we deliver it. We run good tournaments and good events and we represent people honestly and well. We don't steal their money and a lot of agents have gone to jail for that or been scandalized because of it."

No one can argue with McCormack about the awe-inspiring scope of IMG, but there are plenty who question his and his firm's tactics, attitude, and scruples. Those skeptics include plenty within Arnie's inner circle who question just how straightforward IMG deals even with Arnie, its star client and apparent minority owner.

In a lengthy 1990 feature on McCormack and IMG, *Sports Illustrated* writer E. M. Swift reported that "except for a small interest held in some IMG businesses by Arthur J. Lafave, the chief financial officer, IMG is entirely owned by McCormack." However, Arnie has made no secret that he owned 10 percent of the firm. Whom do you trust? Did McCormack mislead Swift? Or did Arnie need to review his stock certificates?

"Arnold's relationship with me and my company is totally between us and I have no comment on that," McCormack said at Bay Hill. Giving McCormack the benefit of the doubt, he could merely be trying to shield Arnie from possible legal fishing expeditions by the various individuals and entities who either file or threaten IMG with lawsuits at an ever-increasing frequency.

Protecting Arnie from financial liability exposure seems an overriding goal of McCormack, Johnston and other IMG moguls,

while protecting his image and good name appears to be somewhere farther down the list of priorities. Some of IMG's actions
suggest the credo is to always go for the bottom line with gusto
even if Arnie's golden image takes a hit or two.

The years 1990-91 brought to a head a trio of messy
imbroglios that thrust Arnie into a quagmire of embarrassing lawsuits and public ridicule—problems that shouldn't be furrowing
Arnold Palmer's brow, say his family and friends, at this stage of his
celebrated life.

- At IMG's urging, he approved the highly unpopular sale of Bay
  Hill Club to a group of Japanese businessmen, igniting a spate
  of litigation and a storm of public outrage from many in Arnie's
  Army—and even in Arnie's family—still fighting World War II.
- Under IMG guidance, his visible role and equity stake in the
  posh Isleworth Country Club development in Orlando yanked
  him off the course and into the courtroom for a humbling $6.6
  million environmental judgment that drove his lifetime dream
  club into receivership.
- Finally, his auto empire was rocked by soap-opera infighting
  and more lawsuits connected to the failure of partner Jimmy
  O'Neal's attempt to form a publicly-held megachain of dealerships under the banner of Arnold Palmer Automotive Group.

That Arnie's image withstood such an onslaught speaks volumes for the solid bond he has forged with his public. Few celebrities could have recovered from such a broadside of controversy to
enjoy the widespread embrace that once again is his.

In a dot-and-dash column during this procession of disturbing
headlines, I offered this throwaway line: "If Mark McCormack and
his International Management Group are supposed to be keepers of

Arnold Palmer's image and finances, how would you score them right now? . . . "

Before noon on the day that column appeared, Johnston was on the phone transatlantic from Scotland, whining to me about the comment. For some thirty minutes, he made a case for how efficiently IMG was representing Arnie. Mostly, his arguments dealt with IMG's success at sheltering Arnie from significant financial losses in the three disasters. But he also offered the fractured logic that Arnie's image hadn't suffered in the auto deal "because Arnie has nothing to do with APAG."

Arnold Palmer has nothing to do with Arnold Palmer Automotive Group? No matter what it may say on stacks of legal documents, don't try to sell that one to the guy on the street.

True, what had begun with Arnie's permission as Arnold Palmer Automotive Group legally became only the acronym APAG after Arnie and O'Neal emotionally ended their partnership and close friendship for reasons detailed in the next chapter. But national news magazines obviously weren't buying Johnston's twisted rationale, as was painfully apparent in the headlines on accounts of the fifty-four-dealer smashup.

"THIS BOGEY HAS ARNIE'S NAME ON IT," screamed heavy black type over *Business Week's* March 1991 spread on APAG's legal jam. "PALMER'S MEGA FLIES OFF COURSE," *Auto Age's* July 1991 issue shouted.

The aborted Bay Hill sale to WDI Systems Inc., a Japanese holding company, is the perfect example of how persuasive money-hungry IMG can be with Arnie even when his family and closest friends argue that a profitable deal is a public relations time bomb. Arnie admits that Winnie and most of his close friends were upset with him over the attempted sale.

"That's basically right," he said. "She's very attached to this place."

Winnie: "You have to keep in mind that I'm my father's daughter. He still has a great influence on me and he was quite upset that the club was about to be sold to the Japanese group. Some of my boyfriends around here felt the same way. Newt Cox and Admiral [Joseph] Fowler live here at Bay Hill and they felt pretty strong about that. They influence my thinking a lot.

"Plus, I have a tremendous emotional attachment to Bay Hill. Isleworth is very nice and a wonderful club. But I'm not a country club socialite. I feel more at home at Bay Hill. This is a toy to me. Arnie has his planes and I have Bay Hill. There was a time when our kids were telling us that Bay Hill was sort of a mom and pop thing and needed more sophisticated management. So we did that for a while and that was the year when Arnie and I moved to Isleworth. I thought I could handle that better if I was over there most of the time. But now I'm back involved and it just will take some time to overcome some of the mistakes that were made."

Arnie says he wasn't that anxious to sell, but McCormack (who owns roughly 20 percent of Bay Hill) and Johnston kept mouthing the offer: twenty-five million dollars for the club with its twenty-seven holes and seventy-two-room lodge, plus another twenty-three million dollars in endorsement and course-design commitments to Arnie from WDI. "When you get a number like that—forty-eight million dollars—you've got to take a look," Arnie reasoned. A tentative agreement was reached and WDI put up three million dollars in earnest money. When the pending deal became public a few days into 1990, Arnie was darkly cast as a turncoat defector to the Rising Sun.

Johnston ignored his own grasp of the PR fallout: "To many people," he said, "Arnold Palmer selling Bay Hill to the Japanese is like John Wayne selling the prairie."

Said Arnie: "A lot of my friends were upset at me. I heard from everybody. Jeez, I got reports from everyone. I think what got to me most was the speculation on what would happen at the club after the new owners took over."

They never took over. WDI backed out of the deal, citing asbestos insulation and buried tanks that would have to be removed. WDI claimed Johnston had hidden those expensive problems. Johnston claimed WDI had failed to raise the money and was simply trying to recover the three-million-doller deposit. WDI sued Arnie. Arnie countersued WDI. The matter went to arbitration and the three million dollars was split.

The week before the sale was to close, O'Neal was in Arizona participating in an annual golf reunion of friends including such luminaries as former baseball commissioner Peter Ueberroth and San Francisco Giants owner Bob Lurie.

"Jim, aren't you involved as one of the owners of Bay Hill?" Ueberroth asked O'Neal over dinner that night. O'Neal nodded.

"Well, you know that deal's not going to close, don't you?"

"Yes it is," O'Neal corrected. "They were all in Orlando last week. Arnold played golf with them at Isleworth and gave them a putter and they were all happy."

"Well, I can tell you no matter what you think, I know the guy who was to buy it," said Ueberroth. "I played water polo against him in the Olympics."

After dinner, O'Neal called Johnston, who argued that Ueberroth didn't know what he was talking about.

"As it turned out, Peter Ueberroth knew exactly what he was talking about," recalled O'Neal. "The Japanese group didn't have

their money together. The deal didn't happen. But it was a PR disaster. Even my dad, who had been in the Navy, was furious that we were selling to the Japanese."

During negotiations, Ed Bignon, then head of Arnold Palmer Golf Management Company—which ran day-to-day operations at Bay Hill and dozens of clubs around the world—kept pressing Johnston for an assurance that the deal would include a long-term extension for APGMC to continue as overseers of Bay Hill. In trying to fend off all the concerns of members, Arnie assured one and all that little would change after the sale and that he would continue to run Bay Hill Club and its annual PGA tour event.

"Alastair was dealing with the Japanese group and I kept asking about what terms and conditions would be in place for the management contract," Bignon recalls. "Alastair kept telling me not to worry, that it would be taken care of."

Shortly thereafter, Bignon was speaking in Palm Springs at a golf seminar. In the audience was a representative for WDI, who introduced himself to Bignon after the session and advised there was no provision for APGMC to run the club for any significant length of time after the sale closed.

"I came home and screamed to Arnold about there being no management contract as part of the sale proposal. He called Alastair who insisted there was," said Bignon. "That was just life with Alastair. Caught him again. If the sale had gone through, Arnold would have had about two months of control and after that, nothing."

Johnston filed an offer in Orange County court proposing certain management rights for Arnie after the sale, but WDI didn't sign off on it.

Bignon would discover that complaining to Arnie about Johnston or McCormack could be fatal to one's job security. In addition to the terms of the Bay Hill sale proposal, Bignon had also opposed Johnston on several other matters—not the least of which was Johnston's veto of an offer by Prudential to give Arnie the golf course at its Turtle Bay resort in Hawaii. "Why do we want to own a golf course in Hawaii?" Johnston asked, arguing that having the 5 percent management contract was better than running the risk of the course making a profit. In 1992 the twenty-seven-hole Turtle Bay golf operation grossed seven million dollars and in 1993 APGMC's management contract would expire. Indications were that APGMC, which could have had all the profits from that seven million dollars, wouldn't even have its 5 percent after 1993. Bignon howled to Arnie about the ill advice Johnston was giving him.

"One thing I've learned over the years," says Dave Harman, an independent contractor who did the earth-moving for most Arnie designed course projects, "is you don't ever want to be the messenger of bad tidings going into Arnold's office. You'll wind up with a bullet between your eyes. It might not come there. It might be a week later, but you will have been shot."

Bignon's bullet arrived in December 1990 when, at Johnston's urging, he was fired.

"You do anything at all to tick off Alastair," said former Isleworth general manager Carter Speer, "and he'll stay after you until he gets you."

According to Bignon and myriad other current and former staffers, Johnston was not only into managing Arnie's business affairs, but also managing how much Arnie knew about them.

Said Ed Bignon: "If I heard it once, I heard it a thousand times from Alastair and the others at IMG: 'Arnold doesn't need to know about this.'"

Apparently Arnie didn't need to know about the lowball settlement opportunity that could have averted the $6.6 million judg-

ment that rocked Isleworth. Before the case went to trial Arnie was asked about whispers of fifty thousand dollars, one hundred thousand dollars, and two hundred thousand dollars settlement offers variously stiff-armed by Johnston, Isleworth attorneys, Arnie's Isleworth partners, and perhaps, Isleworth general manager Peter Fox in the early stages of the dispute. Arnie said he didn't believe there were any such offers. "I'm sure I'd know about that if it had happened," he said.

Alas, it did happen. And McCormack didn't deny it, though he said he didn't recall the offers ever being that low.

"We had done nothing wrong, so we felt why should we pay a couple hundred thousand dollars to somebody for nothing?" he said. "I suppose hindsight is always good. What if I had hit a 4-iron instead of a 3-iron? I didn't pay much attention to it."

The 1987 suit centered around Isleworth's drainage system that was dumping stormwater and nitrate-laced golf course runoff through a forty-two-inch drainpipe into landlocked Lake Bessie, a pristine, 175-acre lake straddling one boundary of the development. Dotting the opposite shoreline are a number of comfortable old Florida homes that are not part of Isleworth. Those residents claimed the runoff was raising and polluting Lake Bessie. The creeping shoreline was destroying their docks and lakeside trees and shrubs.

John Robertson, a trial lawyer and one of those Lake Bessie residents, led the fight. It became clear that Johnston had convinced Arnie that Robertson was virtually the devil incarnate. In truth, he is a kindly man and accomplished artist whose oils of his dogs and Florida scenes adorn his airy home with its dock and gazebo overlooking Lake Bessie. He vows he had no desire to harm Arnie, only to stop the pollution and overflow of Bessie. With trial experience in cases involving some of the country's most prominent developers, Robertson knew the territory. Early on, he tried to arrange an audience with Arnie, hoping to effect a solution that would avoid a costly and senseless legal fight, but Arnie's underlings refused to allow it.

Robertson said the first settlement offer to drop the suit involved no cash at all—simply a request that Isleworth plug the offending drainage pipe. "Fox said they'd never change it, that they'd break me first," he recalled. "They began to stonewall and lie about everything."

As expenses for legal and engineering spadework grew, the offer increased to: fix the problem, plus fifty thousand dollars. Then one hundred thousand dollars. Then two hundred thousand dollars. The latter offer was tendered both by phone and in writing August 9, 1989, to Tallahassee attorney Chris H. Bentley, a state regulatory specialist that Isleworth attorney Bill Doster had hired to help fight the Bessie residents. With each offer, Doster, after checking with Johnston and/or Jay Eddy (president of Arnie's development partner Concord Corporation), haughtily told Robertson and his neighbors—as one Orlando lawyer so quaintly put it—to go pound sand.

Despite the grim knowledge that losing the suit could send him and neighbors into financial ruin, Robertson decided to take up the fight. "I didn't feel I could hold myself out as a lawyer if I couldn't protect my own property and the property of my neighbors," he said.

Three years and mountains of depositions, exhibits, and engineering studies later, at the conclusion of the longest civil trial in Orange County Circuit Court history, a six-member jury found for the Lake Bessie residents and ordered Isleworth to pay them $2.7 million. Judge Bernard Muszynski tacked on $3.9 million in legal

Associated Press

Howdy Giles

(Above) Golfing greats Jack Nicklaus, Arnold Palmer and Greg Norman share a laugh during practice for the Masters in 1990.

(Left) A pensive Arnie contemplates his next move.

(Top right) Arnie with his unofficial dentist and photographer, Howdy Giles, with the elegant Isleworth clubhouse in the background.

(Bottom right) Arnie and George Bush became frequent golf companions, including this day at Cave's Valley C.C. outside Baltimore on the weekend the President asked Arnie to run – but not as his V.P. He autographed the picture for photographer Howdy Giles.

Courtesy of Bay Hill Club

(Above) This cherished photo of a younger Arnie and his dad, Milfred "Deacon" Palmer hangs in the Bay Hill clubhouse. *(Below)* Winnie Palmer has been standing behind Arnie for nearly 40 years.

Howdy Giles

developers, Robertson knew the territory. Early on, he tried to arrange an audience with Arnie, hoping to effect a solution that would avoid a costly and senseless legal fight, but Arnie's underlings refused to allow it.

Robertson said the first settlement offer to drop the suit involved no cash at all—simply a request that Isleworth plug the offending drainage pipe. "Fox said they'd never change it, that they'd break me first," he recalled. "They began to stonewall and lie about everything."

As expenses for legal and engineering spadework grew, the offer increased to: fix the problem, plus fifty thousand dollars. Then one hundred thousand dollars. Then two hundred thousand dollars. The latter offer was tendered both by phone and in writing August 9, 1989, to Tallahassee attorney Chris H. Bentley, a state regulatory specialist that Isleworth attorney Bill Doster had hired to help fight the Bessie residents. With each offer, Doster, after checking with Johnston and/or Jay Eddy (president of Arnie's development partner Concord Corporation), haughtily told Robertson and his neighbors—as one Orlando lawyer so quaintly put it—to go pound sand.

Despite the grim knowledge that losing the suit could send him and neighbors into financial ruin, Robertson decided to take up the fight. "I didn't feel I could hold myself out as a lawyer if I couldn't protect my own property and the property of my neighbors," he said.

Three years and mountains of depositions, exhibits, and engineering studies later, at the conclusion of the longest civil trial in Orange County Circuit Court history, a six-member jury found for the Lake Bessie residents and ordered Isleworth to pay them $2.7 million. Judge Bernard Muszynski tacked on $3.9 million in legal

ment that rocked Isleworth. Before the case went to trial Arnie was asked about whispers of fifty thousand dollars, one hundred thousand dollars, and two hundred thousand dollars settlement offers variously stiff-armed by Johnston, Isleworth attorneys, Arnie's Isleworth partners, and perhaps, Isleworth general manager Peter Fox in the early stages of the dispute. Arnie said he didn't believe there were any such offers. "I'm sure I'd know about that if it had happened," he said.

Alas, it did happen. And McCormack didn't deny it, though he said he didn't recall the offers ever being that low.

"We had done nothing wrong, so we felt why should we pay a couple hundred thousand dollars to somebody for nothing?" he said. "I suppose hindsight is always good. What if I had hit a 4-iron instead of a 3-iron? I didn't pay much attention to it."

The 1987 suit centered around Isleworth's drainage system that was dumping stormwater and nitrate-laced golf course runoff through a forty-two-inch drainpipe into landlocked Lake Bessie, a pristine, 175-acre lake straddling one boundary of the development. Dotting the opposite shoreline are a number of comfortable old Florida homes that are not part of Isleworth. Those residents claimed the runoff was raising and polluting Lake Bessie. The creeping shoreline was destroying their docks and lakeside trees and shrubs.

John Robertson, a trial lawyer and one of those Lake Bessie residents, led the fight. It became clear that Johnston had convinced Arnie that Robertson was virtually the devil incarnate. In truth, he is a kindly man and accomplished artist whose oils of his dogs and Florida scenes adorn his airy home with its dock and gazebo overlooking Lake Bessie. He vows he had no desire to harm Arnie, only to stop the pollution and overflow of Bessie. With trial experience in cases involving some of the country's most prominent

Courtesy of Howdy Giles

To Howdy
Must have been
one great shot
Arnold

Howdy Giles

Mike Zizzo/The Orlando Sentinel

(Left) Caddie Royce Nielson tests wind direction for Arnie, a man Nielson said is one of the hardest working people he's ever been around.

(Below) Arnie and IMG agent, Alastair Johnston.

(Top right) Some of the tour's younger players surprised Arnie with a cake during a rain delay at Bay Hill in 1991. Present at the emotional tribute were: Peter Jacobsen (with cake), Paul Azinger, Leonard Thompson, Greg Norman, Ray Floyd, Jeff Sluman, Bill Kratzert, Wayne Grady, Bob Tway, Robert Wrenn, David Frost, Tom Kite and Tom Seickmann.

(Bottom right) Q.B. Palmer "sacked" by Oklahoma State defense during a Citrus Bowl publicity stunt. As a kid, Arnie loved to sneak in sandlot football games because his father didn't want him to jeopardize golf.

Howdy Giles

Howdy Giles

Red Huber/The Orlando Sentinel

The Orlando Sentinel

Courtesy of Bay Hill Club

(Above) In something of a tradition, Arnie often plays host to the head coaches of the Citrus Bowl teams. Here he's with then Ohio State Coach Earle Bruce (left) and Brigham Young Coach Lavell Edwards for a game of golf before the '86 bowl game.

(Left) Arnie and The Great White Shark, Greg Norman. This photo hangs in the Bay Hill clubhouse.

(Top right) At this stage of Isleworth construction, Arnie didn't envision the legal hassles that would plague the project.

(Center right) A time for celebration: A grand opening for the Arnold Palmer Hospital for Children & Women, and Arnie's 60th birthday, in 1989.

(Bottom right) Arnie and Winnie at the hospital's groundbreaking.

Dennis Wall/The Orlando Sentinel

Tom Spitz/The Orlando Sentinel

The Orlando Sentinel

George Skene/The Orlando Sentinel

Eileen Samelson/The Orlando Sentinel

(Above) A 1985 photo captures the warmth of family as Arnie and Winnie take time out for granddaughters Emily and Katie Saunders, then 4 and 2.

(Left) Even during tournament rounds when autographs are supposed to be taboo, Arnie has trouble resisting the younger fans.

(Top right) "…You slash at it as hard as you can, then hitch your pants."

(Center right) Arnie's Army comes in all sizes, shapes and ages.

(Bottom right) Arnie with former Nestle USA CEO Jim Biggar and Nestle Invitational tournament director Jim Bell at a pro-am party prior to the 1991 tournament.

Mark Losey/The Orlando Sentinel

Bobby Coker/The Orlando Sentinel

Joe Burbank/The Orlando Sentinel

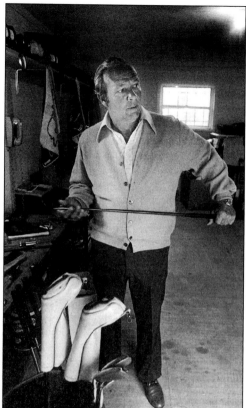

The Orlando Sentinel

(Left) Tinkering with his clubs in his shop on an almost daily basis is therapeutic more for Arnie than his clubs.

(Below) Winnie and Arnie on a float boat ride on the chain of lakes at Bay Hill.

(Top right) A newspaper's playful composite of Arnie being sworn in as "Prez."

(Bottom right) This picture of Arnie the golf star and Joan Collins the screen star hangs in the Bay Hill clubhouse.

Howdy Giles

Orlando Sentinel composite

Courtesy of Bay Hill Club

Howdy Giles

(Left) The one place he can find sanctuary from the phones and the autograph hounds – in the cabin of N1AP.

(Below) Arnie and O.J. Simpson teamed up for fun and a commercial. Another of Arnie's favorite photos, this hangs in the Bay Hill clubhouse.

(Right) The famous Swing.

Courtesy of Bay Hill Club

The Many Faces of Arnie ...

Howdy Giles

Howdy Giles

Red Huber/ The Orlando Sentinel

The Orlando Sentinel

fees and waded back into his caseload of embattled couples fighting over the house and custody of the children.

A multimillion-dollar suit involving a famous golfer and some of the county's most powerful figures jousting over the clarity and level of a little lake had been much more stimulating. "This is much better than a divorce," Muszynski said at one point in the proceedings.

It was not much fun for Arnie, however. The "couple hundred thousand" that McCormack thought unreasonable had become $6.6 million and financial apocalypse for the Concord/Palmer partnership. Concord defaulted on loans, taxes and other obligations, and Mellon Bank sued to foreclose on Isleworth.

Johnston proudly announced: "Arnold Palmer has no exposure, no liability." But plenty of ulcers.

Arnie's avowed dream club had become one of his worst nightmares—one that could have been averted with a few bucks and a little less arrogance by those charged with handling his affairs.

At the Masters tournament three months before the trial, McCormack had been introduced to Orlando attorney Victor Woodman, who related a telling exchange.

McCormack: "What sort of guy is this Robertson fellow?"

Woodman: "He's a competent lawyer and if he feels he has a case, you would be wise to take it seriously."

McCormack: "Ah, we're gonna crush him."

Robertson said Isleworth's downfall in the case was just that sort of attitude and arrogance.

Dave Harman thinks Arnie's advisors should have brought him to the raging inferno when it was only a brushfire. "My thought has always been they should take advantage of Arnold's ability to negotiate with people," said Harman. "Take advantage of the fact that people respect Arnold and that integrity is what he's all about. Put him in that situation, and even if it comes a cropper, you're going to get kicked in the ass a lot softer if he was there to help, than keeping him hidden. There have been so many times where there have been mistakes or problems, some understandable, where had Arnold stepped in and said, 'Hey we made a mistake or we're gonna correct this, it's no big deal,' it wouldn't be a problem. But they purposely keep him in the dark."

The crippling Isleworth suit was the perfect example.

"If Arnold had walked into a meeting one day and said, 'Hey, I've been on the road playing golf. What's this I hear about a drainage problem? How can we work it out?' he would have worked out a solution and they'd all have ended up in the bar having a beer and laughing."

Instead, Arnie's own court testimony revealed his IMG advisors and Isleworth lieutenants initially had told him nothing of the offending drainpipe, downplayed it when he first heard of the flap, then falsely told him the problem had been fixed as he had ordered. "Arnie," said Robertson, "was surrounded by a bad group of people. We would have been happy to have let him come in and be the hero. 'Arnold Palmer, big ecologist, comes in and saves the lake.' We'd have hugged him on TV."

Isleworth is located on five hundred acres of rolling Central Florida grove land with frontage on Bessie and six other lakes. During the Civil War, the property was used as collateral to secure payment on scrip issued to Confederate soldiers. In 1894, Joshua and Sydney Chase tracked down and bought enough of the scrip from former Confederate soldiers to acquire the first major parcel

Larry Guest

of what would become the Chase Groves, one of Florida's most respected and innovative citrus operations.

Arnie said the site first caught his eye in 1948 when, as a member of Wake Forest University's golf team, he played Rollins College in nearby Winter Park. Later, he and his father boated on the Butler chain of lakes and talked about what fun it would be to build a course there on the banks just a few hundred yards from his own Bay Hill Club.

"I just fell in love with it," Arnie said. "It's one of the most beautiful pieces of property in the world."

He was thrilled in 1984 to acquire the land on behalf of his development partner Concord, a San Antonio-based company owned by one of Mexico's most prominent families. For arranging the purchase, designing the golf course, and lending his name and TLC to the project, Concord would give him two prime lots and a minority equity share in the development.

Arnie had designed more than one hundred golf courses — but all for other people. "I had never built one for myself," he said, "built one that was going to be just right." He hailed Isleworth as "the potential capstone of my career. I want the entire facility to be a credit to the game of golf and to me personally."

As promised to Frank Chase when they bought the property, Arnie and Concord dressed the old girl in finery. The development would have lush landscaping including some ten thousand azaleas. Parts of its main boulevards would be paved in crushed pink granite and imported Mexican stone, leading to sprawling houses that range up to and well beyond one million dollars. The centerpiece is a sprawling, three story, 63,000-square-foot, Mediterranean clubhouse. Arnie's office featured a leather floor, and the men's grill is adorned by a massive refrigeration door from one of the old Chase warehouses. The woodwork in the main bar, dining room, and elegant ballroom is a deep-brown Brazilian walnut.

Just up the shoreline from the clubhouse, Arnie intended to build Winnie's dream house, where they would retire to spoiling grandchildren and leafing through scrapbooks of Augusta National triumphs.

The Golden Pond storyline first took a wrong turn when, during construction of the course, the drainage plan was improperly altered to route some stormwater not into the vast Butler chain where it could be absorbed, but through the added forty-two-inch pipe into land-locked Lake Bessie. Robertson and his neighbors on the opposite shore soon discovered their homesites were being flooded. When they felt their complaints were being ignored, they filed suit but made the early offers to drop the action in exchange for relief and modest expenses.

Robertson was saddened that he couldn't seem to get the attention of Isleworth's development team of Doster, Fox, and Arnie's main man, Alastair Johnston. He was also saddened when Doster thumbed his nose at the settlement offers. But sad turned to mad when Polly, his twelve-year-old Old English Setter, slipped off his half-submerged dock and drowned—a tragedy that drew little compassion from his ritzy new neighbors across the lake.

"When Peter Fox told Robertson he didn't give a crap that the dog had drowned," Johnston said, "I think the die was cast."

"That's an outright lie. I never said anything like that," Fox said angrily. "I don't want to say anything negative about Arnold. But Arnold knows nothing about real estate and Alastair and those people know less. IMG is beautiful. They never make a mistake. It's always someone else's fault."

Robertson affirmed that Fox never said anything unkind to him about his dearly departed dog.

Larry Guest

The Lake Bessie judgment was soon joined by other headaches. "It was Developer 101," said Bignon. "Every mistake to be made, they made it."

The state discovered that the main entrance to the development, complete with electronic gates and security hut, had been illegally built on state land. In a letter on his law firm's stationery, dated January 9, 1985, Doster remarkably advised the other principals that the gate site was on state land but suggested they illegally "take the risk" that state officials would not discover the encroachment.

The risk cost $162,000 in fines by the state Department of Natural Resources, one of the steepest ever levied by the DNR.

Approached by reporters, Bill Doster refused comment.

A few months after the Lake Bessie trial, the ITT Hartford Insurance Group sued Isleworth, charging, remarkably—there's that word again—that no one from the development informed the insurance company of the Lake Bessie suit until after the judgment had been rendered. The Hartford company, which wrote at least one million dollars in liability insurance covering buildings and grounds at Isleworth, balked at paying the claim.

The insurance company said it did not receive notice about the suit from Isleworth until November 1990—three-and-a-half years after the suit was filed. Thus, Hartford never had a chance to represent itself or attempt to settle the suit.

Isleworth attorney Bill Doster did not tell Hartford to pound sand. He declined to comment.

Just before leaving on a business trip to Japan in March 1991, Arnie gave Winnie a portable cellular phone for her birthday.

Winnie is not much into contemporary electronics. Computers, calculators, cellular phones give her the willies. She appreciated the thought, she told Arnie, but doubted that she would use the phone very much. Arnie said she would be surprised just how handy the little fold-up phones are. Neither fathomed just how quickly that would be underscored.

A few days later, Winnie had a board meeting at the Arnold Palmer Hospital for Children & Women in downtown Orlando. Afterward she had lunch and decided to slip away and do what she occasionally does—take in an afternoon movie by herself. She went to the artsy Enzian theater that day to see Cyrano, starring a French actor she had been wanting to see.

Ten minutes into the film, a strange chirping sound could be heard. Other moviegoers began shuffling at the noise and craning toward Winnie, who belatedly realized with great embarrassment the chirping was coming from her purse. The cellular phone.

She scurried out into the lobby and took the call from Judy Furman, Arnie's longtime secretary and family confidante. Furman was frantic. She had just received word that sheriff's deputies were being dispatched to Isleworth with a court order to seize anything that wasn't nailed down. None of the $6.6 million judgment had been paid and the Lake Bessie residents were growing impatient. Perhaps a scavenger hunt through the Isleworth clubhouse would serve as a down payment. "Ohmigod," Winnie thought. "Arnie's trophies! My grand piano!"

Winnie bolted from the theater and raced across town, furiously punching numbers on the little cellular phone. She called Kathy Merrill, the Palmers' houseperson, with instructions to gather up all the bags she could find and get over to the Isleworth clubhouse pronto. She put in an emergency call to a furniture mover. Help! Help!

Arriving at the club, Winnie quickly cleaned out the trophy cases of assorted glittering and prestigious baubles that Arnie had collected along the golf trail. "I still have all of them locked up in a closet here at Bay Hill," she said, nearly two years later.

The furniture movers arrived to help shift all of the furniture out of Arnie's posh, third-story office and into a friend's garage. The piano was transported to Bay Hill for safekeeping.

Winnie had bought the Steinway grand piano and loaned it to the Isleworth Club shortly after the clubhouse was completed. The club featured an elegant ballroom that cried out for a grand piano, but the initial budget stopped short of such an accessory.

"My thought was to one day give the piano to one of our children," says Winnie. "If the sheriff had taken it, I could see it being put in some holding pen. I wasn't going to let that happen to a Steinway."

Robertson said he had instructed deputies not to touch anything in Arnie's office. Little did he know at the time that about all Winnie had left in Arnie's office to be taken was the light switch.

Robertson wasn't after sentimental mementos, he said. He was just weary of Arnie's underlings and partners thumbing their noses at the court order just as they had at Robertson and his neighbors for more than three years.

The Orange County deputies seized forty golf carts, six riding mowers, four other vehicles, and merchandise from the pro shop, including golf balls, clothes, and umbrellas. The club had to be closed, but the course reopened the next day when Arnie, trying to put out the fires from Japan, sent crews from Bay Hill to mow the fairways and greens. Nothing he could do, though, about the club's planned Easter dinner that Sunday.

"It was going to be a great weekend for our members," club manager Ed Blakely said. "We had more than three hundred reservations. It's unfortunate."

In November 1991, more than a year after the Lake Bessie trial, all parties resolved the dispute. Robertson, et al., let Isleworth off the hook with a confidential, reduced settlement believed to be in the neighborhood of five million dollars, which was used to restore the lake. Further, Isleworth had to hire Harman's company to rebuild one fairway and revise the drainage to keep the runoff out of Lake Bessie.

"The cost was $250,000 and everybody's happy," Harman said. "Now, if that's all that was needed, you tell me why they lost a $6.6 million judgment and ran up $1.5 million in fees to their own lawyers."

As the controversy faded, Isleworth began to rebound and blossom again even before Mellon Bank unloaded the development in a 1993 auction. Million-dollar homes once again began to spring up around the course, many of them purchased by sports stars. The neighborhood athletic who's who now includes pro golfers Tiger Woods, Mark O'Meara, and Craig Parry; Orlando Magic stars Penny Hardaway and Dennis Scott; and baseball superstar Ken Griffey Jr. Golfers Payne Stewart and Scott Hoch are Isleworth members and live nearby. Just off Isleworth's fifteenth hole, basketball's Shaquille O'Neal bought and expanded a sprawling lakefront mansion, which he kept as his prime residence even after jumping from the Orlando Magic to the Los Angeles Lakers in the summer of 1996.

The new owner, wealthy and golf-crazed British financier Joe Lewis, who submitted the $20.64-million winning bid to Mellon Bank, promptly invited Arnie to take a significant but nonequity role in the new management of the club.

However, Arnie, embarassed and angered by the turn of events that cost him his stake in the posh development, not only declined Lewis's offer, but systematically divorced himself from the club. He sold a tenth fairway spec home in which he and Winnie lived briefly and moved back into their condo at nearby Bay Hill Club. He sold the Isleworth property he and McCormack acquired from O'Neal in the auto partnership breakup. And he began to play less and less at the club with the several close friends who had moved there at Arnie's urging when the development first opened. For a period of time, he even refused to set foot inside the clubhouse, having his playing partners bring out a sandwich to the patio area for him if they stopped at the turn for lunch.

Arnie completed the retreat in 1996 when he sold those two prime lots—where Winnie's dream home was intended just up the shoreline from the clubhouse—to Orlando Magic president Bob Vander Weide. That Isleworth golden pond scenario faded into but a painful memory of troubled water.

7

Arnie's Mutt and Jeff Sidekicks

As key supporting characters in Arnie's life saga, Dick Tiddy and Jimmy O'Neal represent a study in stark contrasts and mirror similarities. They are similar in that for years they have been extremely close colleagues and confidants of Arnie's, sidekicks as trusted as anyone in Arnie's solar system. Tiddy, the college teammate and twenty-five-year staffer, and O'Neal, the business partner and intimate travel companion, are outspoken advocates of Arnie and remain fiercely loyal to and supportive of their celebrity golfing pal. Both are hale fellows well met, upbeat souls whose personalities and presence routinely lifted Arnie and made his life even more enjoyable.

THERE WAS ALWAYS a physical contrast between the two. O'Neal is a pint-sized elf of 5'5"; Tiddy a giant of a man at 6'6" and, during most of his life, more than three hundred pounds. But their differing status in Arnie's Army widened dramatically when O'Neal was banished as an outcast from the inner circle after his and Arnie's auto-dealer partnership dissolved in a flood of red ink and criminal charges against O'Neal. (In 1995, O'Neal was acquitted of the more serious charges and convicted and fined only on a misdemeanor tax evasion matter involving the sales tax collections at one of the Arnold Palmer Automotive Group dealerships.)

Like Tiddy, O'Neal remains an enthusiastic Arnie advocate even in the wake of their massive business fender-bender and resulting friendship split. However, Tiddy and O'Neal remained good friends through the messy auto episode. The two men represent windows of intimate observation into the man they call "King."

Mention of the "King" around the Bay Hill Club is a common reference to only one man — that international golfing legend in residence, the famed proprietor, Arnold Palmer. But additional royalty could be typically found padding about the prestigious club for years, adjusting stacks of sweaters in the pro shop or scrutinizing somebody's swing on the practice tee.

The Prince of Bay Hill. That's the combination rank and personality assessment long accorded Dick Tiddy, Arnie's longtime Bay Hill head professional and, more recently, director of instruction for the Arnold Palmer Golf Academy headquartered at the Orlando club. "Prince" is invariably the word that emerges each time Tiddy's name pops up. As in, ". . . what a prince of a guy."

Here's a man even Don Rickles would like. An easygoing giant with a gentle, unassuming manner that has endeared him to colleagues and clients alike. A pro's pro whose unpretentiousness is greater even than his grain elevator dimensions. It's a rare personality that can make someone with such an imposing silhouette seem part of the woodwork, but Tiddy would rather blend in and serve than flex his own ego—if he has one.

Although "prince" fits nicely with Tiddy, his principal handle with close friends is a lifetime moniker gained while a rumbling, 260-pound football fullback at Charlotte (N.C.) Central High School. He answered to "Train" long before Arnie reflexively blurted that very nickname at first sighting of his very large new freshman golf teammate at Wake Forest College in North Carolina. The year was 1948.

"A teammate on my freshman team was Mickey Gallagher, now a pro at PGA National in West Palm Beach," Tiddy said of that initial encounter with Arnie. "I was about 6'6" and weighed about three hundred. Mickey was maybe 6'5" and weighed about 130. Arnie looked at us and said, 'Here we have the "Train" and here we have the "Human One-Iron!" So those names stuck with us through the years.

"From that day, through college, and through the years, Arnie and I have remained close friends. Another team member, Bubby Worsham, was his very closest friend at Wake. They roomed together and after Bubby was killed in a car wreck, Arnie lost interest in college and left school before graduating."

Prior to the tragic accident, Arnie and Worsham played 1-2 for Wake in the dual-match collegiate format of that era, which called for a team's No. 1 player to play the No. 1 of the other school in individual three-point match play, No. 2 vs. No. 2, and Nos. 1-2 vs. Nos. 1-2 in a simultaneous three-point, two-man team match play. Tiddy and Gallagher did likewise as Wake's 3-4 combo. With that 1-4 murderers' row, Wake cut a wide swath through 1949-50 college golf, winning the 1950 Southern Intercollegiate and back-to-back conference championships.

"I had heard a little about Arnie before I got to Wake," Tiddy said. "But I could tell from the first day I played with him in practice that he was really an overpowering player. Of that era, he was like Tiger Woods or John Daly today—very long compared to other players. I was long, but I was surprised a guy that size—Arnold wasn't very big in those days—could hit it so far.

"He always drove good, but the best part of Arnie's game back then was long irons—2-, 3-, 4-irons. He could nail those in there time after time. He was very aggressive, very confident in himself.

"We got along so good, we were very close. All the guys on the team were close. Bubby Worsham had the only car, a real pile of bolts, and we all piled in there and ran around together. For our golf team trips, the school had an old four-door DeSoto we'd travel in. We'd stuff all six of us and our little cloth golf bags in there and off we'd go. It was fun. We had a great time. Arnold was the leader. He was the take-charge guy. Several weekends, he went home with me to Charlotte. Back then, we'd hitchhike the 150 miles. My family liked him a lot. We shot a lot of pool, went to a lot of movies. We even studied some."

One spring, the Wake team drove the DeSoto all the way from North Carolina to Winter Park, Florida, for a match against Rollins College at Dubsdread Golf Club, then a fashionable facility which now serves as the City of Orlando's public, municipal course.

The Washington Senators trained in Orlando at the time and the Wake golf team was awed their first night at Dubsdread by a chance encounter with the Senators' star pitcher, Bobo Newsome. During the trip, Arnie was awed more by a Rollins women's golf

team member, who so turned his head that he approached the Rollins golf coach about transferring to the Central Florida school. Thrilled with the idea, then golf coach Joe Justice was turned down by Rollins administrators when he requested scholarship assistance for young Palmer. For but a small investment, Rollins might have reaped a lifetime of lucrative returns and prestige that have, instead, been enjoyed by Wake Forest.

The Rollins coed, now Mrs. Betty Probasco of Chattanooga, Tennessee, is a former Tennessee women's amateur champion and remains a prominent amateur golfer. She is married to banker Scotty Probasco.

In the national college finals that spring at Albuquerque, Arnie was the individual medalist for the second year in a row and Tiddy won the long-drive contest. But although Wake had handed the North Texas State juggernaut its first defeat by winning the Southern Intercollegiate at Athens, Georgia, the Demon Deacons couldn't disrupt North Texas State's four-year title string at Albuquerque. The Texans were anchored by future tour pros Don January and Billy Maxwell.

Contrary to a number of accounts, Tiddy and Arnie, though genuinely close, were never roommates at Wake. "Supposedly, about 950 guys roomed with Arnie at Wake," muses Tiddy. "But I only remember two—Bubby Worsham and a basketball player named Al McCotter. Even on the road, Arnie and Bubby roomed together and I roomed with Mickey Gallagher."

The legendary Peahead Walker was the football coach at Wake, where the football practice field was directly between the athletic dorm and the nine-hole campus golf course. Recalled Tiddy: "We had to walk right by the football team working out every day, our golf bags over our shoulders on the way to practice while they were beating heads. We got a lot of kidding from the football players in the dining hall."

Though Arnie was of relatively slight stature, Walker openly envisioned his strong arms and shoulders covered by a set of Wake pads. But Arnie's father had a clearer vision and wouldn't hear of Arnie subjecting his bright golf future to the perils of football.

In the first few years after college, Tiddy and Arnie were reunited just once, at the inaugural of a long-running charity tournament in Bethesda, Maryland, in memory of Bubby Worsham. Arnie was in the Coast Guard at the time. It was a match-play affair that boiled down to a championship final between Dick and Arnie. "We both wanted to win. I never will forget that match," says Tiddy.

Both players boldly hit their opening tee shots over the trees to cut the dogleg on the first hole, a feat that remains part of Bethesda Country Club lore. Arnie won, two-up, and Bubby's brother Lew, who went on to PGA tour fame, presided over the awards presentations.

"I'd hear from Arnold occasionally," Tiddy recounts. "I went to work and Arnie went on the tour. Then five of my members at Charlotte C.C. sponsored me to go out on tour in 1959, starting with the Rubber City Open in Akron, Ohio. By then, Arnie was in his heyday."

The two old college chums occasionally were paired in tournaments but mainly renewed their friendship over evening beers and regular practice rounds. The most memorable of those for Tiddy was a practice round at Hartford, Connecticut, when Arnie and Dick had an informal match against Gene Littler and Ted Kroll. "Arnold and I shot a best-ball of 59 because he shot 60 by himself. I managed to cut him one shot. And I think we won a total of six bucks," laughed Tiddy, who remained on the tour just two

years before being offered the head pro job back home at the Charlotte Country Club.

"I did all right on tour. I finished fifteenth at Tucson one year, which was my best finish. I won $275 for that, my biggest check. But those were fun days. We all had a good time. We were on the road, driving, all the time. You might have to drive from Salt Lake City to San Antonio for the next tournament. I was driving a green-and-black '54 Buick, and two other players, Jimmy Riggins and Mac Main, rode with me most of the time."

Tiddy returned home in 1961 to resume his career as a club professional, first as head pro at Charlotte Country Club and then across town at Cedarwood Golf Club. He and Arnie maintained their friendship through occassional talks and pro-ams. In the summer of 1971, Arnie asked Tiddy to consider moving to Orlando as head pro of the Bay Hill Club that Arnie had acquired a few years earlier and established as his winter home. Arnie flew Dick to Bay Hill and sealed the deal with but a handshake.

"We never had a contract. I moved to Orlando six months later, January 1, 1972." In 1988, Dick became director of golf, then later moved into his current role as Director of Instruction for the Arnold Palmer Golf Academy, which is based at Bay Hill.

"For all the years I was the head pro, Arnold would just tell me to do what I thought was right. I never called him, never asked him a question. Never did." But he used his privileged, point-blank vantage point to develop his own observations on why his old college teammate had become one of the most compelling sports personalities on the planet.

"Arnie is an everyday guy. Gets up early, works out, plays with the guys. He makes himself available. That's what I like about Arnie. He's there. He's an aggressive person. He plays golf aggressively. He doesn't shy away from people. He's very outgoing.

"And he's worked hard. We had some guys on that team in school—we were all good. But out of golf season, I might play fraternity football or some of us might play in a pickup softball game or something. But Arnie was out working on his golf game. He made those sacrifices great players make and I think that made him better."

Tiddy typically migrates to Augusta National each spring as a spectator at the Masters to renew hundreds of golf-related friendships and follow the exploits of his famous friend. He recently flashed back fondly to a scene on Friday of a recent Masters, Arnie's nostalgia-laced and historic thirty-fifth appearance at the storied tournament. Though he had disappointingly missed the thirty-six-hole cut despite a back-nine charge that included three birdies and an eagle, Arnie lingered in the parking lot, thanking hundreds of those nameless but familiar faces who had made up Arnie's Army year after year. "He told them how much he appreciated all that they had done for him and their support," Tiddy recalled sweetly. "To me, that was fantastic. Those people were really moved."

The son of an insurance salesman, Dick Tiddy was born July 14, 1929, two months ahead of his future pal Arnie. Remarkably, this hulk of a man was just five pounds at birth, but he quickly made up for that. As a first-grader, he was larger than his teacher.

Young Tiddy's storied appetite suggests he needed a fork with racing stripes. Says John "Lefty" Tiddy, one of Dick's two brothers: "We never had anything left on anybody's plate. Thanks to Dick, Mom never had much dishwashing to do."

In an interview a few years before Lucille Tiddy died, she recalled that the lunch she packed daily for her largest son rarely reached school. She affirmed an oft-told tale about the basket of chicken she fried for Dick's third-grade picnic. Seems he paused

Larry Guest

under a shade tree on the way to school, was overcome by the magnificent aroma, and only the basket arrived at the picnic. "I didn't sit down from the third grade through the fifth grade, my daddy whipped me so bad over that," he recalled.

Dick became the champion of just about every country club and ice cream parlor in North Carolina. While still in high school and wearing overall pants and a white T-shirt, according to Lefty, Dick defeated famed U.S. Amateur champ Harvie Ward in a tournament at sophisticated Charlotte Country Club. It was there at C.C.C. where one of the most respected golf club professionals in the business would later get his start as an apprentice.

A gifted and well-coordinated athlete for a lad of his immense proportions, Tiddy naturally included football among his boyhood activities. As an underclassman at Charlotte Central, he played tackle but also put his uncommon coordination to work as an impressive placekicker and punter. For his senior season, he was switched from tackle to fullback and became sort of an unstoppable early version of the lovable Bill Cosby character, Fat Albert. Thus the nickname — "Train."

Tiddy's career as a ball carrier ended in a game against Miami Edison in the Orange Bowl where he incurred a serious knee injury that required extensive surgery. Still, his football coach, Bill Brannin, urged Tiddy to accept a football scholarship to any one of several major colleges as a punter. Dick averaged 44.7 yards per punt during his senior year at Charlotte Central. That would typically rank among the top five punters in most any recent NFL season.

Tiddy's impressive resume as a high school football, track, and golf star was compiled for this book only through diligent sleuthing and research; a tower of modesty, Tiddy is not one to toot his own trombone.

"I was a good kicker. I was big and strong and could kick it a long way," Tiddy admitted, almost sheepishly, when pressed. "Coach Brannin thought I was a better punter than anything else."

But his first love was a more genteel sport, and he was off to Wake Forest on a golf scholarship and what would become a lifelong relationship with Arnie.

"We became close friends, and I probably taught Dick all of his bad habits," Arnie once mused. "He came to Wake as a ministerial student and left as a golf pro, if that tells you something. He was one of the boys—he played golf, shot pool, drank beer, and ate hot dogs."

As the head pro at Charlotte's Cedarwood Country Club for eight years and later at Bay Hill for more than twenty years, Tiddy's pro shop operations became models of the industry—frequently leading golf merchandisers from around the globe would study his methods. And his reputation as an effective instructor—with every golfer from tour stars to beginners with hiccup swings—eventually earned him *Golf* magazine's acclaim as one of the nation's top hundred teachers.

"I love to watch him give a lesson," former Bay Hill assistant pro Dave O'Connor once gushed. "He has such a knack of putting people at ease. And he has a keen eye for spotting some flaw and correcting it in a simple, easy-to-grasp manner. Invariably, the student will go, 'Oh, yeah!' It's like a light comes on."

Overshadowing his professional expertise, however, has always been the embraceable Tiddy persona—ever sunny and gracious, never complaining despite a staggering litany of medical setbacks ranging from that knee surgery and meningitis as a youth to a string of challenges in recent years that included losing part of one foot to diabetes, four hip operations culminating in hip replace-

ment, a heart attack requiring open-heart surgery, and two carpal tunnel operations on his wrists.

Each time, he has returned to work accompanied by a wide smile and occasionally a walker or a cane he could use as both a prop and a pointer while correcting some loop or lurch in a faulty backswing.

A certain Charlotte hospital never had a visitor limit before young Tiddy was confined for six weeks with spinal meningitis. After the initial quarantine was lifted, so many Charlotte High classmates filled Dick's room each day, the hospital board assembled in emergency session.

But the most dramatic evidence of Tiddy's popularity with his fellowman came shortly after Arnie talked him into leaving Charlotte to become head pro at Bay Hill. Dick's friends in Charlotte quickly announced a little farewell dinner/tribute. As reservations poured in, the compelling affair had to be twice shifted to larger halls until the guest list was finally cut off at four hundred.

"Arnold flew in for it and they put on a *This is Your Life* type of program. It was very emotional for me," recalled Tiddy.

At forty-six, Jimmy O'Neal is an elfish man of 5'5" with a winsome spirit. He's an avid golfer, energetic businessman, and impish prankster who moved his young family to Florida and quickly became one of the most popular residents and members at Arnie's Bay Hill Club.

By age twenty-seven, he commanded a chain of seventeen small newspapers in the area of Indiana where he was born. He sold the newspaper group and set out in search of a new business venture. Jim and Sally O'Neal and their small son at first rented a place in the Pompano-Boca Raton area on South Florida's east coast. They hadn't considered Central Florida until a clip on the local TV news caught their eye one evening: Then-Vice President Spiro Agnew was being interviewed during a visit to Arnold Palmer's Bay Hill Club in Orlando.

"So we got in the car one day and drove up to Bay Hill to see what it looked like," O'Neal recalled. "We liked it immediately. It was overbuilt. There were seven homes on my street that were vacant. So we bought a home for seventy-three thousand dollars and moved in. It was great."

Disney World had just opened on the outskirts of town, Orlando was exploding with opportunity, and he got a steal on a house just off the first hole of the prestigious golf club where one of his neighbors would be Arnold Palmer, his father's lifetime hero. O'Neal put his newspaper cash-out into rental real estate, buying the first of numerous apartment complexes he would accumulate over the next dozen years.

"The first time I saw Arnold, I had gone over to the practice tee because I saw a Cadillac in the parking lot that said 'Arnold Palmer' on it," O'Neal recounted with a laugh. "I had no idea Arnold had a Cadillac dealership then, so I figured that had to be Arnold Palmer's car."

It wasn't. But there on the practice tee were Arnie and a friend, central Florida corn magnate Foley Hooper, warming up for the Bay Hill "shootout," a daily ritual in which Arnie, other pros and select members play in friendly team competition. O'Neal stood back and watched, excitedly observing what he thought was a major national news story.

"I heard Arnold say to Foley Hooper that he had quit smoking. I thought, 'Jeez, I just heard that Arnold Palmer hadn't

smoked in twenty days! Nobody knows that but me!' I watched them play the first couple of holes from a distance then went back home to tell Sally the big news."

O'Neal soon made the approved shootout roster and landed on Arnie's team one day. O'Neal and Arnie hit it off instantly. Sally O'Neal and Winnie Palmer also hit if off instantly. Their friendship was sealed on the occasion of Jimmy's thirtieth birthday when Sally invited the Palmers to join them for a dinner celebration at LaCantina, Arnie's favorite steak house in Orlando. That evening, Arnie pulled up at the O'Neals' front door driving an old black limo that was owned by the club and jocularly referred to as the Bay Hill Bus. One of the club's assistant pros, Ted Beisler, a favorite of Arnie's, and his wife, Janie, joined the party.

"We had a blast," O'Neal recalled. "After dinner, we came out with six bottles of the cheap red house wine that LaCantina serves and drank it all going back across town to Bay Hill. Arnold was supposed to be flying out the next morning, but that got postponed because of the cheap red wine."

That summer, O'Neal and another Bay Hill shootout regular, Cecil Glover, planned to make their first trip to the British Open in 1977 and follow Arnie at Turnberry. When Glover became ill and died of a heart attack, Arnie invited O'Neal to go along with him and stay in the adjoining room at the Turnberry Hotel. The trip started a long-running, globe-hopping tradition. For the next dozen years, Arnie and his fun-loving, little red-haired pal O'Neal seemed at times almost inseparable, showing up together at every golfing port from Scotland to Palm Springs to Hawaii to New Zealand, enjoying a camaraderie heavily laced with laughter.

O'Neal's apartment business was flourishing and didn't anchor him to Orlando. He had the money and the freedom to go along for the ride, typically keeping Arnie loose with playful repartee and pranks. This was one pal who gave him his due respect but didn't grovel at his toenails, and Arnie liked that. Part of why Arnie so enjoys playing in the daily Bay Hill members' shootout between tournaments and business trips is that the group treats him like one of the gang, cajoling with put-down humor. In O'Neal, Arnie found an entertaining shootout buddy he could take along on the road.

Instead of genuflecting, O'Neal would enliven the day by doing things like taping the button down on the telephone in Arnie's hotel room with a small strip of cellophane tape. He first did that at Turnberry, strategically waiting until he knew Arnie was in the bathtub before dialing the room from next door.

"I could hear him saying, 'Hello! Hello!' but the phone would keep ringing. He'd say, 'Goddammit!' and slam the phone down. Five minutes later, it would be ringing again. It took several times before he saw the tape," O'Neal said.

When Arnie would discover he'd been had again by O'Neal, he would typically confront his small pal with a menacing glare. Then they'd break up in laughter and frolic off to the bar like two playful Boy Scouts.

"I short-sheeted him all the time. Generally, he'd act like it didn't happen," said O'Neal.

When Arnie first started wearing a hearing aid, O'Neal and pros Bill Kratzert and Leonard Thompson—often Arnie's practice-round partners—would conspire to pull Arnie's chain by continuing to move their lips in mid-conversation with no sounds coming out. Thinking his hearing aid had gone on the fritz, Arnie would start fiddling with the contraption until he realized the ruse and voiced puckish threats of bodily harm to all three.

On the road, O'Neal grew weary of becoming the handy photographer for every member of Arnie's Army that walked up in a hotel lobby with a camera, wanting a snapshot with their hero.

Often, O'Neal's playful revenge was to aim the camera with Arnie out of the frame. Around the world today there must be dozens of Arnie fans trying to convince friends that the shoulder or arm there next to them in the photograph really belongs to Arnold Palmer. "Arnold would not condone that, but after it was done, he'd laugh along with us," said O'Neal.

One O'Neal prank Arnie didn't laugh about came at Bay Hill's traditional year-end shootout, dubbed Cecil Glover Day after Glover died. In addition to the usual team competition, Cecil Glover Day featured a raucous luncheon beforehand and a kangaroo court in the locker room afterward, "Judge" O'Neal imposing an assortment of sniggering fines on various shootout regulars. The fines made up a holiday bonus fund divided among the pro shop staff. On Cecil Glover Day, all courtesies were suspended among shootout members, turning it into a bonding festival of good-natured insults.

O'Neal had a dilly up his sleeve on one particular December 31. He had heard IMG officials joking about a promotional photo for an Arnold Palmer line of jewelry in Japan. To showcase as many of the items as possible, a Japanese fashion photographer had talked Arnie into unbuttoning his shirt almost to the waist to expose an array of gold chains and medallions. He had bracelets on each wrist and a flashy pinky ring in addition to a couple of other gaudy rings. Arnie was uncharacteristically transformed into sort of a cross between Sylvester Stallone and Deion Sanders East.

Working clandestinely with a couple of IMG staffers, O'Neal and Charlotte businessman John Harris managed to obtain a rare copy of the photo ("To this day, I would never tell who got us the picture") and spent four hundred dollars to have it blown up to near-billboard size, six by eight feet. They squirreled it into the Cecil Glover luncheon with a heavy cloth draped over it at the front of the dining room. At just the opportune moment and with appropriate fanfare, the giant photo of "Arnie Stallone" was unveiled to the hooting joy of all but one shootout member.

"I played with Arnold that day," O'Neal recalls impishly, "and he didn't talk to me the whole round. My understanding is he had club employees destroy the picture, literally sawing it up in small pieces."

Arnie was always considerate of O'Neal. If the day's game was a social foursome with President Gerald Ford in Palm Springs, it became a fivesome, at Arnie's insistence, to accommodate Jimmy. O'Neal was given a long-running, point-blank intimate look at the most compelling golf figure of this century and he still likes the view he was afforded.

"As his friend, you learn there aren't two different Arnold Palmers. The Arnold Palmer you see and know as a friend is the same Arnold Palmer the fan in Hawaii or Augusta sees. He doesn't have what I've seen as stage presence in people like Bob Hope or Kenny Rogers," said O'Neal, who observed a scene on the beach in Hawaii that said volumes about Arnie's thoughtfulness toward people.

Rogers, staying at the same hotel, was sunning on the beach a few yards from where O'Neal and Arnie sat. A knot of kids ran up to Arnie to get his autograph, mostly at the prodding of their parents. Arnie, in his bathing suit, signed every autograph. The cluster of autograph hounds moved on to Rogers, who refused, saying he doesn't sign autographs while he's on vacation.

On another occasion in Hawaii, O'Neal said he and Arnie were sitting in the lobby of the Kahala Hilton, sipping Pink Squirrels, the specialty concoction of the house. A busload of Japanese tourists unloaded and spotted Arnie. Said O'Neal: "They started bowing from the time they got off the bus until the parade

finally reached Arnie. This is 11:30 on a Friday night. He's missed the cut and he's disappointed. Yet he signed every autograph and had his picture taken with every one of those Japanese. Probably took him forty-five minutes. That's his public image and also his private image. He's just as thoughtful to strangers as he is to friends. With caddies, car park people, anybody. I have never seen Arnold be rude to a person in my life. And I have been with him from the period of 1977 through 1990 as much or more than anybody."

Before the proliferation of Skins games and other made-for-TV events that now dot the golf calendar in November and December, Arnie used to devote that period to international activities — an appearance in Japan, a course design project in China, the Australian Masters, some tournament elsewhere on the Pacific Rim. He developed the habit of taking along a half-dozen close pals and associates for what O'Neal began to label as "trips of a lifetime."

"At least that was our sales pitch to our wives," O'Neal mused in recollection. "I think there were about five 'trips of a lifetime.'" The traveling party typically included O'Neal, Foley Hooper, Ed Seay, Alastair Johnston, Charlotte businessman John Harris, and Arnold Palmer Cadillac dealership partner, Gar Laux. The first of those trips contained more excitement than had been bargained for. The group was rousted out of bed in the middle of the night by the piercing wail of fire alarms in a small hotel in Rotorua, New Zealand.

The fire alarm went off at four in the morning, and Arnie's best friend and closest confidant, Jimmy O'Neal, rushed out of his room wearing only boxer shorts. His instincts were to get the hell out of the hotel, but he didn't see Arnie and knew how solidly he sleeps and how poorly he hears.

O'Neal recalled: "Do I get the hell out of the hotel before it burns up, or do I see if Arnold's gone? So I go pound on his door, for a long time, for as hard and loud as I can pound and yell. 'Arnold! Wake up! Are you in there!?'"

After a few moments that seemed an eternity to O'Neal, Arnie finally came to the door in his undershorts, still groggy with sleep.

"Arnold! We gotta get outta here!" O'Neal shouted. "There are fire trucks down in the street! This place is on fire!"

Arnie grabbed a sheet to throw around him and out they went.

The hotel was full of Japanese businessmen and they were all outside, dressed, with their suitcases and their cameras in hand. (Apparently used to such nocturnal emergencies, many Far East travelers typically go to bed with their suitcases packed and a change of clothes laid out.) They were all standing in the street like that when Arnie and O'Neal burst out of the hotel nearly naked.

"Even then," remembers O'Neal, "they wanted autographs. 'Palmer-san, Palmer-san . . .' They have a way of queuing up, even in that environment. It turned out the fire was a small one in some remote area of the hotel and they said it was safe for us to go back in. But Arnold stayed there and signed their autographs and posed with them for pictures, like he had just walked off the eighteenth green and was hanging around the clubhouse. How many public people would do that?" What started as a life-threatening scare developed into yet another chance for Arnie to show his fans how much they mean to him.

O'Neal's ill-fated transition from a happy-go-lucky friend to business partner/friend took seed on another of those "trips of a lifetime" that touched down in New Zealand. Before hooking up with Arnie in the Charlotte auto dealership, Laux (pronounced "low") had headed Ford's Lincoln-Mercury division at a time Arnie was doing Lincoln-Mercury commercials. Laux left Lincoln-

Mercury a few years before Lee Iacocca was fired as head of the Ford division. Gar later teamed up with Arnie to buy the Charlotte dealership.

"As far as Gar and Arnold, it was a fine relationship," O'Neal recalled. "Where the mixing of gas and oil was concerned was Gar and McCormack; they didn't get along at all. Plus, Cadillac would have rather had Saddam Hussein than the immediate former head of Lincoln Mercury running one of its Cadillac stores. All of that made it a cat-and-dog fight for four or five years. I heard all this constantly. When you're Arnold's friend, he tells you about everything in his life. And Gar would come down to Bay Hill and we played golf and became friends."

On a trip to New Zealand in December 1978, Laux and O'Neal were in adjoining rooms separated by paper-thin walls. They could hear one another's conversation and even talked to one another through the walls, laughing about it.

"Iacocca was calling Gar every two or three hours from the U.S. trying to entice Gar to come with him to take over Chrysler. I couldn't help but hear the conversations and Gar and I talked about the dilemma he had. He had the chance to be the No. 2 man at Chrysler and restore the company. It was very tempting. He said, 'If I were to leave, would you buy my part of the Charlotte dealership?' I said I would love to, but that was up to Arnold. He said he thought Arnold would like that."

The conversations between Laux and Iacocca continued and, once back in the States, O'Neal flew to Charlotte to scout out the dealership. "I determined I would absolutely be thrilled to have a part of it and be Arnold's partner. God, what a dream!" he said. "But Gar turned down Iacocca and everything seemed to be settled."

But a few weeks later came thunderclap news while Jim and Sally O'Neal and Arnie and Winnie Palmer were dining at Nick's Fish Market in Honolulu on the eve of the 1979 Hawaiian Open. An acquaintance walked up to the table and mentioned seeing in *The Wall Street Journal* that Laux was going to be the No. 2 man at Chrysler.

"No, he was talking about that," Arnie said, "but Gar turned them down."

"The hell he did," said the man. "It was in the paper today that he accepted the job."

Arnie got up from the table at ten o'clock at night, went to the phone, called Laux in Charlotte where it was three a.m., and woke him up. Laux confirmed the newspaper account.

Three months later, Arnie invited the O'Neals to fly with him and Winnie to Charlotte where he would be playing in the Kemper Open at Quail Hollow Country Club. "While you're there," Arnie told him, "I'd like you to think about buying into the dealership."

Cadillac hadn't relished Laux running one of their dealerships, but with him out, the notion of Arnold Palmer running it himself was equally unappealing because he wasn't a car man. Arnie was a professional golfer. Although immensely popular and respected, he was still a professional golfer and Cadillac had pushed Arnie for a face-to-face meeting to discuss the management of the Charlotte store now that Laux was gone. The meeting was set for the next day after the Kemper Open. Arnie could play in the tournament and stay over and meet with them at the dealership on Monday.

"In the meantime, I come into the picture," said O'Neal, "spend the weekend with Arnold in his house right on the course at Quail, play in the pro-am. He took me down and showed me the dealership. On Sunday night he asked if I was going to do it. I said, 'Yeah, hell yes!' My deal was to buy a third of it. He could have

offered me any portion. I would have jumped out of my jeans to be Arnold Palmer's partner."

Arnie, McCormack, and O'Neal would each have a third of that and five later dealership acquisitions, with O'Neal managing the group. But first came that sticky Monday meeting with the Cadillac execs. It was agreed that O'Neal would stay over and attend the meeting and Arnie would fly their wives back to Orlando.

At one o'clock the next day, two large cigars followed by Cadillac bigwigs paraded into the executive offices of Arnold Palmer Cadillac, announcing to the receptionist they had an appointment with Mr. Palmer. The receptionist informed them Mr. Palmer was not on the premises, but "our new general manager, Mr. Palmer's new partner," awaited them. Two pairs of eyebrows raised over the two cigars.

O'Neal recalled the comical scene. "They walked in and sat down with me. It was Charlie Chenowith, Cadillac's head of the eastern half of the U.S. and he brought with him Robert Henning, the southern regional head. At first, I think their interpretation of Arnold's new partner was pretty positive. 'Nice to know you, Mr. O'Neal. What dealerships have you been with?' I said, 'Well, actually, I've never been involved with a car dealership in my whole life. I do happen to own a Cadillac, but that's about all I know about the company. I don't know any of the people or know anything about Charlotte, but I've become Arnold's partner, so I guess we'll be working together.'"

Within minutes, the two Cadillac execs were on a forced march out the front door, billowing black smoke of anger rising from their cigars.

O'Neal: "Sometime later, I remember Chenowith saying at a public meeting that he had 'fourteen hundred Cadillac dealers, a golfer and a race-car driver. Everybody is a Cadillac dealer except Arnold Palmer and Roger Penske.' I remembered thinking what a foolish statement. I mean, who better could you have than Arnold Palmer and Roger Penske? But his thinking was they weren't traditional car people, so what right did they have to be dealers? I told Arnold we would never be accepted in that industry until people accepted us as dealers. I wasn't living off the dealership. I was living off my apartments and off my investments. Arnold and Mark certainly weren't depending on the dealership for their income. The only way for us to become accepted was to sell big volumes of cars." Hello, Hertz.

McCormack was close to Frank Olson, chairman of Hertz, and the three partners worked that relationship for an order of two hundred Cadillacs from Hertz. The golf pro's dealership that had been selling five hundred new cars took a sudden jump to seven hundred and the cigars started to take notice, especially when the Hertz order quickly grew to two thousand a year. By the mid-'80s, Arnold Palmer Cadillac had grown to be the No. 3 Cadillac dealer in the country, by volume, and all was harmony and joy among its three equal partners. Arnie became a spokesman for Hertz, which in turn became the title sponsor for Arnie's Bay Hill tournament in addition to his largest auto customer. It was a cozy arrangement with smiles all around the circle.

Soon came the opportunity to buy Latrobe Motors, the failing Cadillac/Oldsmobile dealership in Arnie's hometown. It was an appealing thought, and O'Neal was told to go for it.

"I met the dealer, Sid Rosenfeld, the day after all of his cars had been picked up by the factory," said O'Neal. "It was strange with no cars in the showroom, no cars on the lot. Nobody in the building but me and Sid. He took me in a back room, sat down at

a conference table and we talked about a sale. The phone rang and he asked me to answer it. 'I'm not here,' he said.

"It was a collect call from the Pennsylvania State Penitentiary, a guy calling for Sid. I repeated the name and Sid told me to talk to him. It turned out to be a guy getting out of the pen two weeks later and he had paid for a car two years before. He wanted to pick up his El Dorado in two weeks.

"I don't know whatever happened on that, but I can't imagine the guy was very happy when he got out and discovered the car he had paid for wasn't available. But Sid and I made a deal. That was typical. If we decided to do something, I generally went ahead.

"Of all the time I was Arnold's auto dealer partner," said O'Neal, "that was our most fun store. It was in his hometown, always clean as a whistle, and the work ethic of the Latrobe people who worked there was superb. Those are good people. We hired twenty-two start-up employees in 1981 and when I left in 1990, twenty-one of them were still there. The other one had let us move him to run another dealership we bought."

Arnie's friend Joe Tito, who owned a small Buick/Pontiac dealership across the street from his Rolling Rock brewery, offered to sell his franchise to be merged into what had become Arnold Palmer Motors. Now it was a four-way store, better suited for the small Latrobe market. But more importantly, Arnie, McCormack, and O'Neal could now sell Hertz not only Cadillacs, but Oldsmobiles, Buicks, and Pontiacs, too. The Hertz order quickly escalated to twenty thousand cars annually.

A minor thorn was a California law that required rental car companies to buy from California dealerships. O'Neal scoured the state and snapped up a small dealership in northern California that had all seven GM franchises—Cadillac, Chevrolet, Pontiac, Oldsmobile, Buick, GMC, and Geo. It became an outlet to sell thirty thousand cars a year in California. Adding a Chevy-Buick dealership in Cave City, Kentucky, filled the need for a Chevy outlet in the eastern half of the country.

Oops. Ford Motors bought Hertz in the late '80s. Hertz now has a taste for Fords and the Arnold Palmer group has only General Motors flavors. No prob. O'Neal picks up Fairway Ford-Lincoln Mercury in Hilton Head, South Carolina, for the partnership and that store explodes to sales of $421 million in 1988—highest volume of any dealership in the nation, according to *Ward's Auto Dealer*, an industry journal.

By now with six car stores, the Palmer group became the No. 1 megadealer in sales in 1988. The next year, sales would nearly double again to $1.6 billion with the Hertz order pushing one hundred thousand cars. O'Neal was running the chain, but like his partners, Arnie and McCormack, drew no salary out of the company. "I had sold all of my apartments in Orlando for several million dollars, so I didn't need cash," he said. "Our idea was to keep putting the money back into the dealerships and letting the equity grow."

O'Neal said the three-way partnership that had begun with an out-of-pocket investment of only a few hundred thousand dollars acquired the additional stores through cash flow and loans. By 1990, their six dealerships were collectively valued at upwards of fifteen million dollars.

But O'Neal already had begun working on an even grander plan: a massive holding company—Arnold Palmer Automotive Group—that would buy the six dealerships and dozens of others across the country, then go public with a stock offering. Publicly held dealership chains were in place in several foreign countries, but Detroit automakers were cautious. In a costly, time-consuming campaign, O'Neal began screening dealerships and found forty-eight prime stores that were profitable, audited, state-of-the-art computerized and willing. He obtained approvals from the automakers, reached tentative agreements with General Electric Credit and GMAC for floor-plan and real estate financing, and romanced Banker's Trust, a giant New York investment bank, for the necessary capital to complete the $250 million megadeal.

But the targeted closing for the megadeal was delayed twice, just long enough for the whole project to collapse. Clouding the attempt was emerging sales tax problems with APAG's pending seventh dealership, Orlando's Braun Cadillac, and a massive, failed buyback arrangement with Hertz that involved tens of thousands of rental cars and millions in losses for the Palmer/O'Neal/McCormack triumverate. Though Arnie and McCormack helped arrange the deal, O'Neal took the fall and agreed to cover his former parters' losses.

While the Isleworth flap and the aborted sale of Bay Hill were items of courtroom embarrassment and momentary tarnish on Arnie's golden image, the devastating developments he experienced in connection with his far-flung automobile empire went far beyond mere financial or image setbacks. The messy dissolution of his relationship with primary auto partner Jimmy O'Neal deeply affected Arnie and left emotional scars both he and O'Neal may carry to their graves.

O'Neal was family. For more than a decade, he was without question Arnie's closest friend and confidant. Arnie is godfather to O'Neal's children. O'Neal was a constant companion, business partner, and playmate on assorted continents. There was such mutual trust they made one another executors of their wills—a painful and embarrassing blow to Mark McCormack, who had been the designated caretaker of Arnie's estate to that point and whose staff had processed the paperwork necessary for the change.

But all of that chumminess came to a sudden and stormy end in December 1990, when O'Neal was banished from Arnie's inner circle, cloaked in innuendo that he had not only plunged the auto partnership into suffocating debt, but—at the very least—used Arnie's friendship and name and—at the very worst—perhaps diverted hundreds of thousands of dollars from the company to his personal use. Two weeks later, O'Neal was briefly hospitalized with "stress related" problems.

Was O'Neal a spurious opportunist guilty of massive skimming? Or was he merely the latest and most calamitous in the procession of friend/business associates who became too close to Arnie for IMG's comfort? Was O'Neal a rat? Or did McCormack and IMG seize an opportunity to poison Arnie's mind on O'Neal and sweep him aside? That is the lingering debate among those in Arnie's inner circle. Even his family is divided on the issue.

One faction, including most of those who worked alongside O'Neal in the auto business, remains convinced O'Neal is an honorable, if incurably fast-lane Arniephile, guilty of nothing more than a megadealership dream and a disastrous 1988 buyback arrangement with Hertz that cost the three-way auto partnership (O'Neal, Palmer, McCormack) thirteen million dollars. The opposite faction accepts the McCormack/IMG portrait that paints O'Neal as a calculating scalawag who avoided criminal prosecution only by signing over to Arnie and McCormack his show-stopping, $4.5 million Isleworth home, his nearby farm, his third of the auto partnership, and his 14 percent stake in Bay Hill Club.

O'Neal insists he voluntarily handed over those assets as a moral obligation to help offset the multimillion-dollar losses Arnie

and McCormack sustained as a result of his ill-fated Hertz deal. Obviously, Arnie chose to embrace IMG's dark portrait, though he curiously allowed O'Neal full use of the farmhouse as an office for the next two years.

"I considered him my best friend. I am the godfather to his children," Arnie said early in 1993 in a rare comment on the painful matter. "To have something like that happen was very traumatic and emotional."

Did O'Neal betray that friendship?

"I'm not going to get into that. I'd just as soon not get into that whole thing at all," said Arnie.

O'Neal, who has moved back into the more modest Bay Hill home he bought when he moved from Indiana to Florida in 1972, openly discusses Arnie and their fractured relationship.

"Arnold has an inherent magnetism with people and it goes both ways. It still does with me," said O'Neal at the start of a three hour, often emotional interview. "The trauma in my life—my midlife crisis—was I lost my business, my mother, my home, and my best friend in December of 1990. That kind of overloaded me. I came close, healthwise, mentally, to disaster.

"The close friendship Arnold and I had, where he knew everything about me and vice versa, all of a sudden that daily conversation we would have—every day, Christmas, whenever, it didn't matter—was gone. I probably feel that loss as much as I feel any loss in my life. Somehow I hope to get over that rainbow and reestablish that relationship. It's probably a hopeless dream on my part."

O'Neal still harbors hope of resurrecting the megadealer concept and, recovered from his legal bouts, was moving closer to another possible closing of a similar nature in late 1996, independent of Arnie or McCormack. Against all legal advice, he has steadfastly refused to file for bankruptcy protection. His massive debts to Arnie and McComack have been mostly satisfied.

"Whatever money that would have come to me as their partner goes into the company to pay off the debt to Hertz. I'm at Mark and Arnold's mercy to tell me the numbers. I trust Arnold. If Arnold tells me the number is X, it's X," said O'Neal, who holds out hope that he may one day laugh again with Arnie.

"I just feel for fifteen years I got the privilege of an experience that anybody my age in the world would have exchanged places with me. Being Arnold's best friend was a gift. Unfortunately, it didn't last. And it didn't last because of mistakes that I made, not because of mistakes that he made."

8

Political Pitchman

It was one of those magnificent Central Florida autumn days that inspires your golf clubs to rattle in the trunk, crying to get out. The piercing blue sky was embossed with a few fleecy, white clouds, and there was just the proper mix of warm sunshine and gentle breezes to send young boys and old men into delicious fantasies of a creek bank and a cane pole.

TOSS IN THE MANICURED EMERALD of Arnold Palmer's Bay Hill Club late that Friday morning, and I was regretting the noon flight that would whisk me off to a weekend football assignment. My mission at Bay Hill was only a brief errand en route to the airport.

The stop was extended, however, when Arnie insisted I switch to a late-afternoon flight in order to complete his noon foursome. I have had the pleasure of sharing a round of golf with Arnie on dozens of occasions, but this was especially memorable for two reasons. First, I enjoyed a career round from the championship tees, a fortuitous 75. Arnie, experimenting with two drivers, found himself in assorted trouble and settled for a 77.

But overshadowing even an asterisk victory over Arnold Palmer was a charming little moment not long after the round was complete. There was a frantic dash to the airport to make the later flight, including a sprint down the concourse and an Olympic triple jump onto the plane just before the door was closed. I flopped into my seat, exhaling mightily. From force of habit, I reached for the airline seatback magazine, which flopped open magically to a full page color ad in which Arnold Palmer's photogenic smile was beaming from the page, hawking the virtues of a Lanier microcassette tape recorder.

The reflexive impulse was to turn to the man in the adjacent seat and brightly announce: "See this guy? I just played golf with him and beat him by two strokes."

I resisted the urge, thus preserving a lifetime of amusing conjecture as to what the man's response might have been. No. 1 in my little guessing game is that the man's face would have settled into a skeptical leer as he replied: "Oh, yeah? And I bet Winnie came running out at the turn with a batch of fresh-baked cookies."

The story is retold here not to boast of having played and beaten Arnold Palmer. The scores were an aberration and the next time I improve on what must be a lifetime 1-50 record head-to-head against Arnie will no doubt occur when he is rolled out to the first tee by a male nurse. What was not such a longshot, however, was opening a seatback magazine to discover Arnie's mug grinning out at me on behalf of commerce.

For more years than any other before him, Arnie has endured as the preeminent spokesman for Madison Avenue, the crown prince of athletic pitchmen. Were you to switch on a TV most any evening in the past twenty years, you likely would see one or more

commercials or public service announcements featuring Arnie Palmer touting any one of more than thirty major corporations and organizations. Pennzoil, Sears, National Home Life, Paine-Webber, Toro, Hertz, United Airlines, Lanier, Pro Group, Loft grass seeds, Beltone, Cadillac, March of Dimes, United States Golf Association, Annedeen Hosiery, Arnold Palmer Golf Academy, NBC-TV, Humphrey's Leather Goods, Kellwood Company, Atlantic Optical, Oxford Industries, Pacesetter Industries, John Peel clothier, Westin Hotels, Swank, Robert Bruce, Cessna, *Golf* magazine, Johnson and Murphy golf shoes, *Ladies' Home Journal,* Rolex, Woodard Furniture, Trace Publications: just for starters. And that's just in the U.S.

Such lists make Alastair Johnston edgy. Johnston, a top executive at Mark McCormack's well-connected International Management Group, is in charge of most of Palmer's business deals. "It's a race we're glad to be in," he said of the who-has-the-most commercials derby. "But it's not necessarily one that we want to win. That implies that he is overexposed, and we have worked very hard to prevent that."

Really? The impression of most insiders is that IMG rarely turns down any suitor willing to pay the big ticket set for Arnie's time, resulting in the endless list of endorsements.

"We turn down about 90 percent just at the first approach," Johnston insists. "Some are due to potential conflicts with current Arnold Palmer licensees. Some are controversial products that might not be good for Arnold's image."

For example, Arnie says he will do no commercials for any alcoholic beverages. "I drink beer, a lot of it," he concedes. "But I don't want children portraying me as someone who drinks a lot of beer or would tell them that it would be good for them to drink."

Madison Avenue moguls confirmed that Arnie, for years, was the runaway leader in active national commercials. Assorted runner-ups like his close pal Bob Hope were often distant blips in his rear view mirror. "Phil Harris likes to joke that I've driven Bob Hope to do Amway commercials," Arnie muses.

The result is a huge stack of fees for Arnie, and a handsome commission for IMG. The record shows that in his long and glorious golf career now in its fifth decade, Arnie has earned roughly $3.5 million in official money from the regular and Senior PGA tours through 1996. By the late '70s, he was earning that much each year from endorsements alone. By the mid-'80s he was doubling that each year and estimates suggest his endorsement income has been in eight figures in each of the past four years.

As late as 1992, *Forbes* magazine was still listing Arnie as the top earner among golfers even though he hasn't won a regular PGA tour event in twenty years and hasn't won a major since the 1964 Masters. *Forbes* listed his 1991 earnings from commercials and appearances alone at eleven million dollars, down slightly from its estimate of $12.5 million for Arnie a year earlier. Even with the dropoff, he was two million dollars ahead of Jack Nicklaus.

Specific fees for individual sponsors are a closely guarded secret. However, Johnston indicated that Arnie's minimum fee for a single, national commercial had risen into the six-figure category as far back as 1984. Getting Arnie to do a single-commercial deal, however, is almost impossible. Johnston crafts most endorsement affiliations into multiyear, complex packages that include not just the TV commercials, but print ads, golf outings with the company's executives and top clients, and even motivational talks at the company's conventions. Arnie entered into an agreement with Toro that encompassed all of those elements. A Toro top executive confirms the deal paid Arnie seven figures.

The price might be less if the deal includes business for one of Arnie's other companies. An example: In 1988, Hertz paid him "only" four hundred thousand dollars for being a company spokesman but also bought more than sixty thousand cars from his dealerships.

Advertising executives insist he is well worth it, noting that Arnie is one of the precious few spokesperson/celebrities who requires no identification and is swathed in an aura of trust. When his face comes on the screen, people know who he is and they believe him.

The megabucks for Arnie's public stamp of approval began rather modestly, with a Wilson Sporting Goods contract when Arnie first turned pro in 1954. In return for using Wilson Clubs and posing for print ads, he was paid two thousand dollars for the first six months, which came in handy in the days when PGA tour pros had to go through a six-month apprenticeship during which they were ineligible for prize money.

"Even in those days, two thousand dollars wouldn't cover your expenses to travel the tour for six months, so I had to borrow some money," Arnie recalled. "But it helped to get me started without having a [personal] sponsor."

Analysts unfailingly gravitate to the word "trust" when trying to explain why so many companies stand in line to have Arnie stump their products and services. "Arnold Palmer," said Rick Adams of the Scally-McCabe advertising agency that handled the Hertz account, "is one of the most respected and popular people in the United States. Hertz was late getting into the gift-giveaway program, and we needed to immediately increase awareness. We wanted someone who has awareness among the business-type renters. We teamed Arnie with O. J. Simpson, and what we discovered was that we had one heck of a team."

Madison Avenue has its own measuring stick for the effectiveness of TV commercials, called an "impact score." The typical average for all commercials hovers around a score of thirty. The impact score for the first O. J.-Arnie Hertz bit was a phenomenal seventy-four, according to Adams.

"First, Arnold is a very well-known personality who transcends both golf and the demographics," Johnston explained. "He is appealing to the steelworker in Pittsburgh and to the very elite in Palm Springs. He is regarded as having very strong, credible credentials. He has a well-earned reputation of honesty and credibility."

If those attributes can sell motor oil and tractors, it's reasonable to assume they also could attract massive blocks of voters. But when asked about the assorted serious and not-so-serious attempts to draft Arnie into running for political office, the charismatic golfing millionaire usually twists his face into a smirk and dodges the issue. Just like a politician.

"If I were going to run," Arnie once chortled, "I'd go all the way for president so I could get some things straightened out. I always say if you're going to make a mistake, make a big one."

A birdie in every pot and an E-Z Go in every garage?

Most within the Arnie inner circle think it would, indeed, be a mistake for Arnie to get involved in politics. But few doubt that this popular, international celebrity grandfatherly baby-kisser could attract the necessary votes to become, say, a governor or congressman.

The most serious attempt to persuade Arnie to throw his hat into the political ring was led by Pennsylvania Governor Raymond Shafer in the late '60s. Shafer wanted Arnie to be his successor in the state mansion and had more than one million dollars in pledges already mustered for Arnie's campaign. When Shafer and Arnie

Larry Guest

played an exhibition near Harrisburg, the state capital, a group of fans burst onto one green waving banners imploring, "Arnie for Gov."

Arnie graciously declined, as he has similar attempts in Pennsylvania, North Carolina and Florida. "I'm flattered, but I have not given any of them serious consideration," Arnie said in 1982 when Florida Republican leaders dropped his name as a possible U.S. Senate entry. "Not while I'm still active on the tour. Maybe in a few years I might consider it."

Spoken like a veteran politician: graciously firm, but conveniently noncommittal. The door was left ajar for any future change of heart.

Doc Giffin, Arnie's longtime administrative aide, sees other viable political attributes in the boss. "In my opinion, he's got some sound and valid conservative views," Giffin said. "He would make a very good president from that aspect. He certainly would be a very good vote-getter. And the nature of his day-to-day schedule — the constant traveling—would make him well equipped to handle that type of hectic schedule that seems to go with a high political office."

Yet, Giffin agreed the boss would have problems in politics by the very nature of the word.

"He'd have trouble with the patronage and the deal-making," said Giffin. "He's so damned honest, that would drive him crazy."

One area in particular that would severely tax President Palmer's diplomacy would be in dealing with gay rights activists. In Deacon Palmer's home of the '30s and '40s, good, old-fashioned values prevailed and things like bisexuality and homosexuality were regarded as repugnant. Thus, when young U.S. Coast Guard Seaman Arnie Palmer experienced his first approach by a homosexual, he reacted with disdain.

Arnie shared the encounter one evening over dinner thirty years later on a day when sexual preference was in the news. The sports world was abuzz that day in May 1980, when tennis star Billie Jean King had gone public with confirmation that she had a female lover.

Arnie dropped out of Wake Forest and enlisted in the U.S. Coast Guard in January 1951. Assigned to Cape May, New Jersey, Arnie often hitchhiked home across the length of Pennsylvania to Latrobe, about three hundred miles. There on the shoulder of the Pennsylvania Turnpike would stand Seaman Apprentice A. Daniel Palmer with thumb out, golf clubs across his back and a duffel bag over one shoulder.

It was on one of these junkets in the early fall of 1951 that young Arnie had a ride offer that turned out to be a distasteful, though memorable, chapter in his education. A large man in a red Cadillac convertible stopped right outside Philadelphia and Arnie asked how far he was going.

"Harrisburg," said the man.

Arnie was thrilled. Not only was he about to fulfill one of his life's dreams—to ride in a red Cadillac—he was catching a ride that would cover a significant, seventy-five-mile portion of his trip.

"Son, do you have a driver's license?" the man asked and Arnie nodded. "Good. I'm a little tired and I think I'll let you drive."

Wow. Excited simply that he was about to ride in a red Cadillac, now he was about to actually *drive* one. It was almost too good to be true.

Arnie tossed his clubs and duffel bag in the back seat and settled in behind the wheel. He guided the gleaming, luxury car out onto the turnpike and quickly accelerated to the speed limit, a sense of power and affluence sweeping his innards.

Larry Guest

All was wonderful for the first few miles as the man engaged Arnie in small talk. Arnie didn't notice his host had inched closer across the seat until the man reached out and placed a hand on Arnie's right thigh. "You don't mind, do you?" he asked.

Arnie remembers becoming flush with, first embarrassment, then anger, as he assessed the situation. "I had been to college and had been in the Coast Guard nearly a year at this time, so I knew about women," he said in recounting the predicament. "But I didn't know about men."

After a brief moment to collect himself, Arnie pressed the accelerator, balled his left hand into a fist, and issued this dark warning: "If you don't get your hand off me, you and I and this Cadillac are going over the side of this mountain!"

Arnie's "suitor" quickly retreated to the far side of the seat and a period of silence ensued as Arnie began to feel in control of the awkward situation.

Finally, the guy broke the silence and mumbled something about changing his mind about his destination. "I think I'm going to get off up here at the next exit," he announced.

"No you're not," snorted Arnie, now in full command. "You said you were going to Harrisburg, so we're going to Harrisburg."

The man sat, scowling but docile, for the next sixty miles as young Arnie Palmer roared across southeast Pennsylvania in the fanciest car he had ever experienced. At the Harrisburg exit, Arnie picked out a good spot to resume his hitchhiking, pulled off onto the shoulder of the turnpike, and hopped out with his golf clubs and duffel bag. "Thanks for the lift," Arnie said cheerfully, managing to keep a straight face. The guy said nothing, wheeled onto the eastbound lane, and disappeared back toward Philadelphia.

Arnie was reminded of the story when President Clinton became embroiled in the issue of gay rights for members of the military. "I'd probably be very difficult," Arnie concedes of his presidential style. "But I'd improve the country. I'd be pretty strict, I'm afraid."

There could never be a more gracious first lady than Winnie Palmer, but Arnie's charming bride of more than forty years sees a somewhat ironic problem for President Arnie: the press. Winnie thinks he would overreact to negative White House coverage.

A faithful, outspoken Republican, Arnie not only voted for George Bush—one of his many Oval Office golf pals—but flew himself and baseball legend Ted Williams to Houston on Election Eve in November 1992 to lend their presence to the closing Bush rally.

The next day, he was back in the Bay Hill grill room, reminding one and all to go to the polls. I assured him that I already had voted that morning, but ventured a guess that my daughter had canceled out my Bush vote with one for Bill Clinton.

"If either of my daughters voted for Clinton, they're out of the will," he scowled, pausing for an afterthought: "On second thought, I don't guess it matters. If Clinton wins, I won't have anything left to will."

The last time I checked, it appeared Arnie will continue to limit his presidential activities to that of playing partner to the men in the White House. He has been a fairway companion to Eisenhower, Nixon, Ford, Bush, and even Clinton

"And no," he said icily, one step ahead of a needling scribe, "I didn't play with Washington."

Arnie became particularly close to Bush during his administration, often showing up to share a round of golf with the president and attempt—unsuccessfully—to talk President Bush out of using that elongated Pole-Kat putter you've seen him waving in so many wire photos out of Kennebunkport.

For all his affinity with Bush, however, there is little doubt that when pressed, Arnie will confess his favorite occupant of the White House was Dwight Eisenhower. In the prime of Arnie's career, he became close to Eisenhower through the conduit of Ike's affection for and membership in Augusta National Golf Club. That Arnie won the Masters four times during and immediately after Ike's tenure in the White House no doubt helped spawn the long-running relationship. They played and socialized often, at Augusta and Palm Springs in particular. Arnie's evening-long visit to Ike's house at El Dorado during the Bob Hope Desert Classic became an annual ritual.

In 1990, Arnie was proud and honored to be picked among a select group of five to address a joint session of Congress to posthumously honor Ike and mark the one-hundredth anniversary of his birth. Joining him were Walter Cronkite, Winston Churchill III, Ike's son John Eisenhower, and Senator Bob Dole, a Republican from Kansas, where Eisenhower grew up.

The House and Senate convened a rare commemorative joint session to honor the farm boy who became supreme commander of Allied Expeditionary Forces during World War II, the nation's thirty-fourth president, and a leading advocate of his favorite pasttime — Arnie's game.

For his part, Arnie chose to remember the devoted duffer he first met at the 1958 Masters. After the third round, Arnie, just twenty-eight at the time, was told the winner would be asked to play golf with the president. "So you will understand the pressure of the final eighteen holes," he chuckled to the Congress.

When Arnie arrived in Washington to participate in the Eisenhower salute that day, there was an incident that shows just how devoted some of his fans are. The limo driver assigned to Arnie and his party was a man about Arnie's age who was beside himself with the opportunity to ferry his longtime hero. Initially assigned by his company to Cronkite, he had begged to be switched to Arnie. "I just wanted you to know, Mr. Palmer," he said proudly, "that I've driven heads of state and congressmen of all sort. But this is the biggest thrill of my life."

Arnie and Ike became so close that Ike even agreed to be the surprise for Arnie's birthday in 1966. At Winnie's invitation, Ike and Mamie agreed to be smuggled into Latrobe for what was supposed to be a quiet birthday celebration that evening with a few neighbors.

Smuggling in an ex-president, just five years removed from the White House, is no simple task. Secret Service officers had to be consulted and apprised of all intended movements. They had to whisk in and scope out every area where Ike might be exposed.

Ike, seventy-five at the time, was living at his Gettysburg farm near York, Pennsylvania. Mamie and Winnie's longtime mutual friend, Phoenix spa operator Mollie Cullen, helped Winnie with the arrangements, which included bringing Arnie's principal copilot at the time, Darrell Brown, into the loop. Brown would be dispatched to pick up Ike, and his task would be to come up with some plausible story to tell Arnie why he had to take the plane out of town that Saturday.

Before landing, Brown and Ike flew right over the Latrobe Country Club and Arnie spotted the plane. Efforts to keep him bottled up inside the house had failed. Arnie was out tapping balls on the putting green his father had built in his backyard when his plane whisked overhead. He was telling Mollie Cullen about his airplane when he looked up and said, "As a matter of fact, it's just like that one." Brown's final approach was purposely high to keep Arnie from recognizing that it was his own plane.

Twenty minutes later, Arnie answered the doorbell, swinging open the front door to discover Dwight David Eisenhower, standing alone with a bag in one hand, asking: "Any chance an old man can spend the night here?"

For the quintessential man-who-has-everything, Ike had the perfect gift which still hangs today in a position of prominence in the foyer of Arnie's Latrobe home: a small painting of simple beauty and serenity that Ike had done, depicting a barn, corral, and horse at his Gettysburg farm. Though it is an original, there is no signature, only initials: DDE.

After an early evening dinner party with a dozen friends at the fancy Rolling Rock club in nearby Ligonier, the Palmers and Eisenhowers returned to Latrobe for a quiet night.

"Mamie and Ike were very comfortable people, like the Bushes," Winnie picks up the story. "They were delightful to be around. Ike demanded his respect and we always called him 'Mr. President.' But he was like your grandfather. That evening, there was a football game on TV and the guys started watching that. But Mamie said, 'I'm going to watch the Miss America pageant.' Arnie was a little startled. He's used to having his way, but he gave in on this one. After awhile, Mamie and I watched Miss America on the TV in the living room and the boys went back to our bedroom to watch the football game.

"The next morning, we had breakfast in our kitchen and wound up sitting there until noon, just talking. It was a pleasant, sunny morning and we just enjoyed one another, talking all morning. When they left, I gave Ike a bouquet of carnations, which he carried out in his hat. I remember that because we have a wonderful picture of him standing next to Arnie's plane as they were about to leave, the carnations in his hat."

Arnie flew Ike back to York, more than pleased with his birthday surprise.

Three years later, Ike died. Arnie and Winnie had visited him in the hospital a month before his death and flew back into Washington for the funeral.

"President Eisenhower had more integrity than most people you would ever hope to meet," Arnie remembers fondly. "He really was a no-nonsense man. He liked a joke; he liked a good clean joke. He was not much on profanity.

"Unless he missed a short putt."

9

Care and Feeding of Caddies

Ernest "Creamy" Caroline, a former Vaudeville performer with a terminal case of the jabbers, was easily the best known of the various regular caddies who worked for Arnold Palmer. Creamy carried The Bag for more than a decade at the height of Arnie's career.

IRONICALLY, it was Arnie's previous caddie, Bob Blair, who had opened the door for this dumpy and talented little man by hiring him to carry the bag of Arnie's agent, Mark McCormack, during the old Bing Crosby Pro-Am. McCormack was so impressed with Creamy's work that when Arnie and Blair parted company a short time thereafter, he recommended Creamy as the new man.

Arnold's primary challenge, though, was to figure out a way to interrupt Creamy's incessant babbling long enough to squeeze in a golf shot. Otherwise, Creamy was a skilled caddie. Prompt. Never bothered the boss with personal problems. Stepped off precise yardage. Knew the rules. Ever alert for gallery distractions as Arnie settled in over a shot.

Creamy made a science of measuring the courses, even to the point of producing little, multicolored charts of each hole, showing the traps, water hazards, and yardages to various key points on the green. He safeguarded the charts in plastic, waterproof sleeves for use in subsequent years, making changes only as course alterations were made at any of the regular tour stops.

Several TV commentators of the day sought out Creamy to purchase copies of his charts for the closing holes covered in the telecasts. When you heard Chris Schenkel tell you on one of the early telecasts that Gene Littler's drive came to rest next to a shrub 157 yards from the pin, chances are the surveying was the work of Ernest Caroline.

As was inevitable in most all player/caddie relationships, Arnie fired Creamy in 1975. Those close to Arnie say it was the chatter that finally got to him, though Creamy injected some mystery into the "divorce" by refusing to specifically reveal what provoked the pink slip.

"It was just a misunderstanding," Creamy said in 1975 not long after the split. "You won't get me to say anything bad about the man, but I was hurt deeply. I will say this—Palmer is a very demanding man."

Most caddies who worked for Arnie early in his career agree. Once, at the 1964 U.S. Open at Congressional in Washington, D.C., Arnie changed caddies three times before the tournament even started.

Before the Masters relented and allowed players to bring their regular caddies, Arnie's man out of the Augusta National pool was a rugged, veteran black man named Nathanial Avery, known to his

colleagues as "Iron Man." All four of Arnie's Masters victories came with Iron Man carrying The Bag.

Iron Man said of Arnie: "He just jerk on his glove, hitch up his pants, start walkin' fast and says, 'The game is on." Arnie terminated him in the early '70s when the Iron Man forgot his station. The word among the other caddies was that Arnie felt Iron Man was "getting too big for his britches," bragging about "Arnie and me a corporation."

It's hard to think of any caddie in corporate terms. But unlike most other tour caddies, Creamy managed his finances well and neither smoke nor drank. He just talked. Talked so much, in fact, it made Arnie's skin crawl.

Arnie might turn around on the tee to ask Creamy for a club and the caddie would be twenty yards down the restraining ropes reciting Arnie's life history to a group of enraptured fans. In a way, he was upstaging Arnie—a fatal error.

Creamy similarly stole the spotlight with his habit of shagging Arnie's practice range shots with a baseball glove, which he kept tucked away in a plastic bag. In more recent years, range balls are provided at each tour stop and the caddie remains on the practice tee with little more to do than clean each club after the pro progresses to another. During most of Arnie's career, however, pros provided their own practice balls and their caddies stood downrange, collecting them in leather shag bags.

Like most pros, Arnie typically begins warming up with short, soft wedge shots, which Creamy would one-hand with the baseball glove and drop into a shag bag he held with the other hand. As Arnie progressively ran through his irons, Creamy retreated twelve paces for each longer club. It was all rather simple with the shorter, more accurate irons. But as Arnie moved into the long irons and woods, Creamy became more of a centerfielder, often making long sprints to snare errant shots.

Practice tee spectators routinely became engrossed as much in Creamy's outfield play as in Arnie's golf swing, even to the point of erupting in applause for particularly spectacular catches. Irritated, Arnie would mutter to the gallery, "Watch this," and alternately hook and slice the next few shots, sending Creamy on several long dashes. Or, he'd feather a few short shots, leading Creamy to think the boss had switched clubs. When the old caddie made the adjustment to the "shorter" club, Arnie would rip the next shot over Creamy's head, sending the grandstander in puffing pursuit.

Nobody upstaged Arnold. Not his pilot, not his agent, not his secretary, and certainly not his caddie. Over the years, he has frequently admonished the help with this terse declaration: "There's only room for one prima donna around here." There was little doubt about who he had in mind.

That working relationship came through loud and clear at the 1981 Houston Open when I caddied for Arnie for the purpose of writing a *Golf* magazine piece on the experience.

We were at the trunk of his loaner automobile, preparing to embark on the weeklong folly of a newspaper columnist working as Arnie's caddie, when he launched into the special instructions for the week.

"I just want to say that I want to play really well here" he began, his voice trailing off, the famous face retooling into a look of uncertainty.

He would later say he merely wanted to underscore the seriousness of playing in a PGA Tour event such as the Houston Open and review such items as courtesy toward other golfers, paying attention, staying close, keeping the clubs clean, etc. He had obviously decided to skip the crash course of basics, and we waded off

into the Houston humidity, his sixty-three-pound bag of equipment tugging against my virgin shoulder. In addition to fifteen clubs (twenty-one during a practice round) and a dozen balls, the bag's inventory included a sweater, rain suit, visor, floppy hat, large umbrella, a squirt bottle of grip treatment, contact lens lubricant, spare contact lenses, a jar of Coppertone Noskote, granola bars, pencils, a couple hundred tees, spare gloves, Band-aids, tape, and a jackknife.

Neither the weight of his bag nor Houston's balmy 92 degrees would prove the most difficult part of the assignment.

Sixteen years as a journalist had conditioned me to observe sporting events in a dispassionate, objective demeanor. I had been able to hide my feelings behind a facade of indifference that now seemed a liability as a golf caddie.

A caddie is expected to show outward support for his man, and since Arnie would step off his own yardage and make his own club selection on this particular week, it seemed my primary contribution would be limited to a series of back flips immediately following well-played shots, or at the very least well-timed, inspirational phrases.

Instead, the first inspirational gem was ill-timed.

Arnie was surveying an eight-footer on the second green during the first round when I recalled a catch-phrase he had uttered during the previous day's pro-am. "First birdie of the day!" I blurted in encouragement.

After missing the putt, he assailed me with scolding eyes. "Don't say anything when I'm about to address a putt."

On the next tee, I vowed aloud to introduce a whole new technique to the art of caddying.

"What's that?" Arnie inquired.

"Just carrying the bag and keeping my mouth shut," I said.

"That would be new," he said, laughing.

It would still be new. I spoke up often, but never again after handing him the putter.

At least one utterance helped.

When the hostess in the clubhouse dining room blocked Arnie's entrance one morning, he became flustered. "You're kidding me," he snorted. "We've been in here every day."

She held her ground. "You have to have a badge like that one," she said, pointing to my PGA tour media pin.

"It's okay," I interjected with a straight face. "He's with me."

On the course, Arnie was accorded his just recognition. Even to the point of a burst of applause when, on a secluded tee, he turned his back to the pro-am gallery and unhooked his pants to tuck in his shirttail.

An hour later, with fans around the final green applauding Arnie's approach, my vow of silence was overcome by another of those inspirational phrases as we closed in on the green. Eyeing the birdie putt there ahead, I implored: "Give 'em a thrill!"

"What do you want me to do?" he deadpanned playfully. "Make the putt or unbuckle my trousers again?"

He did neither.

At least I didn't make the mistake Bob Blair made many years earlier by showing up Arnie on the course in front of his adoring Army. That incident occurred during the 1967 Florida Citrus Open at Orlando's Rio Pinar Country Club and prodded Arnie into an ill-fated decision that may have cost him the title.

The tournament was winding down to the final decisive holes with easy-swinging Julius Boros looking down over his middle-aged paunch at a one-stroke lead. Looming formidably in the challenge position, and in the next-to-last threesome, was none other than the champion of the masses, A. Daniel Palmer.

The card-carrying Orlando members of Arnie's Army sensed victory. Thundering through the long-leaf pines of Rio Pinar Country Club, the Army startled sleeping tree frogs as it jockeyed for the best vantage points to witness its hero once again pulling off the improbable. By the time Arnie reached Rio Pinar's par-five fifteenth, his worshipers had assembled in division strength, completely encircling the tee, fairway, and green of this critical, 510-yard hole.

The fifteenth at Rio is a sweeping dogleg, gently bending to the right, with a creek protecting the smallish green. A well struck tee shot skirting the pine thicket at the corner left Citrus Open contenders with a soul-searching, go-for-it-or-layup decision. Several titles were squeezed to a dry pulp on this very decision.

Not even his most devoted legions could have conceived a more suitable stage for Arnie's swashbuckling flair for the dramatic. Certain that his dashing stroke at the improbable would happen right there at the fifteenth, the Army clamored into position to witness more golf history in the making.

A slight depression runs across the fifteenth—the result of a buried TV cable—just beyond the bend of the dogleg and about two hundred yards short of the creek. Tour players came to regard that cable depression as the "go or no-go" line.

Arnie caught his drive that tense Sunday afternoon a hair off-center. The ball streaked low down the right side, narrowly averted the pine trunks, kicked up a little puff of dust, and began its roll past the corner of the dogleg. At last, it wobbled to a stop on the edge of the fairway about fifteen yards short of the buried TV cable. Decision time.

Bob Blair, Arnie's regular caddie at the time, was first to reach the spot and wasted no time pulling the headcover off of Arnie's 3-wood. A handsome ex-Marine with a sailor's vocabulary, Blair exuded excitement each time Arnie nibbled at victory and often injected the boss with an extra dose of adrenaline

With the group ahead still on the green, Arnie stalked his position for several anxious moments, wrestling with the alternatives. He knew a huge 3-wood would be required to clear the creek. The gallery knew it was far from their general's nature to resist just such a challenge. Yet, Arnie knew he didn't want to hand the trophy to Boros on a foolish shot.

He decided to layup with an iron, quietly announcing that to Blair. "No, no!" the caddie protested. "A good 3-wood and you can reach!"

The Army buzzed, reading the conflict on the faces of Arnie and his caddie. Arnie stepped back to reassess the next shot.

When he stepped back to the bag and reached for a club, two thousand heartbeats echoed through the pines. He pulled out an iron.

Blair reeled in animated protest, throwing one hand aloft in blatant dismay. The mutinous gesture stunned Arnie. Half astonished, half-angered, he glared at Blair for a long moment, then jammed the iron back into the bag. "Okay, you s.o.b., I'll show you!"

He yanked out the 3-wood—to the guttural and joyous approval of the Army—and unleashed a mighty swing.

In a low, white streak, the ball screamed toward the green, rising majestically as the Army implored: "Go! Go! Go! . . ." It hung there against the brilliant blue Florida sky for several seconds before falling with a thud against the sloping bank just short of the putting surface. The ball seemed to pause for a tantalizing instant, then tumbled down the bank and disappeared into the creek.

Forty minutes later, Arnie stalked out of the scoring tent. Boros was a one-shot winner, Arnie was livid, and Bob Blair was

Larry Guest

an endangered species. Arnie stormed through the locker room, jerked his gear out of his assigned locker, and was still steaming when the entourage retreated to Rio Pinar's rear parking lot. As Blair loaded the clubs into the trunk, Arnie silently glared at his insubordinate caddie.

Arnie slid behind the wheel, slamming the door to underscore his continuing unhappiness. Blair hopped in the back and two Palmer business associates eased gingerly into the car, being careful not to set off the nitro there in the driver's seat.

In his prime, Arnie abhorred auto air conditioning, which he blamed for his onetime hip ailment. So unless it was a day when birds sweat and scorpions pant, Arnie typically rolled down the windows for natural ventilation. As he pulled out onto the dirt driveway skirting the rear of the clubhouse, the car was filled with a deathly silence you could have broken with a marshmallow sandwich. It was shattered, instead, in a more novel way.

An automatic sprinkler head sprang to life just as Arnie pulled near and scored a direct hit through the open window—a real-life duplicate of a Laurel & Hardy skit. In a split second, the brooding countenance of the new 1967 Citrus Open runner-up was thoroughly drenched. The car jolted to a stop and the first words came spontaneously from the back seat. "Well," snorted Blair, "maybe that will cool off the s.o.b."

The business associates flinched in disbelieving horror, perhaps mentally reviewing their Blue Cross policies. Arnie pivoted ever so deliberately, water still dripping from his eyebrows, to face the insolent caddie. A frozen moment in the history of sporting slapstick. A little smile began forming at the corners of Arnie's mouth.

"Dammit!" he exclaimed, unable to contain his spreading smile. "I told you I couldn't knock that 3-wood on there!"

The car rocked with laughter as it pulled away from the club leaving a little trail of water on the asphalt.

▼

"Arnie always told me Blair was the best caddie he had, but also the meanest," said Royce Nielson, a quiet, well-mannered Minnesotan who became only the third man to carry Arnie's bag for any extended period of time. Nielson worked for Arnie for nine years after accidentally becoming a caddie in 1984.

A young Chariot golf cart salesman in Orlando at the time, Nielson found himself out of work when Yamaha bought out his company. Visiting Bay Hill one day, Nielson was recruited by caddiemaster Paul Johnson to carry the bag for "some big shot from out of town. I played a little golf and had caddied a little in high school, but I never gave any thought to that kind of work. But Paul said he was desperate and kept insisting. He guaranteed me forty dollars if I did a good job. I figured what the heck."

The big shot paid him $167 that day and thanked Johnson for providing such a hard-working and pleasant caddie. Suddenly, Nielson was reassessing his low view of the caddie profession and was more receptive to Johnson's invitation to return the next day for another "top" assignment.

The next morning, Nielson grew impatient as Johnson doled out bags to other caddies. Finally came the assignment: Arnold Palmer.

"I couldn't believe it. He walked down the steps of the pro shop, stuck out his hand and said, 'Hi! I'm Arnold Palmer.' I was like, well, yes, of course you are."

Pleased by Nielson's neat appearance and polite manner, Arnie soon had his new caddie handling a myriad of duties in addi-

tion to carrying his bag in social rounds at Bay Hill and most tournament appearances in the United States and Canada. Between caddie duties, Royce became a gofer for Arnie and Winnie, fetching people from the airport, tending bar at private gatherings in the Palmer home, performing odd chores for Winnie. He was added to the Bay Hill payroll at two hundred dollars a week, plus what he earned as caddie for Arnie. When the Palmers moved to Latrobe for the summer, Royce went along and continued his duties there until the shift back to Bay Hill each fall. He often rode to and from tournaments in Arnie's jet and even began playing himself as an extra in some of the commercials Arnie made.

Talk about being in the right place at the right time . . .

"I felt like I had hitched a ride on a space shuttle," Nielson said of his first few years in the Arnie lane. He didn't care that his financial deal was less than other tour caddies. He didn't care that he wasn't getting paid like other extras in the commercials. He was just happy to be along for the rocket ride and Arnie was happy to have a caddie who was neat and trim, polite and quiet. Royce didn't say boo. Except for, "Yes, Mr. Palmer." Or, "Good morning, Mrs. Palmer."

When Royce did have a spurt of conversation, Arnie would teasingly call him "Creamy." But that was rare, which made his outburst during a Senior tour event at Naples, Florida, in early 1992 all the more amazing. After the two conferred on club selection for a layup shot on a par-five hole, Arnie's shot slithered down the left side of the fairway and came to rest in a funky lie next to a water hazard. Shaking his head over the ball, he groused to Nielson about the club selection that had left him in this predicament.

Nielson isn't sure to this day how or why it happened, but the next thing he knew, his mouth flew open and out blurted a biting rejoinder. "Goddammit, I didn't know you were going to hit it over here!" snapped Nielson. "I thought you were going to hit it over there where everybody else lays it up!"

Arnie blinked in shock.

Nielson blinked in shock.

"It scared me that I had yelled at him. He didn't say another word the rest of the round," Nielson recalled. "In fact, after the round, I told Miller Barber that I thought I had just gotten fired."

He was wrong. When he boarded Arnie's jet that afternoon, Arnie laughed about the exchange, and all was right with the world again. "That's the way he is. Once something like that happens, it's over," said Nielson.

Nielson continued for the rest of 1992, then resigned after Arnie's final tournament. Arnie was paying him $350 a week plus five percent of purse money—about half that of most other top regular caddies. After expenses for motel rooms, food, and the few airline tickets necessary when he didn't fly to a tournament in Arnie's plane, Royce said he was clearing only about ten thousand dollars a year. He did finally earn a stipend from one of the commercials, but the shuttle ride had lost its luster. He left with no hard feelings.

"He's the hardest working guy I've ever been around," Nielson said of Arnie three months after the break. "To the public, he was the most accommodating of all the pros out there. People would hand me letters and notes to give him about some relative in the hospital, dying, who would be lifted by a call from him. He just about always did that for them. It was fun working for him. It was a great experience."

Nielson later signed on again for an additional eighteen-month stint at an increased pay, but again parted amicably in 1995.

Larry Guest

10

Air Arnie

Well-chronicled is that Arnie's principal mode of transportation has improved dramatically over the years. Currently part-owner of six automobile dealerships, luxury sedans are at his beck and call. He is better known, however, for his mode of personal air travel, progressing from the twin-prop Aero Commander 560 he began flying from tournament to tournament at the height of his career in the mid-'60s to his latest toy—a fifteen-million dollar, ten-passenger Cessna Citation X executive jet.

IN BETWEEN were a procession of various Jet Commander, Lear and Cessna Citation 500, II, III, and VII models, all of which have borne his specially-approved FAA registration number: N1AP. He typically flew them all from the command seat in a style not wholly different from his golf. Though an accomplished and calculating pilot, Arnie is sometimes bored by over-cautious procedures and has been known to cut corners on a familiar approach.

That style was reflected in a brief dialogue with buddy Joe Tito during one of those thousand moments when Arnie paused on a golf course to observe some passing aircraft. In this instance, the craft was another private jet making a conservative, by-the book approach into Latrobe Airport.

Arnie: "That guy doesn't have any guts."

Tito: "Maybe it's not his jet."

Arnie, laughing: "You know, Joe, maybe you've got a point."

Flying to Arnie is as much a passion and release as it is a business convenience. Behind the yoke of his plane or helicopter, he is away from the phones, away from the tugging business associates, away from the autograph seekers, doing what is fun to him. At forty thousand feet, he is allowed at last to retreat within himself to mindlessly fiddle with the instruments, plot the course, or simply savor yesterday's string of birdies.

The planes also allow him to take along close associates and friends, which he routinely does on most trips to give him something of a "family" on the road. He is the ultimate airborne host, always making sure guests in the opulent cabin are comfortable and provided drinks and snacks—everything except smoking materials.

In the cabin of the Citation III was a little plastic sign that advised: "If You Want to Smoke, Please Step Outside." At forty thousand feet, you get the message.

Arnie's aviation career has included a number of ticklish moments. He once blew an engine during the critical moments of takeoff from a small airport just outside of Miami. He unknowing-

ly took off from a grass strip in South Georgia in a plane that had lost its rudder, clipping tree limbs as he became airborne. He had to grab the controls from a chopper pilot who froze in the path of an oncoming commercial jet. He completed a Hawaii-to-California hop virtually on fumes due to headwinds that had him actually reviewing ocean-ditching procedures during initial approach.

The latter close call came while Arnie was returning from China in November 1986. After a refueling stop in Hawaii, Arnie pointed his Citation III jet to Palm Springs, California. However, after encountering unexpected and severe headwinds, he was forced to divert to the closest terra firma—Monterey, California, where Arnie landed on little more than fumes. Arnie confided with friends that he mentally reviewed his will and brushed up on emergency procedures for ditching at sea as the fuel gauge dropped lower and lower. After Arnie taxied to a stop and shut down, attendants at the Monterey flight service manually checked the tanks and reported there wasn't enough fuel inside to register on their measuring sticks. "All that counts is that we made it and I'm here now," Arnie said, glossing over the close call.

Another harrowing experience that ended up being more comical than life-threatening was Arnie's impulsive, all-night return to Latrobe a day after the 1970 Bing Crosby.

On the Monday evening following the tournament, Arnie had a speaking engagement at Modesto, California, where he and Winnie planned to spend the night and jet home on Tuesday. During the function, he decided to make the four-hour flight home right after dessert. With the three-hour time difference, Arnie, his copilot and Winnie descended into western Pennsylvania that cold January dawn a half-hour before the Latrobe Airport tower would open at 7:00 A.M.

Since no one was on duty to advise about ground conditions via radio, Arnie made a low pass over the winter setting to observe what appeared to be a perfectly clear runway ringed by snow banks. Little did he know the "clear" runway had been covered during the night by a half-inch sheet of ice. "But you couldn't tell that from the air," he recalls.

When Arnie's seemingly uneventful landing touched down, the jet began sliding sideways across the "rink." Dramatic efforts to steer the craft under control overpowered the nose-wheel circuit breaker. The wheel began flopping like a boated mackerel, causing the runaway jet to dart here and there as it hurtled across the ice. Using the rudder, Arnie managed to keep the plane on the runway surface until diminished speed rendered the rudder ineffective. Finally, the plane veered to a thudding stop in a small snowbank.

A visual check indicated all was in order with the landing gear. The circuit breaker was snapped back into place and the decision was made to rev the engines to taxi the plane out of its snowy prison. With Arnie outside, giving hand signals and filling the chilled air with little white puffs of shouted instruction, the copilot managed to swing the craft back around toward the runway. An extra surge of power was needed to free one wheel from the snowbank.

As Arnie intently concentrated on the entrapped wheel and motioned thumbs-up to increase power, the wheel suddenly broke free of its snowy rut and the plane lurched forward directly at him. What Winnie and the copilot saw there for an instant was a scene right out of most any Saturday morning cartoon: Arnie's eyes became horrified saucers, his legs became a frantic propeller going nowhere atop the frozen runway. An instant before being impaled by his own jet, Arnie went down in a heap, his noggin cracking

Larry Guest

against the ice. The plane skated over him as he managed to roll over and dodge the landing gear.

Damage report: Only a large bump on his head and a small laceration to his pride.

The damage could have been far more serious the night Arnie took a few shortcuts to the prescribed landing procedure and, on an uncharacteristically poor landing, touched down ten yards short of the Latrobe runway. Thankfully, the wheels bounced over the lip at the end of the runway and Arnie completed the landing without further incident. Had his wheels hit the lip, the landing gear could have been sheared off.

Flying out the next morning, Arnie taxied to that end of the runway and was startled by the sight of the two fresh and ominous ruts in the mud just a few yards short of the pavement.

Two months later, as Arnie was taxiing out for takeoff, a Lear landed short and scraped down the runway with one wingtip tank dragging the ground. Upon his return, the Lear was still at Latrobe undergoing extensive repairs. On the flawed landing, the right wheel had hit the lip of the runway and knocked the strut up through the wing. The sobering sight got Arnie's attention and the ensuing thousand or so landings have all been well onto the runway.

Arnie enjoys flying all types of aircraft and has piloted everything from the McDonnell-Douglas 500E, four-passenger helicopter he has owned since 1985 to an Air Force fighter jet to jumbo 747 and DC-10 airliners.

Arnie's love of flying is well-known among plane manufacturers. McDonnell-Douglas invited Arnie to fly the DC-10 from its plant in Long Beach, California. So after an evening in the Beverly Hills Hotel, Arnie and pal Foley Hooper, a Central Florida corn baron, downed a huge breakfast and took off in a DC-10 that

McDonnell had manufactured but not yet delivered to its destined airline. After being up an hour, Arnie decided to put the big plane through its paces, shooting touch-and-go landings and going into stalls and steep banks.

All went well in the cockpit. Back in the cabin, the passenger list of one wasn't faring as well. When Arnie finally completed the joy ride and parked in front of a McDonnell hangar, he was confronted by an ashen Hooper, holding two barf bags now containing the large breakfast.

When Arnie graduated from the prop-driven Aero Commander to the Jet Commander in the mid-'60s, he had to get type rated by the Federal Aviation Administration. This meant a crash course—no pun intended—at LaGuardia where officials helped him compress a normal ten-day school into two intense, twelve-hour days. He passed the written test with flying colors and was ready for the critical flight test, which was administered by none other than the head of the FAA at the time, Jack Shaeffer.

Shaeffer took a crew to Orlando and stayed in the lodge at Arnie's Bay Hill Club. The test involves being run through all emergency procedures, including having an engine shut off during takeoff.

The FAA is a government-funded agency that does not customarily send out its flight inspectors to give tests. *You* go to *them*. Arnie's friendship with Shaeffer, who was about to go out of office at the time, cut through much of the red tape.

This is not to suggest Arnie passed the test because of special treatment. All of his various copilots over the years attest that he could have passed it anywhere. Arnie is an accomplished pilot. But there was no doubt that when Shaeffer and his crew flew to Orlando and stayed at Bay Hill, Arnie would pass the test.

Larry Guest

If Arnie has a fault as a pilot, it may be that he becomes a bit overconfident or bored at times and is given to either lapses of concentration or playful aerobatics. If a pilot is talented enough, he can execute a slow roll, gradually turning the plane upside down and on over to the original position without the passengers "feeling" the roll.

Orlando businessman Paul Polizzi and former PGA tour star Dow Finsterwald can attest that their buddy Arnie is one of those pilots. Returning from a tournament a few years ago in Arnie's jet, Polizzi and Finsterwald were engaged in conversation when Polizzi was startled by something odd he saw through the porthole window.

Chuckling, he advised his fellow passenger: "Dow, I think we're upside-down."

Finsterwald checked his window and indeed the ocean was "above" them.

"The amazing part," Polizzi recalls, "is that I had a beer sitting on the table and not a drop was spilled." After landing, Polizzi said something about the roll and Arnie put on his best "who me?" expression of feigned innocence.

Until the recent surge of European talent, the Ryder Cup Matches offered little mystery on or around the course. An exception was the 1967 matches that provided more than a little excitement and intrigue, thanks to the renowned aviator and most hospitable host on the Yanks' team. Taking Tony Jacklin and some of his British teammates aloft for a joy ride and aerial view of the Champions Golf Club course was merely Arnie's idea of livening up a routine practice day.

He didn't imagine the gesture might very nearly touch off an international incident and jeopardize his own private pilot's license.

In simplest terms, Arnie recalls he "took the British Ryder Cup team up and gave them a real ride. The FAA said I was flying too low. They questioned it, and I had to write a letter stating the situation. They found no fault."

From David Wayne Hooks Field, a private strip not far from Champions, Arnie took off with the Brits in his Jet Commander and playfully buzzed the golf course. Just how high—or, more to the point, how low—Arnie made his two passes of the course, became an item of touchy debate. Even by the most liberal interpretation, five hundred feet was the legal minimum in the area of the Champions club. A high-speed pass was followed by a low-speed pass with flaps and landing gear down, causing a stir at the club. Arnie punctuated the ride with a few acrobatic maneuvers, then returned to Hooks Field, satisfied he had properly entertained his foreign guests.

Taxiing back to the hanger also used by legendary golfer Jimmy Demaret, Arnie suddenly found himself in an aviation brouhaha. A Champions resident had been startled enough by Arnie's aerial mischievousness to log a complaint with the FAA, whose investigators were on the phone to Hooks Field by the time he deplaned.

Arnie thought the call was a gag by the playful Demaret and fully expected Demaret's Texas twang on the line, giving Arnie a hard time about skimming so low over Champions, when he was handed the receiver. The impish grin quickly gave way to concern as Arnie motioned for pen and paper to jot down the official addresses and procedural appeals the investigator was reciting.

There had been various estimates from players and spectators at the club as to the altitude of Arnie's flyovers, including "below

Larry Guest

treetop." Houston sportswriter Dick Peebles offered to "help," saying a *Chronicle* photographer had snapped one of Arnie's passes and the photo clearly showed the jet was not below treetop. Indisputably, the plane was *even* with treetops.

Uh, thanks, Dick, but would you mind keeping the photos out of the paper? Peebles and the *Chronicle* obliged.

Arnie wrote to the FAA, crossed his fingers, and swore that he didn't fly below one thousand feet on the pass. The British Ryder Cup members, thankful to be back on the ground, and even Jimmy Demaret, who hadn't left it, gave similar testimony to the FAA.

Six weeks later, the FAA decided there was too much conflicting testimony to make a case and dropped it, thus saddling Arnie with only a valuable lesson.

Even at recommended minimum altitudes, Arnie's habit of a flyover as he's leaving a tournament has not always met with universal approval. Pro Bob Murphy let it be known that he was distracted when he was still competing on the course at Hilton Head one year when Arnie buzzed overhead on his way out of town.

He flashed back to that Hilton Head exit a few years later as he was leaving the 1976 Tallahassee Open. Arnie had been among the early players in the final round and the leaders were grinding down the closing holes when N1AP flashed overhead, its wings dipping ninety degrees to one side, then just as dramatically to the other.

The crowd and even the leader, Gary Koch, enjoyed the show. Up in the Lear's cabin, Foley Hooper and a freeloading columnist were trying not to lose their cookies. From the captain's seat, Arnie turned and looked over his shoulder, laughing at the consternation his aerobatics had caused his two passengers. "I haven't done that in more than a year," he laughed. "I had to lay off awhile ever since

Murph complained that time. But he's already off the course today and, besides, I didn't get down too low."

He was not always so comfortable with such hotdogging himself. The first man with whom he had flown happened to show up in his gallery at the Tallahassee tournament. That brought back memories of Arnie's very first time aloft.

"It was back during World War II and I was about twelve years old," Arnie recounted. "The guy had been washed out of cadets and was a glider pilot. He took me up in a Piper Cub and did a few loops and rolls. I thought it was all over. When we got down, I told him thanks, but I didn't want to ride in an airplane again."

His next flight was not much more encouraging. Arnie was a twenty-year-old amateur when he took a trip to Chattanooga in an old DC-3. Already nervous about the experience, Arnie looked up in horror to watch a ball of fire—he result of static electricity combustion—racing down the aisle past his seat.

"That," Arnie still says with raised eyebrows for emphasis, "scared the hell out of me."

But realizing the convenience private air travel would mean to his career, Arnie began taking flying lessons at Latrobe in his late twenties. Within a few years, he was flying himself to many tour stops and developing a hobby that has served him well as a luxury and as a form of mental refreshment for three decades.

In 1990, ABC-TV aired an hourlong special titled, "Arnold Palmer: The Man and the Legend." It followed the pattern of so many other video profiles before it—a mix of poolside reflections from Arnie, black-and-white footage of Ike-era glory in Opens and Masters, and the usual collection of adoring testimony from colleagues, competitors, and historians.

What may set this one apart is the pleasing, eloquent narrative of almost equally enduring Jim McKay and an enlightening off-

Larry Guest

course glimpse into Arnie's demanding business schedule. The latter was portrayed by tracking Arnie, day by day, through a multi-faceted September trip to the Far East that included playing appearances, business meetings, and course construction in Japan, Korea, the Philippines, and Borneo.

The profile's dearth of anecdotal spin could have been spiced simply by including even a basic account of the near misadventure Palmer experienced when being ferried by helicopter from a course-design site one hundred miles across mountainous Korean terrain to Seoul. McKay told his audience only that "weather almost grounded the chopper," delaying Palmer's return to the city for yet another appointment.

In truth, the consequences might have been far more grave than a mere disruption of Arnie's itinerary. Thump-thumping along at 110 knots and suddenly socked in by zero visibility, the Korean chopper pilot had to switch to instrument flight and became momentarily disoriented. As a licensed helicopter pilot himself, Arnie fully recognized the peril revealed by the lurching gauges and dials for a few harrowing moments before the pilot recovered.

The same nerve under fire that Arnie employed on the golf course came in handy more than once in the air. And one time, it was only a few feet in the air.

Arnie had flown into Charlotte for a photo shoot at the TPC of Piper Glen Club, one of his design courses that became the home for the Senior tour stop in that city starting in 1990. At the time, the course was in the final stages of completion and Arnie would be posing for promotional shots at the club.

From Douglas Airport, he would be shuttled to and from the course by helicopter. He and caddie Royce Nielson hopped aboard the chopper, which was being piloted by a Vietnam veteran.

When the rotors were up to speed, the pilot lifted a few feet and sought clearance from the tower. Clearance given "any direction west," Arnie expected the pilot to proceed upward and west, away from the nearby runway.

Instead, nothing happened. The chopper continued to hover a few feet off the ground and began drifting closer to the runway. From the back seat, Nielson could sense something wrong and noticed the concerned look Arnie was flashing at the pilot. As the chopper continued to drift, Nielson instinctively leaned forward to get a clear look up the runway and was stunned to see a commercial jetliner bearing down on them.

Arnie lurched toward the pilot and grabbed the control stick, pulling the chopper upward and clear of the runway. Once safely in the air, the pilot recovered and flew to Piper Glen without further incident, but with a flurry of apologies.

"The guy was so embarrassed," said Nielson. "He said he was nervous about flying Arnie and knew Arnie was a helicopter pilot himself. He said in all the missions in Vietnam, he had never frozen before.

"When we got out at the golf club and walked away from the helicopter, Arnie looked at me and asked, 'You want to fly back with that guy?'"

Remarkably, they did.

Larry Guest

11

Those Memorable,
Maddening Majors

The first year Arnold Palmer competed at Augusta National's cathedral of golf, he and Winnie pulled a tiny travel trailer into the charming little Georgia city and paid eleven dollars to hook it up for the week. In more recent years, Arnie and Winnie typically spend the Masters week residing in spacious estate homes, paying upwards of four thousand dollars rent.

THE ELEVEN BUCKS in 1955 were tougher to come by than the four grand today.

"We were broke when we showed up for our first Masters," Arnie recounted a few springs back, sipping a beer in the shade of the sprawling landmark just behind the Augusta National clubhouse that has come to be known as, simply, The Tree. A soft smile of fond recollection eased across his face. "That was during my apprentice period."

For those unfamiliar with medieval golf tour history, the pros once had to play for six months before becoming eligible for PGA prize money. An apprentice tour player could pick up a few bucks from pro-ams and a few non-sanctioned events outside the country, but those earnings were all but depleted when the young Palmers made it to Augusta. Since that tournament is not operated by the PGA tour, the Masters was Arnie's first opportunity to collect a check from a regular American tournament.

"And I played pretty well," Arnie noted. "I finished about ninth or tenth, I think, and won nine hundred and some dollars."

"Six hundred ninety-five," corrected Winnie Palmer, the family bookkeeper before Arnie's later millions would require the services of professional beancounters.

If Arnie has been golf's big show, the Masters has been his center stage. Arnie hitched his pants to four Masters victories, captivating national television audiences that were just discovering the game as a living room spectator sport.

Though little threat now to add a fifth green jacket, his annual strolls through Augusta's enchanted gardens of blooming dogwoods and azaleas nonetheless underscore his enduring popularity. Each April at the Masters, Arnie is engulfed by autograph seekers even in the early-week practice rounds on his short walk from the lockers to the driving range. He obliges another hundred or so en route to the putting green back on the other side of the clubhouse. Dozens more are rewarded between each hole, as assigned Pinkertons provide interference to the next tee.

They cheer his good shots. They applaud his arrival on each and every green. They even applauded one year when he shed his sweater on the fifteenth tee. Two men lurched in competition for a

broken tee Arnie discarded at the sixteenth. And those incidents were only in a Tuesday practice round—a rehearsal as Arnold Palmer groped for the magic of bygone years.

He has not won at Augusta since 1964. The spurts of solid play onto the early leaderboards have become distantly spaced. The most recent was in 1983 when Arnie bolted out of the blocks to a first-round 68. Arnie's Army has grown more nostalgic than hopeful. But they're still there, every year, in numbers only marginally diminished, tromping through the pines, drawn by this man's magnetism and the cherished memories of glories past.

Each year there is cause to embrace the dream that just one more time, someway, somehow, he'll revive the echoes of those stirring triumphs. In 1979, on the occasion of his twenty-fifth Masters, that hope was tethered to a slump-busting spree in the weeks prior to the tournament. With his fiftieth birthday lurking in the fall, Arnie had opened the year by missing the cut in his first four tournaments. Then he qualified for weekend play in the next three—his own Bay Hill Classic, the Tournament Players Championship, and the Heritage at Hilton Head—to rekindle fantasies among the diehard Palmerites.

"I'm playing better. I'm putting better," declared Arnie, who had slipped into Augusta three times earlier in the spring for practice rounds. He was obviously determined to be a factor in his silver anniversary Masters, to hush the critics who were saying the flame had died.

"To win again here? Ooooooo . . ." He repeated the question and emitted a low tone, smiling and savoring the dream of breaking his then six-year tour-victory drought on this most celebrated playground. "That would be super. Yeah, I guess it would."

Winnie Palmer smiled demurely at the daydream. In another era, she had tried to make Arnie's Masters victories happen, following a mild superstition brought on in 1958.

"The tournament always gives the players' wives a gift, something Mr. [Cliff] Roberts picked out," she began, alluding to the late Masters chairman. "In '58, they gave us a gold charm, and I went downtown the day before the tournament started and splurged for a bracelet to go with the charm. I think it was twenty-two dollars, and I was so nervous about it because we really couldn't afford it."

Winnie stuffed the receipt in her pocketbook and fretted all week over her jewelry store indulgence. She didn't tell Arnie about the purchase until that Sunday night—hours after he had been fitted for his first Masters green jacket, the symbolic spoils for Augusta winners.

"So for many years after that, I'd go downtown shopping early in Masters week and buy something I couldn't afford," Winnie said with a laugh. "But I don't do it anymore. I found out that didn't work."

Besides, there is hardly anything for sale in downtown Augusta that the wife of Arnold Palmer can no longer afford. Although she said she came close one recent year.

"Yeah," she laughed. "I bought groceries."

Alas, Arnie missed the cut in that 1979 tournament for only the third time in his twenty-five tries to that point. Then the exception, Arnie's missing the cut has become almost the rule in recent years. Through the '96 Masters, Arnie had missed the thirty-six-hole cut thirteen straight years. During that stretch, his stroke average at Augusta was 77.3—this by a man who had averaged 70.8 during one ten-year stretch of Masters.

Larry Guest

Nevertheless, the fall-off in his Augusta galleries has been ever so slight. In equal parts hopeful anticipation and nostalgic appreciation, Arnie's fans have stood by their man at the Masters, traversing the east Georgia hills with him each year. "They aren't fans," he said one day under The Tree. "They are friends. The people I see out here, most of them I know. But I'm amazed they keep coming out."

After watching the usual herd of two thousand agonizing along with Arnie during a round of 81 a few years ago, golf writer George White observed: "It's no secret that people would much rather watch Arnold Palmer shoot 81 than to watch Nick Faldo shoot 68."

Arnie's love for the Masters and its lore and dignity is such that he will defend it from all attack — even when, as in one year, the source of affront comes from the tournament chairman himself.

Hord Hardin served as Masters chairman for thirteen years through 1991, quickly branding himself as something of a cartoon character with his infamous post-round TV interview with newly crowned champion Seve Ballesteros. "Tell me, Seve, something people are always asking me —" Hardin began, pausing when distracted by a CBS voice in his earpiece, "uh, how tall are you?"

In the Palmer camp, as well as most golf inner circles, the space cadet chairman was known derisively as "Hard Hordin." But his image as a harmless buffoon suddenly changed to something more threatening when Hardin began making public threats on the eve of the 1988 Masters that he might discontinue the tournament due to pro golf's runaway commercialism and mushrooming purses. Even routine stops on the PGA tour were beginning to pay more than the Masters. Hardin said he could see the demise of the Masters if the trend continued.

To Arnie and others who so loved the Masters, Hardin's shallow threats were seen as a gross departure from the dignity of the club and the Tournament. The prize money was secondary to all of the other things that the Masters represented to the players and golf's public. To make an issue of it was seen as Hardin's most offensive gaffe.

"That's ridiculous, and I told him so," Arnie bristled. "I told him, 'I can't believe you said something like that.' I don't know why Hord Hardin is giving press conferences, anyway. He should stay in his office and keep his mouth shut.

"It's a tragedy, some of the things he's doing to the tournament and the course. There's too much integrity at this club for these things to be happening. Commercialism? Bull! The only guy who can 'demise' the tournament is Hord."

Under Hardin's leadership, Augusta's severely sloping greens, already crusty and frighteningly quick during most Masters, were steadily being made harder and faster to protect the tournament records against the onslaught of young talent. In that year, 1988, the greens went right off the scale, producing a batch of embarrassing four- and five-putt disasters by some of the game's finest players.

Arnie charged that Hardin's regime had turned the hallowed Augusta course into "Disney World. I don't think the fans want to see that."

Even after shooting a 66 to move into second-day contention, not even ebullient Fuzzy Zoeller was a happy camper. He joined Arnie's chorus. "You don't hear the cheers out there anymore," he lamented. "The greens are so hard and dry they won't hold a shot. I get angry because when I hit good shots I like to be semi rewarded, not see them bounce over the green."

And what would it take to get the greens in good condition?

"An eight-hour thunderstorm," Zoeller quipped. "Seven hours wouldn't do it. Hopefully somebody will wake up and get us some good surfaces to putt on. Everyone says, 'Be positive. Be positive.' I'm an upbeat guy, but I'm fed up. I know Jack Nicklaus and Tom Watson say, 'Everyone has to play under the same conditions,' but that's the problem. Those two guys don't complain, so nothing gets done. But, damn it, someone's got to speak up."

Someone did. At Arnie's urging, adjustments were made prior to the '89 tournament, taking the "goofy golf" factor out of some of the more treacherous greens.

Arnie verbalized his love for the course and the tournament in a letter to Augusta National icons Bobby Jones and Clifford Roberts. The letter, which is proudly reprinted each year in the tournament record book, reads as follows:

January 10, 1961

Dear Mr. Jones and Mr. Roberts:

It is extremely difficult, if not impossible, for me to put into words what I feel about the Masters Tournament and the Augusta National Golf Course. I can recall that as a young boy, prior to attending Wake Forest College, the Masters was something I read about in the papers, and it was my burning ambition to some day be able to play this great course, particularly as a participant in the tournament. One incident in particular stands out in my memory. The Wake Forest golf team was scheduled to play a spring match in Georgia. In an effort to get to see the Masters, we offered our services to the officials in charge. Unfortunately for us, arrangements had already been made, and our offer was turned down. To say that we were disappointed would be a mild understatement, but it made us all, and myself in particular, even more desirous of finding a way to be invited to your great classic.

I finally achieved this honor, and have had the pleasure of competing in six Masters, and the good fortune to win on two occasions. I realize now why participation in the Masters meant so much to me, and why it undoubtedly affects many other young golfers with similar feelings today. As far as I am concerned, there will never be another tournament to equal it. Even today I retain a longing to win it again and again. I know this feeling will stay with me for years to come and when I am no longer able to compete, I hope to be there to watch the expressions of happiness and pride as each new participant walks off the eighteenth green after he has played his first round at the Masters.

Therefore, to you, Mr. Roberts, to Mr. Bob Jones, and to each member of the Augusta National, I want to personally express my sincere and humble thanks for this great course and tournament, and for the many wonderful memories it will always have for me.

Most sincerely,

Arnold D. Palmer

Arnie was so enamored with the Masters that he incorporated some of Augusta's best ideas into his own tournament at Bay Hill. For one, he used the Masters-type practice of eliminating walking scoreboards, instead creating a scoreboard at each green to post the progress of the group playing that hole. The move eliminated part of the unseemly clutter inside the ropes.

Another is Augusta's fabled champion's dinner. Or at least a version of it.

On the eve of each year's tournament, Masters tradition calls for the reigning champion to host all other past champions—even selecting the menu. Sandy Lyle's choice of that old Scottish nightmare, haggis (a goat stomach stuffed with unspeakable horrors), ranks as the most dramatic departure. When there is a food indigenous to a champion's homeland, he is given more latitude than normal. If Lyle is ever in contention again, watch for assorted past champions to step on his ball or wheeze in his backswing.

During the four years in which he was the esteemed host, Arnie usually gave the champs alternatives, either chicken and fish or chicken and steak. I once playfully suggested if he had selected a menu item indigenous to the little western Pennsylvania mill town where he grew up, it might have been shots and beer.

"Actually, it would have been stew. We had a lot of stew at our house," he said.

How about hamburger?

"Oh, noooooo," he said. "That's way too expensive. More often, we had whatever we could raise or hunt. We raised chickens, so we had chicken. We could hunt, so we had pheasant and rabbit. My mother fixed rabbit a lot."

He never treated the Masters champs to a rabbit dish.

A man who truly feeds on the traditions and history of his beloved sport, Arnie regards his PGA tour stop at Bay Hill as he would a favored child and is ever alert to any tactic or dressing that might make it even more prestigious and memorable.

In 1989, the past Bay Hill champs were invited to bring along their winning gray blazers and break bread on the eve of the tournament. Except, unlike at Augusta, where the dinner is restricted to the current tournament chairman and green jacket winners, Arnie's IMG advisors turned it into a mini-sponsor bash, stuffing the guest list with tournament angels, committeemen, various IMG execs, and one interloping columnist.

In a column the next morning on the historic occasion, I expressed appreciation to Arnie for having me there to chronicle the inaugural dinner for the archives but publicly suggested he shouldn't invite me again. Or anyone else except the champs, himself, and perhaps the CEO of the title sponsor and that year's tournament chairman.

The invitation list for a similar champions' dinner at one Texas tournament grew to the point that it became just another social affair where the players had to shake hands with a lot of people they didn't know. Feeling exploited, most of the past champs of that tournament began skipping the affair.

At the Augusta fete—the brainchild of the great Ben Hogan—Masters champs hoist a glass of wine, share dinner, push back and light up a stogie, and just rap. Gilded yarns of golf.

Constructive criticisms of the course. Suggestions for the tournament policy. Persimmon heads, square grooves, perimeter weighting, the price of unleaded, whatever.

"I love it. I really love it and look forward to it every year," said Tom Watson, a man who has come to lust for golf's unique lore and camaraderie. "You don't often have a chance to see Claude Harmon and Herman Keiser and Arnold Palmer and Sam Snead all in one room and talk golf. I don't have to read golf history; for one night a year, I can live it."

Many improvements in the Masters—indeed, all of golf—have emanated from the freewheeling exchanges in that past-champions' dinner. But not all is fairway seriousness.

"Sam Snead," Arnie recounted, "always tells a joke and usually it is the worst joke you can imagine.

"Somebody will say, 'Sam, you got any jokes?' And Sam will start," Arnie mused, lapsing into his best cackling, West Virginia impression of the Slammer: "'There was this old guy who had two pigs . . .'"

Arnie's shoulders began bouncing in laughter as he revisited the special mood of those Augusta dinners. For the same mood to live in Orlando, the Bay Hill champs would need the sense of intimacy that would permit them—without feeling "on stage"—to tell Arnie the new green on such-and-such hole is a disaster or that some locker room policy has been a wonderful addition.

Or, if the mood strikes, to tell a raunchy joke about an old guy with two pigs.

Winnie Palmer was a demure young flower when she and Arnie made their first trip to St. Andrews for the 1960 British Open, booking into the ancient Rusack's Marine Hotel overlooking the famed eighteenth on the Old Course. Thirty years later, much was made of Arnie and Winnie staying in the hotel's Royal Suite on the second floor (at about five hundred dollars per night) for his "last" crack at the British Open.

It was alleged to be the same digs they had used in 1960. But, actually, the Palmers had occupied the Royal Suite in 1964 for filming of the old "Big Three" television golf matches against Jack Nicklaus and Gary Player. In 1960, the Palmers had more modest accommodations—a single, thirty-dollar room on the third floor with shared facilities down the hall.

Winnie recalls with a laugh her trepidation over the community bath, her first such experience. Upon her initial, cautious approach, the door swung open and a burly man wearing a large towel and larger moustache emerged, obviously fresh from a bath. Startled by the sight of the remarkably thick coat of hair covering the man's upper torso, Winnie blinked and scurried back to her room like a frightened doe. "I never knew who he was, but I wasn't about to get into that bathtub right after he had," she recounted.

Arnie had thought the previous time the Open rota had touched down in St. Andrews—1984—was going to be his swan song. That time, the Palmers had stayed in the remodeled and contemporary Old Course Hotel alongside the seventeenth fairway. Winnie had watched from the balcony of their hotel room as Arnie suffered a second round double-bogey on that daunting "Road Hole" then trod off to the eighteenth tee with little hope of surviving the cut.

He already had begun that famous walk up the eighteenth at the Old Course when the bittersweet realization set in. The knowledgeable fans who had lingered for this seven o'clock hour, half filling the massive banks of grandstands so distinctive to the British Opens, came up with the discovery about the same moment and began rising to their feet. Arnie, then fifty-four, was making his way to the eighteenth green not only for the final time in that tournament, but by all reckoning, for the last time in his long and distinguished British Open career. Even this fading favorite of millions did not entertain the thought at that moment that he would, indeed, make not one but two more curtain bows by playing when the Open rotated back to St. Andrews in 1990 and 1995.

For all he knew, this was the last walk, and one could sense that sobering deduction spreading through the fans as they rose

Larry Guest

and cheered and whistled and applauded—a reception and salute uncommonly warm even by Palmer standards.

It was an electric heart-tugging moment in sports, one that gave this great man of simple dignity a rush. After holing his final putt and acknowledging yet another round of applause and cheers, Arnie paused on the steps of the vaunted Royal & Ancient club-house to send a last, longing gaze back up the revered links and reflect with a friend.

"Yes, I think the crowd knew," he nodded. "This was my last hole here. Oh, I might come back and play here sometime—an exhibition or something—but not in a British Open. Maybe in my next lifetime."

Once the most feared and electrifying man to enter any golf tournament, Arnie had become an aging Henry Aaron, a Stan Musial on a farewell tour. These presumed closing shots at St. Andrews seemed to unofficially launch his final tour of the ball-parks.

While he played the eighteenth, the emotional outpouring from a crowd so grateful for all the magic memories had turned Arnie nostalgic as he made his way between the banks of grand-stands and ancient hotels that flank the final fairway.

"A lot of things ran through my mind. I flashed back to the first time I came here in 1960 and some of the press I met for the first time. That was really sort of a 'press' tournament. Of course, a lot of them are dead now," he said, digging his gold Rolex and a fold of British currency from a pouch in his golf bag.

Having opened with a four-over 76 in the first round that year, Arnie would have had to match par on this day to survive the mid-way cut. He had appeared comfortably on target until his drive at the twelfth found a tiny pot bunker, leading to a double-bogey 6.

He three-putted the next green, admittedly unable to shake the previous hole.

"I lost my cool. I got angry out there for the first time in a long while," Arnie sighed wistfully. "I guess it's just because I really wanted to play two more rounds here. This place means so much to me."

And vice versa.

It was Arnie who had given this sagging championship new life when he brought his bold style and pants-hitching charisma to the Open in 1960 and captivated the Brits with victories in '61 and '62.

During the '61 Open at Birkdale, Arnie struck one of the most dramatic shots of his long career. It was on the sixteenth hole of the final day, and he was clinging to a one-shot lead over Dai Rees. His drive bounded into the rough, leaving him with a terrible lie in knee-high weeds.

"I had hit what I thought was a perfect drive," Arnie recalled. "The ball kicked just a little bit to the right, and it wound up one yard off the fairway. I was actually standing in the fairway when I took my stance. But the rough was so thick I could hardly see my ball."

From 140 yards, he lashed a 6-iron, gambling that he could clear two pot bunkers that would have surely doomed him. "Weeds flew everywhere," remembers Tip Anderson, the angular Englishmen who caddied for Arnie in every British Open. The ball shot out of the hay and came to rest just twelve feet from the cup. Arnie safely two-putted for his par to preserve the one-stroke lead he would maintain for the victory over Rees.

The Birkdale members were so impressed they laid a plaque on the site of the shot. "It was one of the bravest shots I have ever

Larry Guest

seen, considering the position he was in," said Anderson with his clipped British accent.

The shot was one of the reasons Arnie became perhaps the most popular golfer in the United Kingdom, more so than any of the British players of that era. The British golf fans knew his efforts to play their Open boosted the tournament into a position of prominence that it might never have achieved otherwise.

But if the British fans were appreciative of Arnie, the Royal & Ancient didn't seem to be. Arnie submitted to pretournament qualifying before and after each triumph. It was his effective, silent protest against the nonexempt status for all Americans, by skipping the '64 Open—at St. Andrews, no less—that produced an immediate and landmark exemption system to accommodate leading U.S. stars. It paved the way for a flood of Yank celebrities who have both embraced and embellished the tournament, restoring its lost status as, arguably, *the* tournament in world golf.

Why did Arnie cross the Atlantic and take a chance on qualifying when precious few other Americans considered the trip worth the expense for the small prize money offered?

"From the time I was a little boy, my father and I spent a great deal of time talking about the British Open, and he and I both decided that when I had enough money to go to the British Open, we would go," he said. "Because without playing in it, my golfing career would have been minus a very important factor.

"The fact is, it's a championship that is just very important to any golfer who plays for more than just what dollars and cents can get you. You have to play it. You just really must play it if you're a true professional and you love the game. I think anybody who doesn't has missed a lot."

Perhaps his heart had been fueled by that '64 absence or by the fact that this was the site of his last legitimate opportunity to win a major since his '64 Masters triumph. (Two tee shots pushed into the hotel grounds at the seventeenth had relegated him to seventh place in 1978 at St. Andrews.)

As he ended our exchange there on the clubhouse steps in '84, he turned away from the course for what he thought was the final time. Arnie smiled fondly at Anderson. The two, legends in their own right, shook hands warmly and, for a long moment, exchanged nods that said everything about the emotional juncture they had reached.

They parted without a word.

But Arnie is a sucker for The Old Course at St. Andrews, the birthplace of golf and cradle of the game. It's a shrine where history is counted in centuries. A visit to The Old Course, on the windswept coast of Fife north of Edinburgh, is a walk with the ghosts of golf. Six years later, he couldn't resist another crack at a St. Andrews Open, even at age sixty, insisting however that this would definitely be his last entry in the British Open. It wouldn't be.

"This will be a sentimental journey back to St. Andrews—thirty years to the day that I went to my first British Open Championship," he said at the time. Arnie finished second to Australian Kel Nagle in 1960 but won the trophy, the revered old silver claret jug, the next two years.

"Winning those two British Opens was an important step for me, an important part of my career, something I'll always cherish," he said.

The Scots have not forgotten Arnie's contributions to the game they originated, and his final-final walk up the eighteenth,

---

Larry Guest

before the grandstand on the left, certainly figured to produce one of sport's most emotional farewells. It didn't disappoint, although there was a twist.

Grinding his way in with a par 144 through the first two rounds, Arnie and his adoring British regiments thought he had survived the cut, thus delaying the emotional sendoff until that Sunday's fourth round. As he finished just after lunch on the second day, the weather was coming in low and ominous off the North Sea and projections were the cut would be blown to 147 or even 148. But the afternoon skies cleared and the winds abated, permitting a spate of players to shoot good scores and lower the cut mark to 143—one excruciating shot better than Arnie.

His first "bonus" appearance in the Open had been warmly embraced by the fans, the media, and the R&A, which invited him to deliver the sole address that Tuesday night at the traditional past-champions' dinner. Evidence of that passion was clearly spelled out in the words on a T-shirt worn by a dumpy little Scot seated strategically on the front steps of the Rusack's that Friday afternoon after Arnie completed play. "ARNOLD PALMER WILL YE NO COME BACK AGAIN?" the shirt asked.

Arnie smiled broadly at the little man and shook his hand.

As it turned out, the answer to the T-shirt was yes. Arnie returned in 1995 for his final-final-final, another nostalgic appearance the fans and media relished. Alas, he missed the cut again. And again he swore it was his last try in the Open. Stay tuned.

Although all four of golf's majors have been important to Arnie, the Masters and the British Open hold a special place in his heart. He's a traditionalist and those events are pure golf history

---

wrapped in a tournament. The U.S. Open and the PGA Championships are not without meaning to him. He has been a key supporter of the United States Golf Association, which runs the U.S. Open. And he has been especially grateful to the PGA for continuing to give him special exemptions into that tournament.

But the PGA is, after all, the one major that Arnie could never win, leaving a void that the press could never let him forget. And he won the Open just once and cluttered his memory of that event with his frustrating series of failed tries in Open qualifiers. Also, the Open was the stage for Arnie's most notorious collapse, that infamous loss of a seven-shot lead and, eventually, the tournament to Billy Casper in 1966 at San Francisco's Olympic Club.

At the 1987 PGA, he was asked about the one major trophy that never sat on his mantel, and he offered this insightful reply: "I watched Tom Watson this morning on ABC News, and they asked him the same question, the one he hasn't won. He said, 'Arnold Palmer hasn't won it, either.' But I'm still trying. Tom Watson is still trying, and Arnold Palmer is, too. If enough people ask you, 'Does it bother you?' it's going to bother you. When you see all the guys leave the practice tee to go to the Champions Clinic and you're still there, you wonder what the hell's wrong."

Four years earlier, the weekend prior to the 1983 PGA found me in Minnesota poking around on a story that Calvin Griffith was considering a sale of his baseball Twins to a group in Tampa Bay. The Twins then trained each spring in Orlando, thus making such a development big news in Central Florida. After spending a few days on the story, I was checking out of the Minneapolis Hyatt Regency on a Monday morning, preparing to return to Florida when I noticed a familiar silhouette ahead of me in the checkout line.

Larry Guest

I whipped out a personal check, tapped the silhouette on one sloping shoulder, and playfully asked if he could sign this. Arnold Palmer looked at the check and laughed at the coincidence of our meeting.

I explained my mission in Minnesota, and he explained he had been there to appear at a national convention for Toro, for whom he had become a spokesman. He suggested I cancel my flight back to Orlando and instead fly with him to L.A. where he would be competing in the PGA Championship that week. In an hour, he was heading west with a journalist/hitchhiker on board, resulting in this report to Sentinel readers the next morning describing Arnie's bittersweet relationship with the PGA:

Los Angeles — This is a week that is not circled in red on Arnold Palmer's calendar. It's that annual pain in the posterior when a covey of notepads and microphones will hound the enduring king of golf to ask a pointedly negative question.

Why, Arnie, oh why, have you never won the PGA Championship?

As he rehearses today and Wednesday for this, the sixty-fifth PGA at Riviera C.C., Palmer will be dogged by The Question. It'll be phrased a dozen ways, but it'll still be The Question.

Ol' Nosey here bumped into Arnie Monday in Minneapolis, a day ahead of the unwelcome interrogation, and he sighed at a reminder of the broken record he'd be hearing in L.A. I pulled out my notepad, worked up my most penetrating glare, and began on a light note: "Arnie, how come you've never won the PGA?"

Arnie's eyes playfully narrowed to angry slits that quickly gave way to a robust laugh. "Well . . . ," he finally offered, the shoulders dropping a tad as if surrendering to the inevitability of the questioning.

Nobody ever asks J. C. Snead or Kermit Zarley why they haven't won the PGA, perhaps because it has never occurred to anyone that they could. But Arnold Palmer is the man who has won sixty-one tour events and a billion hearts—give or take a dozen. He's won four Masters, a couple of British Opens, and a U.S. Open, but is oh-for-ever in the PGA.

"I guess the PGA is just so late in the year, that I've always spun my wheels by that time," Arnie offered one semi-serious theory. Reminded that one PGA was staged earlier in the year, he deadpanned: "Oh, that one was too late in the spring."

He laughed again.

It's not as if Arnie's swing has become a hiccup during each PGA. He might now own a picket fence of PGA trophies if fate had been kinder. He was tied with Julie Boros in '68 on the last hole and had a ten-foot birdie putt. But the putt failed to recognize its historic opportunity, and Boros nailed a birdie of his own to win in a photo finish. Arnie was runner-up again in '70 when Dave Stockton worked some magic on the closing nine. "And there was that year (1964) in Columbus when Nichols did all those fantastic things," added Palmer. Arnie posted what would have been a tournament-record 274 in that one, but Bobby Nichols, playing out of the Milky Way, shot a 271 that is still the PGA standard.

An hour later, streaking toward L.A. aboard his new six-million-dollar jet, Arnie again flashed back to Nichols' visit to the twilight zone. "Bobby would be in the middle of trees, and I'd look up and here would come the ball. Another birdie. I don't mean to take away from what he did. But I think at the time, no one had ever shot four rounds in the 60s in a major championship without winning, but that's what I did that week."

Ever the gracious diplomat, Palmer will never provide the daily prints with a public wail about the PGA administrative decision

that may well have saddled him with that one "major" vacancy in his trophy case. But you can take it to the bank that Arnie is still irritated that he was excluded from this tournament during his first four years on tour by a five-year apprenticeship rule. He joined the tour in 1954 and already had reeled off ten wins—including a Masters title—before he was permitted to tee up in the PGA for the first time in the summer of 1958. Arnie's absence led to a change in the apprentice rule, but not until after he had missed four PGA chances in the prime of his career.

This week hardly falls into Arnie's prime, but the fifty-three-year-old trouper is ever the optimist. He's drawing on positive vibes left over from his last Tinseltown tournament—the L.A. Open he led last January with just ten holes to play—even though that event was at a different course from the one he'll play this week. And he points to the brief though unsustained contention he enjoyed in all three previous majors this year.

"Can I win it?" he repeated, twisting that famous rubber face into a moment of contemplation. "I think I can, but it's going to take everything I have. I can drive it good enough to win. My irons are good enough to win. And I can even chip and putt good enough to win. But I don't know if I can do all of that for four rounds."

When he had southern California in a frenzy last January, he became something of a recluse all week, virtually hibernating and resting throughout the week. Same game plan this week, he says.

"I've been in good position several times this year; then things sort of slip toward the end of each day. Maybe that's the fate of a fifty-three-year-old."

There's that word again. Fate. Must be the week of the PGA.

But fate was never more of a four-letter word to Arnie back in '66 when he did the unthinkable: blow a seven-shot lead in the final nine holes of the U.S. bleeping Open. That thorn surfaced with renewed pain in 1987 when the Open returned to Olympic, the site of his most celebrated crack-up.

With twenty-one years by then to ponder a solution and the additional experience gained from roughly five hundred tournament appearances to call upon since that disaster, Arnie suggested he knew at last just what he could have done to win the 1966 U.S. Open at Olympic Club in San Francisco.

Chasing Ben Hogan's seventy-two-hole Open record, Arnie had attacked Olympic with trademark, swashbuckling boldness during that last half-lap at Olympic and, as it turned out, played right into Casper's hands. Disdaining layup tee shots and middle-of-the greens approaches, Arnie bulled his way right into agony as he scrambled to a 39 on the incoming nine, opening the door for a playoff that he would lose to Casper.

That day of infamy lingers as golf's version of the Andrea Doria; the water unexpectedly began rushing in, and Captain Arnie, unable to plug the leaks, went down with the ship.

If given an opportunity to turn back the clock, Arnie now confesses what he would do differently on the final nine to win the '66 Open. "I would shoot 38," he said, breaking into that squint-eyed, open-mouthed laugh that has adorned a hundred magazine covers.

Turning serious and, after reflecting for a long moment, Arnie offered what he truly would have changed about his attack of the Olympic back nine that day.

Nothing.

Absolutely nothing.

"I wouldn't do it any differently," he said, a furrowed brow providing several underlines to his resolve. "At that point in time, the one and only thing that could have changed my situation was to make a couple of putts.

Larry Guest

"I'll be very honest. I have never looked back at a golf tournament and said I would have changed the way I played. That's my style. That's the way I got here, and that's the way I'm gonna go out.

"There was a mistake once that I made playing golf, that I felt cost me a tournament," he said. "I was walking up the eighteenth fairway at Augusta on the final day of the 1961 Masters. A friend called me over to the ropes and said, 'Congratulations,' and I shook hands with him. I said, 'Thank you.' And I made six and lost the Masters. Now that was a mistake, one that I would change if I could. That was a bad mistake, one that I shouldn't have done. But any other golf tournament that I lost or won, I accept the conditions in which I won or lost."

He did, however, attempt to clarify the variously retold dialogue between him and Casper as they embarked on the back nine that day. At that point, Casper was seven behind Arnie and two in front of a bulky young star named Jack Nicklaus.

"Bill walked over to me as we headed down the tenth fairway and he said, 'If I don't play better, Nicklaus is going to beat me for second.' He said it casually, no panic in his voice—just sort of making conversation," Arnie recalled.

"I said, 'Don't worry. If I can help you I will.' I didn't mean it in a cheating way. It was just a friendly way, or moral support. Well, I did help him. I helped him win the tournament."

Arnie had blistered the Olympic front in 32 to seize his big lead but ballooned to 39 on the back. Casper shot 36-32.

Casper recently affirmed Arnie's recollection of their tenth fairway dialogue, but says Arnie is mistaken if he interpreted Casper's remarks as indication Billy had run up the white flag.

"When I went to the tenth tee, I was certain I was going to put on a charge on the back nine with birdies and pars," Casper said. "I still felt I could win the tournament. Of course, I'm sure he felt he had it won."

Indeed.

"At the turn, I never thought of losing the golf tournament or even thought it was humanly possible," Arnie said. "But it was, as I found out. I suppose there was some point when I began to think I could lose the tournament and that was the bad part. I never did really get defensive, I kept going strong all the way. If I had gotten a little defensive, I might have won."

For example, at the par-five sixteenth, where he still held a three-shot lead, he could have hit a 3-wood off the tee comfortably into the fairway. "I knew if I hit the driver good, straightaway, there was a good chance of going through into the rough on the far side. But hitting a 3-wood is for someone else, not me. I hit the driver and duck-hooked it," he recounted.

Discretion still could have been the better part of valor on the next shot, but Arnie tried boldly to muscle a 3-iron out of the tangled rough and failed to reach the fairway. Only a fine up-and-down out of the greenside bunker saved a bogey-6, but the damage had been done. Arnie's "insurmountable" seven-shot lead had vaporized to just one, thin stroke.

Dredging up the disaster caused Arnie to lean back in his office chair at Bay Hill and wince a bit. "Up until then, it was no big deal. But on those two holes, fifteen and sixteen, he [Casper] made birdies and I made bogeys, and he picked up four shots. I had forgotten all of this—and didn't even care about remembering it," he added with a chuckle.

"The one thing I remember most is that my friend, Ed Douglas, a Pennzoil executive, kept ignoring me during the final nine because I knew I was disappointing him. He was my host in '55 when I met him and we became good friends. I stayed in his

Larry Guest

home during the '66 tournament. He wanted me to win worse than anything in the world."

"It was interesting to see the crowd," Casper said, picking up the story. "At first, they were all yelling and screaming for Arnold. Then I started to turn it around, and they all switched to become Casper converts.

"At first, Arnold was thinking about Hogan's record. Then when that slipped away and I started gaining on him, he panicked. I've played with Arnold a lot, and that's the first time I've ever seen him what we call choke. He couldn't make a swing. Everything was a pull hook," Casper said.

Dropping another shot at seventeen with a bogey, a dazed Arnie staggered to the eighteenth dead even with Casper. "I made a pretty good par putt there that, at the time, was the biggest putt in my life," Arnie said. "It was about six feet, downhill, left to-right. And I made it."

"He had putted first" Casper said, "and left his twenty-five-foot, downhill birdie try short. He was going to be standing square in my line and asked if I wanted him to spot it. I said, 'Go ahead. You're warm.' I wanted to see what he would do. If he missed, I would have lagged. If he made it, I was still going to lag. I thought I had performed a miracle picking up the seven shots on the back nine and didn't want to throw it all away by doing something foolish."

Casper lagged close and tapped in to complete the darkest chapter of Arnold Palmer's golf life. Casper's 69-73 victory in the next day's playoff was but an unpleasant epilogue that Arnie has erased from his memory bank. "I didn't even remember that I had an early lead in the playoff until a reporter reminded me recently," he said.

But Arnie's collapse at Olympic only served to further endear him to his Army. "People seem led to understand," he said. "The receptions I got in the weeks and months after that were warmer and bigger. It got to the point that I was joking in speeches about the last nine at Olympic Club. But I have fond memories of Olympic. The club and the people there have always been very gracious and nice to me. When asked to pick the top courses in America, I've picked Olympic on many occasions. I have no ill feelings about anything that happened there."

Arnie agrees there has been only one other replay of the Olympic disaster — a time when he similarly blew a huge lead on the final nine holes of a tournament. At the final turn in the 1981 Michelob Seniors in Tampa, he had surged into a seven-shot lead over Don January and Doug Ford.

With the tournament "clinched" at the turn, disaster struck. The stark numbers on the leaderboard began telling the silent tale of horror as he frittered away the cushion with an unfathomable string of six bogeys. He posted an embarrassing 41 on the final nine and lost the tournament to January by a shot.

"Everything just fell apart. My game just went to hell," Arnie concedes. "I can't explain what happened at Olympic or Tampa. I've made some of my best shots that I ever made in the same situations and I won. Thank God that happened more than it did the other way.

"But there's no one totally infallible. There's not a player that ever lived who hasn't lost — whether it's Jones or Hagen or Hogan or Nicklaus or whomever," said Arnold Palmer, a man who occasionally lost but was never defeated.

12

Giving It Back

From one perspective, humanity is segregated into two simple categories: All of us who inhabit this spinning sphere are either givers or takers.

Arnold Daniel Palmer is a giver of the highest order.

Arnie's giving has followed what has steadily fallen into something of a Palmer Pattern: Somebody asks for his help. He agrees to a modest commitment. He becomes attached to the cause. His contribution of time and/or influence and/or money multiplies dramatically.

EXAMPLE: JUST A FEW YEARS AGO, Arnie celebrated his twentieth anniversary as national chairman of the March of Dimes. "They asked me to serve one year," he recalled with a sheepish grin.

Said Winnie Palmer: "After you shoot a 75, you don't really want to go pose with a poster child and spend two hours greeting people who have paid five hundred dollars to attend a function. But Arnie does it time after time and I've never heard him complain."

Orlando businessman Frank Hubbard first approached Arnie about a children's hospital project, imploring him to simply lend his name and make a donation toward the initial ten-million-dollar drive. Arnie tinkered with the project and soon gave something far larger than his name: He gave his heart. The ten-million-dollar target grew to thirty million. As he saw twisted little limbs and premature babies the size of his hand in the Orlando Regional Medical Center's cramped children's wing, Arnie's efforts expanded in every way.

In addition to giving his own time and money, Arnie inspired others from captains of industry to fellow golf stars like Greg Norman and Scott Hoch to join hands in the project—indirectly through simple leadership by example and directly through serious arm-twisting.

In 1989, the Arnold Palmer Hospital for Children & Women opened in Orlando as a monument to Arnie, who then shifted gears toward hustling endowments for the state-of-the-art facility. He started that secondary drive with a $1.6 million endowment of his own in the form of an insurance policy on his life, with the sixty-five-thousand-dollar annual premiums paid as a charitable contribution out of proceeds from his yearly PGA tour event at Bay Hill.

"What everybody has been doing for the hospital has worked out so well—people have been so generous," he said at the time. "I'm happy the tournament can do this."

The endowment package was the brainchild of Orlando insurance exec Tommy Scarbrough, a longtime volunteer for both the Bay Hill tournament and Greg Norman's original Shark Shootout, which also raised funds for the Arnold Palmer hospital. Insuring a sixty-year-old pilot for that much money is no casual assignment,

but Scarbrough said the toughest part was getting Arnie to slow down long enough for the required physical.

In golf, Arnie the Giver has materialized as a volunteer spokesman for the USGA and a living, breathing boost to some of the struggling, off-Broadway stops on the PGA Tour. He kept promising officials in Tallahassee, Florida, and Columbus, Georgia, that he would one day play in their events. He delivered, giving something of himself back to the game.

That habit provides a sharp contrast in the ongoing comparisons of Arnie and Jack Nicklaus. In recent years, the Bear limited his appearances mainly to majors and tournaments played on courses that he either designed or had some other vested interest in. Arnie's habit of showing up at a place like Columbus or Tallahassee monumentally boosted those struggling little tournaments with his mere presence.

He chooses not to criticize other established stars for not following his lead. "You can't put the guys in that position," he insisted. "I do that for a lot of reasons. I did it because I really enjoy doing that. I enjoy being at those tournaments and feeling the success they have. Sadly, some of the guys miss some of the really great things about life and the tour by not going to those places.

"It isn't everything to be up here all the time," he said, holding one hand at eyebrow level. "That isn't the whole name of the game to me.

"It's fun being down here," he said, lowering his hand to waist level, "with some people that are different sometimes, too. I enjoy that. I enjoy hearing them and talking to them. They're not the Bob Hopes and Bing Crosbys and big tournaments. They're just the nice people who go along and want to have a little fun and eat a little barbecue and I like that.

"I was raised in a whole different era than the people playing the tour today. And I know a little more about how things can be a little more difficult and humbling. So I appreciate those things a little more, too."

The Tallahassee Open, in the '70s and early '80s a friendly little alternative for pros who hadn't earned a berth in the prestigious Tournament of Champions staged that same week, offered but a modest purse. Thus, even the game's marquee names not in the T of C predictably stayed away in droves. The most prominent three tour players in most any Tallahassee Open could have stumped the panel on *What's My Line?* At least, that is, until the unpretentious event enjoyed the Palmer impact in 1976. Arnie's surprise entry was measured on every available yardstick.

Attendance more than doubled at Killearn Country Club. Sponsors quickly pledged 1977 renewals. The scope of Tally Open media coverage was unprecedented. And in Killearn's tiny nineteenth hole lounge, bartender Neil Wedewer spoke of still another record.

"On a normal Tally Open day, we'd move about six cases of Budweiser," the barkeep said. "I think the prior one-day record was eleven cases. But when Arnie was here Wednesday for the first time, we broke all records. I think we sold fifteen cases of Bud." What better measure of Arnie's impact?

Even more delirious were the tournament officials, who were so anxious to provide the onetime king of golf every creature comfort, they became flustered when it was discovered the beer provided in the press room was not his favorite. When pressed by one official, Arnie revealed his preferred brand, all the while assuring that the other one was a perfectly satisfactory alternate.

Nevertheless, each day thereafter when Arnie was escorted into the press room for his daily postmortems, perched in front of

his chair was a can of his favorite brew, iced down in a metal water pitcher.

Arnie wasn't in the press room because he was in the hunt. He was there because he was Arnie and because of what he meant to the struggling tournament. Leaderboards carried his name and status the entire week, no matter now many strokes he had drifted off the pace.

A typical leaderboard would look like this:

Koch -12
Eastwood -11
Lott -11
Rodriguez -10
Murphy -10
Palmer - 1

While Arnie expressed satisfaction that his entry had provided a lift for the tournament, he admitted his mission in Tallahassee was not altogether philanthropic. His game was starting to lose its contending mettle. Arnie hadn't survived a thirty-six-hole cut in the previous two months. Not one to sit home and sulk, he was anxious to play his way out of the bog.

Sipping beers with friends at his Bay Hill Club in Orlando the weekend before and feeling "very hollow" after shooting 81 in the Masters to miss the cut for the third straight tournament, Arnie remembered all those times Tallahassee Open officials had asked him to keep their tournament in mind. He decided he and the Tallahassee Open would be good therapy for one another.

Arnold Palmer in the Tallahassee Open smacks of Ruth spending a week with the Richmond farm team, belting baseballs over a wooden fence for the amusement of the locals. It's Richard Burton signing up for summer stock to re-tune his Shakespeare, Sinatra warbling at Charlie's Bar & Grill.

ARNIE

But to the financially ailing Tallahassee Open, it was pure happiness and the critical plasma needed to continue a pulse for the patient. According to tournament director Richard "Moose" Wammock, the event was assured of lasting another two or three years on the residual effects of Arnie's appearance that year alone.

For three rounds at Killearn, Arnie hovered near par amid much conjecture as to whether he would ever win again. By then, his last regular tour victory was some thirty-eight months back up a bumpy highway.

When asked, pro Bob Wynn opined that Arnie's days as a winner were over. His reference was to the regular tour. The Senior tour hadn't been invented yet.

Wynn received an irate phone call that night at his hotel. "I overheard what you said about Arnie and I don't like it," fumed the anonymous caller. "You're paired with Arnie tomorrow. I'm a member of Arnie's Army and we're gonna get you tomorrow." Click.

Wynn shot even-par 72 the next day and if anything "got" him, it was only his own obvious displeasure with the usual lack of courtesy the Army extends to Arnie's playmates.

Chi Chi Rodriguez turned the question around. "Do you think Arnie can win again?" he asked me.

I pondered a moment, then shook my head from side to side.

"I'll bet you a steak dinner he'll win again on the U.S. tour," the engaging Puerto Rican challenged.

"You're on," I said, adding: "And that's one bet I really hope I lose."

"You'll get your wish," Chi Chi assured. "He's got too much pride. There's too much man in him not to win again."

The steak is still sizzling.

Although Arnie was the first to admit he didn't regain championship form in the relaxing, pressureless week in Tallahassee, he

Larry Guest

did view his 71-72-72-69 showing (good for fourteenth place and an inconsequential $1,160) as a return toward respectability. "This wasn't a bad week."

To those involved with the Tallahassee Open, it was a great week.

Doc Giffin, Arnie's longtime aide, keeps an accordion file in his desk with a special purpose. During the course of each year, requests of Arnie for charitable contributions and appearances pour in and are routed to the file. By the end of the year, the accordion file is bulging and Giffin formulates a list of the requests, divided in his own special categories—legitimate, worthy, questionable, etc.

The 1988 list, for example, filled five single-spaced typewritten pages. It was handed to the boss, as is the custom, in early December. He and Winnie pored over the requests, discussing a course of action on each request.

The measure of a true giver is often not chairing the national March of Dimes campaign or helping build a sprawling hospital, but the small, out-of-sight acts like dealing with those 150 personal requests there on that five-page list. Arnie took the list and a red pencil with him to the Mazda Team Championships in Puerto Rico that December, determined to pare it down to a manageable few. But as he read over each agency and individual request, Arnie's compassion kept getting in the way of the red pencil.

"You can't give away something that you don't have—meaning time. That's the big thing you have to explain," he says.

Bottom line: Not a single one of the 250 requests was ditched. Each one received a response of some kind, even if it was a twenty-five-dollar donation and a polite regret that time constraints would not permit him to emcee next year's cake auction.

Is this man simply a soft touch? Arnie grew pensive, his rubber mug reflecting everything from mock pain to impishness. "Not really. But I have a feeling about that. I try to help where I can and when I can and I just wish I had more to give. But I don't think of myself as a soft touch," he said, adding with a laugh: "Just easy, maybe."

Nineteen-ninety was hardly the most rewarding in Arnold Palmer's eventful life. His play on the course gave the Army little reason to rejoice. Business deals went sour or—worse—wound up in ugly litigation and severed close friendships.

The next year, 1991, started out no better. Even his beloved golf tournament, the Nestlé Invitational at Bay Hill, was plagued by rains and had to be shortened to fifty-four holes.

But the gloom that settled in with the clouds scudding in low over Bay Hill that March was temporarily lifted for a most meaningful tribute to all that Arnie Palmer has been. During one of the rain delays, Arnie was asked to report to an "urgent" meeting in the locker room, where most of the players were lying in ambush.

With spokesman Peter Jacobsen doing the honors, the players presented Arnie with a specially inscribed cake, congratulating him for having made the cut the day before and thanking him for all those years as pro golf's leading ambassador.

Honored in countless ways on every corner of the planet, few tributes touched Arnie more. He responded deliberately, trying to cope with the lump that was building in his throat.

"I was trying hard to keep from losing my composure, because I didn't want to let them see me that way," Arnie recounted. "Coming from those guys, most of whom are half my age, it was special, a once-in-a-lifetime thing."

Remember young Larry Alford Jr. back in Chapter 3, the seven-year-old lad who touched Arnie during the blessing before dinner one night at the 1981 Houston Open? During his extemporaneous prayer, the lad offered thanks for this great golfer, jolting Arnie with the tender tribute.

It's ten years later, August 1991. What's left of Larry Alford II has been delivered to the emergency room at Hermann Hospital in Houston. A nasty auto accident has left him with a crushed face, two mangled arms, a collapsed lung, a broken ankle, neck fractures, brain trauma, and the darkest prognosis.

A gifted young golfer and student leader with a brilliant future an hour earlier, young Alford would lose his left arm just below the elbow. Amputation of the other arm was considered and then decided against.

The boy's two months in the hospital, countless reconstructive surgeries on his face and right arm, and months of rehab was one long string of miracles, said a thankful Larry Sr. "His spirit has never been down. He scares me he's so upbeat." Chief among the cheerleaders was Arnold Palmer, who sat down promptly upon hearing of the accident and fired off words of support.

"In the letter, Arnie told me to be sure to keep Larry's attitude up and keep him getting after his goals," said the elder Alford. "He pointed out there are thousands of handicapped golfers. I can't tell you how much that letter meant to Larry."

Nearly a year later, during the '92 Houston Open, the remarkable story of young Larry Alford's miracle recovery went national. As part of its tournament coverage, ABC-TV aired a taped feature on Larry II, including clips of him playing golf with the help of a revolutionary "golf arm," and caddying for Orlando based journeyman tour pro Ernie Gonzalez. (A national magazine erroneously reported that Gonzalez stiffed young Alford, paying him nothing after missing the cut. Young Larry confirmed that he declined payment from Gonzalez.)

"He's a great kid. He was so positive," Gonzalez says. "I'd use him again because he reads the greens so well."

One day not far off, Larry Alford may be reading tour greens for himself. A scratch golfer before the accident, Larry was MVP of his high school golf team. He played in several national junior amateur events in the summer of '91, finishing second to celebrated teen phenom Tiger Woods at Palm Springs, California, to attract overtures from top college golf programs. Then came the car wreck and unthinkable bodily trauma and phantom pains that haunt him still.

But with the help of the expensive prototype prosthesis, Larry was already back in the 70s and competing for his high school golf team before the first anniversary of the wreck. The contraption features an artificial baby's knee joint and a molded hand with Velcro and a pump that tightens the hand's grip on a golf club.

"Sometimes I do have second thoughts," young Alford told the *Houston Chronicle*. "But I feel in my heart that this prosthesis can help take me there. I know I have the will to do it."

Among the convinced is Johnny Miller, the former tour superstar. In 1993 Miller watched Alford hit balls and promptly declared he could become the first amputee to actually play on the PGA Tour. Miller was so moved by this compelling sight that he put on

a benefit tournament in Houston to help defray some of the medical bills that had climbed past a half-million dollars.

Arnie, who marveled at Larry's "golf arm" during a reunion visit with the Alfords at the Masters in 1992, was back in Houston a month later for a Senior tour event. He checked in with young Alford to offer a booster shot of encouragement.

"Just the fact that he is playing golf is pretty amazing," Arnie said at the time. "But he is playing quite well, better than most people with two good arms. He's approaching what I can do and this is my profession!"

You hear his words and his incredulous tones and you wonder who is inspiring whom. The giver was getting back.

▼

A month before Larry Alford's 1991 auto accident, University of Florida punter Jason Hailey was on a family vacation back to rural Oklahoma. He had been a star athlete and decorated scholar there at Hobart High School before the Haileys moved to Lakeland, Florida. Shooting fireworks with friends on a no-rails farm bridge, Jason accidentally stepped off the edge. He tumbled thirty feet, smashing headfirst into the large rocks of a dry creek bed. His right eye socket was crushed, leaving a shard of skull bone protruding into his brain. One lung collapsed. His heart was shifted by the impact.

Emergency skull surgery was performed that night by the neurologist on call who jotted this note on his post-op report: "I just did surgery on a young man who won't make it. It's too bad—he's only twenty and a good athlete." His brain rapidly swelling from the trauma, Jason lapsed into a coma and was connected to life-support apparatus.

In the unlikely event that he lived, he would almost certainly have permanent brain damage, doctors lamented.

In the depressing week that followed, the Reverend Michael Hailey, dynamic pastor of Lakeland's First Baptist Church, sank into the grim mode of deciding how to dispose of his son's effects. Neurologists at the Oklahoma City hospital were outlining the option of disconnecting Jason from the life-support machinery. The Reverend was resolute on one matter: "We were going to have somebody remove Jason's Jeep from our house. If he wasn't going to make it, I didn't want to see that Jeep when we came back to Florida."

On the morning of Jason's eighth day after lapsing into the coma, his grandparents walked into his hospital room startled to discover Jason sitting up, drinking orange juice.

"How is it?" asked Gramps.

"Don't know yet," came Jason's first words of a second life.

Jason's sprint to recovery flabbergasted medics. Within two days, he was out of intensive care. In another week, befuddled doctors could find no reason not to let him return home to Lakeland. Within another week, he was well enough to make brief visits to a Lakeland golf club to chip and putt. Following reconstructive surgery of the orbital bones and fitting for a glass eye, Jason graduated to swatting buckets of practice balls. By late spring, his strength returning and his adjustment to one-eyed depth perception progressing, Jason was approaching his former handicap of 2. In the fall of '92, he enrolled at Liberty University in Lynchburg, Virginia on a golf scholarship.

Among those smitten by published accounts of Hailey's remarkable recovery was an old giver just up Interstate 4 from Lakeland. Arnie made a point of meeting and encouraging Jason and his father in the spring of '92 at Bay Hill Club, where the

Haileys were guests of the club for a playing lesson with Orlando-based teacher Wally Armstrong.

Arnie invited the Haileys back to play a round of golf with him later that year at Bay Hill, a once-in-a-lifetime(s) experience that inspired young Jason to work even harder on his game. Between shots, Arnie kept asking about Jason's recovery, wanting to know if there was anything he could do to help.

He already had.

As you can tell, paybacks are many from this man. Perhaps the one that will live longest as the most visible monument to his generosity and appreciation for the gifts life gave him, however, will be the Arnold Palmer hospital in Orlando.

The grand facility was officially opened and dedicated in August 1989, in ceremonies that said volumes about its namesake. A tough citadel of everything that is macho? The pants-hitching old charger from the rugged steelworker climes of western Pennsylvania? A shots-and-beer, spit-in-your-eye flinty knot of gristle? Hah!

The thousands who attended the hospital dedication—plus the hundreds that night at the glitzy gala honoring Arnie's sixtieth and the hospital's birth—were given a rare public glimpse of the tender inner fiber of this caring man often thought to be just another Old Ironsides.

Joy and pride overcame the hospital's namesake. It had been building, Winnie Palmer confided, each time Arnie visited the crowded old neonatal wing of Orlando Regional Medical Center, each time a construction milestone was reached with the new building. "This has become an emotional thing for Arnie," she said.

So the great golfer's composure already was tottering even before six-year-old Billy Gillaspie, red-haired and vibrant, ripped open Arnie's chest and yanked at his heart. A Disney troupe had just concluded a spirited song about reaching a dream when one of the performers on the makeshift stage at the new hospital's front door poked a microphone at Bill. "Thank you, Arnold Palmer," Billy's clear voice reverberated over the public address, "for building us a children's hospital and making our dream come true."

That's when Arnie lost it.

"I looked over at my daughter [Amy Saunders], and she was a mess," Arnie said later, playfully blaming his tears on hers. "But if you aren't touched at a moment like that, then something's wrong with you." There were a couple of thousand on hand for the ceremonies and hardly a dry eye in the place.

Dennis the Menace creator Hank Ketcham, one of several national personalities on hand for the festivities, joked that Arnie had qualified for a Kleenex commercial.

Arnie told the crowd that that moment, in a different sort of way, was as special as any of his nearly one hundred worldwide golf victories. At least none of those reduced him to tears, Winnie testified. "You have to remember," she said, "that Arnie was raised in an era when men didn't cry. It's more acceptable now."

That children would hold the key to Arnie's vulnerable underbelly is not a surprise. During a busy, globe-trotting career, his two daughters zipped to womanhood, regrettably, almost before he noticed. "As you get older, the more you realize how true that is," says Arnie. However guilty Arnie might have been as an absentee father off on the golf trail while his daughters were growing up, he has more than atoned as a doting grandfather and as a pulsing inspiration in Amy's greatest time of need when she became seri-

ously ill several years ago. At thirty-two and with four small children, she was diagnosed with a very serious form of cancer. Arnie was a tower of support, instilling in Amy his own strong will as if this were just another difficult, dogleg par-four that would not be allowed to defeat them. It didn't.

Arnie coached her into the same defiantly positive mode he would use to successfully bouy architect/partner Ed Seay through lung cancer in 1995 and himself through his own thunderclap discovery of prostate cancer in early 1997. Cancer had foolishly picked on the wrong prostate this time. Doubtless there are lots of prostates that would cower and wither under assault by the deadly disease, but this one is attached to the toughest, most strong-willed fellow I've ever known. Diagnosis had come early, and Arnie emerged from surgery with every indication of a full recovery.

Arnie had brought Amy together with a long-time member of Arnie's Army, a woman stricken with "terminal" cancer ten years earlier. A picture of health despite the grim pronoucement a decade earlier, the woman became Amy's Exhibit A of hope.

Now thirty-nine and again vibrant, Amy lives two miles from Bay Hill with her realtor husband, Roy Saunders, and their four children. They reside in Windermere, a quiet, quaint little suburb of Orlando that she says reminds her of Latrobe's small-town ambiance.

Peggy, forty-one, worked briefly as an executive-trainee with Arnold Palmer Enterprises. She is married to Peter Wears, a stock-broker. They live in Durham, North Carolina.

Although both girls occasionally traveled to golf tournaments with their famous parents while growing up, they were sheltered from the glare of Arnie's spotlight. They liked it that way. Still do. Winnie discouraged me from talking to the girls for perceptions of their father for this book.

In a rare, recent interview, Amy spoke appreciatively of her parents: "They kept us out of the public eye, and I think I had a very typical childhood."

You can't fool animals or children, and the world's little tykes have tuned in to Arnie's abundant love and appreciation for them.

Billy Gillaspie sensed this is a man of genuine concern, and Arnie's working knowledge that life was once a bad bet for Billy made it even tougher to maintain a celebrity millionaire's poise. Bob and Kathy Gillaspie had an earlier Billy, in 1981, who lived just three days. In 1983, Billy II arrived prematurely with cardiac complications. His breathing stopped a few hours after birth, and Billy was rushed to Orlando Regional Medical Center attached to a portable respirator. With the cramped neonatal intensive care unit over capacity, Billy was diverted to pediatrics. He was within a few hours of dying when one of ORMC's miracle makers, neonatal chief Dr. Greg Alexander, returned from vacation to resume his typical hundred-hour work weeks and took charge of Billy's care. He created a makeshift spot for Billy in the crowded neonatal ICU and nurtured the five-pound infant to recovery.

"It would have been a crime not to build a hospital for Dr. Alexander," said Bob Gillaspie. "He's a gift."

The year the new hospital opened, Billy was playing catcher and outfielder for the champion Astros of the Altamonte Springs, Florida, T-Ball Little League. A little small, perhaps, but otherwise normal and happy and extremely alive.

That's why Billy was picked back on that bright, sunny summer day in 1989 to thank Arnie publicly, even at the risk of sending a torrent of tears cascading down those famous bronze leather cheeks. Arnold Palmer is a softie. In these tight-jawed times, thank Heaven there are a few left.

Larry Guest

FOR THE RECORD: ARNIE'S PRO VICTORIES

(*- PGA Tour, **-Senior PGA Tour)

Tournament Year & Location		Score	$ Won
1955			
Canadian Open	Weston GC, Toronto	265	$2,400
1956			
Panama Open	Panama City, Panama	283	$2,000
Colombia Open	Calle, Colombia	280	$1,800
Insurance City Open*	Hartford, Connecticut	274	$4,000
Eastern Open	Mt. Pleasant, Baltimore	277	$3,800
1957			
Houston Open*	Memorial Park GC	279	$7,500
Azalea Open*	Wilmington, North Carolina	282	$1,700
Rubber City Open*	Akron, Ohio	272	$2,800
San Diego Open*	Mission Valley CC	271	$2,800
1958			
St. Petersburg Open*	Pasadena GC, St. Pete, Florida	276	$2,000
Masters*	Augusta National GC, Georgia	284	$11,250
Pepsi Open*	Pine Hollow CC, Long Island	273	$9,000
1959			
Thunderbird Invit.*	Palm Springs, California	266	$1,500
Oklahoma City Open*	Twins Hills CC	273	$3,500
W. Palm Beach Open*	WPB CC, West Palm Beach, Florida	281	$2,000
1960			
Bob Hope Desert Classic*	Palm Springs, California	338	$12,000
Texas Open*	Ft. Sam Houston GC	276	$2,800
Baton Rouge Open*	Baton Rouge CC, Louisiana	279	$2,000
Pensacola Open*	Pensacola CC, Florida	273	$2,000
Masters*	Augusta National GC	282	$17,500
U.S. Open*	Cherry Hills CC, Denver	280	$14,400
Insurance City Open*	Hartford, Connecticut	270	$3,500
Mobile Open*	Mobile Muny, Alabama	274	$2,000
Canada Cup	Portmarnock, Dublin, Ireland	565	$1,000
(partner: Sam Snead)			
1961			
San Diego Open*	Mission Valley CC, California	271	$2,800
Phoenix Open*	Arizona CC, Phoenix, Arizona	270	$4,300
Baton Rouge Open*	Sherwood Forest CC, Louisiana	266	$2,800
Texas Open*	Oak Hills, San Antonio	270	$4,300
British Open	Royal Birkdale, England	284	$3,920
Western Open*	Blythefield, Grand Rapids, Michigan	271	$5,000
1962			
Bob Hope Desert Classic*	Palm Springs, California	342	$5,300
Phoenix Open*	Phoenix CC, Phoenix, Arizona	269	$5,300
Masters*	Augusta National GC	280	$20,000
Texas Open*	Oak Hills, San Antonio	273	$4,300

Tourn. of Champions*	Desert Inn, Las Vegas	276	$11,000
Colonial National*	Colonial, Fort Worth, Texas	281	$7,000
British Open	Troon, Scotland	276	$3,290
American Golf Classic*	Firestone, Akron, Ohio	276	$9,000
Canada Cup	Jockey Club, Buenos Aires	557	$1,000
(partner: Sam Snead)			

1963

Los Angeles Open*	Rancho Park GC, L.A.	274	$9,000
Phoenix Open*	Arizona CC, Phoenix, Arizona	273	$5,300
Pensacola Open*	Pensacola CC, Florida	273	$3,500
Thunderbird Classic*	Westchester CC, Rye, New York	277	$25,000
Cleveland Open*	Beechmont CC, Cleveland	273	$22,000
Western Open*	Beverly CC, Chicago	280	$11,000
Whitemarsh Open*	Whitemarsh Valley, Philadelphia	281	$26,000
Australian Wills Masters	Wills G & CC, Sydney	285	$2,240
Canada Cup	Nom La Bretche, Paris	482	$1,000
(partner: Jack Nicklaus)			

1964

Masters*	Augusta National GC, Georgia	276	$20,000
Oklahoma City Open*	Quail Creek CC, Oklahoma	277	$5,800
Piccadilly			World
Match Play	England	n/a	n/a
Canada Cup	Royal Kaanapali, Hawaii	554	$1,000
(partner: Jack Nicklaus)			

1965

| Tourn. of Champions* | Desert Inn, Las Vegas | 277 | $14,000 |

1966

Los Angeles Open*	Rancho Park GC	273	$11,000
Tourn. of Champions*	Desert Inn, Las Vegas	283	$20,000
Australian Open	Royal Queensland, CC	276	$1,792
Houston Champions*	Champions, Houston, Texas	275	$21,000
PGA Team Championship*	PGA Nat'l Palm Beach Gardens	256	$25,000
(partner: Jack Nicklaus)			
Canada Cup	Yomiuri, Tokyo, Japan	548	$1,000
(partner: Jack Nicklaus)			

1967

Los Angeles Open*	Rancho Park GC	269	$20,000
Tucson Open*	Tucson National, Arizona	273	$12,000
American Golf Classic*	Firestone, Akron, Ohio	276	$20,000
Thunderbird Classic*	Upper Montclair, New Jersey	283	$30,000
Piccadilly			World
Match Play	England	n/a	n/a
World Cup	Club Golf, Mexico City	557	$1,000
(partner: Jack Nicklaus)			
World Cup Int'l Trophy	Club Golf, Mexico City	276 n/a	
(individual title)			

1968

| Bob Hope Desert Classic* | Palm Springs, California | 348 | $20,000 |

Larry Guest

Kemper Open*	Pleasant Valley, Sutton, Mass.	276	$30,000
1969			
Heritage Classic*	Harbour Town, Hilton Head, S.C.	283	$20,000
Danny Thomas Classic*	Diplomat CC, Hollywood, Florida	270	$25,000
1970			
PGA Team Championship*	Laurel Valley CC, Pennsylvania	259	$20,000
(partner: Jack Nicklaus)			
1971			
Bob Hope Desert Classic*	Palm Springs, California	342	$28,000
Citrus Open*	Rio Pinar, Orlando, Florida	270	$30,000
Westchester Classic*	W'chester, Harrison, New York	270	$50,000
PGA Team Championship*	Laurel Valley GC, Pennsylvania	257	$20,000
(partner: Jack Nicklaus)			
Lancome Trophy	Paris, France	202	$20,000
1973			
Bob Hope Desert Classic*	Palm Springs, California	343	$32,000
1975			
Spanish Open	LaManga, Spain	283	$8,750
British PGA Championship	Royal St. Georges	285	$2,484
1980			
Canadian PGA Championship	Mayfair CC, Edmonton	271	$20,000
PGA-Seniors**	Turnberry Isle CC, Miami	289	$20,000
1981			
U.S. Senior Open**	Oakland Hills CC, Michigan	289	$26,000
1982			
Marlboro Sr. Classic**	Marlboro, Massachusetts	276	$25,000
Denver Post Champions**	Pinehurst CC, Denver	275	$25,000
1983			
Boca Grove Seniors**	Boca Grove Plantation, Florida	271	$25,000
1984			
PGA Seniors**	PGA National, Palm Beach Gardens	282	$35,000
Doug Sanders Pro-Am	Memorial Park GC, Houston	134	$20,500
Senior TPC**	Canterbury GC, Cleveland	276	$36,000
Quadel Srs. Classic**	Boca Grove Plantation, Florida	205	$30,060
1985			
Senior TPC*	Canterbury GC, Cleveland	274	$36,000
1986			
Unionmutual Classic	Purpoodock, Portland, Maine	200	$38,000
1988			
Crestar Classic**	Hermitage, Richmond, Virginia	203	$48,750

Total Victories: 92
PGA Tour: 61
PGA Senior Tour: 10

Index

ISBN 1-888952-42-3